P9-CIS-941

Albania
A Guide and Illustrated Journal

by Linda White
and
Peter and Andrea Dawson

BRADT PUBLICATIONS, UK
THE GLOBE PEQUOT PRESS INC, USA

First published in 1989 by Bradt Publications.
This edition published in 1995 by Bradt Publications, 41 Nortoft Road,
Chalfont St Peter, Bucks SL9 0LA, England.
Published in the USA by The Globe Pequot Press Inc, 6 Business Park Road,
PO Box 833, Old Saybrook, Connecticut 06475-0833

Reprinted with amendments July 1996

Copyright 2nd edition © 1995 Linda White and Peter and Andrea Dawson

The author and publishers have made every effort to ensure the accuracy of the information in
this book at the time of going to press. However, they cannot accept any responsibility for any
loss, injury or inconvenience resulting from the use of information contained in this guide.

All rights reserved. No part of this publication may be reproduced, stored in a retrieval system,
or transmitted in any form or by any means, electronic, mechanical, photocopying, recording or
otherwise without the prior consent of the publishers.
Requests for permission should be addressed to Bradt Publications, 41 Nortoft Road, Chalfont
St Peter, Bucks SL9 0LA in the UK; or to The Globe Pequot Press Inc, 6 Business Park Road,
PO Box 833, Old Saybrook, Connecticut 06475-0833 in North and South America.

British Library Cataloguing in Publication Data
A catalogue record for this book is available from the British Library
ISBN 1 898323 10 0

Library of Congress Cataloging-in-Publication Data
White, Linda, 1946-
Albania : a guide and illustrated journal / Linda White, Peter and Andrea Dawson—2nd ed.
p. cm.—Bradt guides
Includes bibliographical reference and index
ISBN 1-56440-697-0
1. Albania—Guidebooks. I. Dawson, Peter. II. Dawson, Andrea. III. Title
DR909.W48 1995
914.96504'3—dc20

Maps *Inside covers* Steve Munns *Tirana and Shkodra* Caroline Crump
Illustrations Peter and Andrea Dawson

Typeset from the author's disc by Patti Taylor, London NW10 1JR
Printed and bound in Great Britain by
The Guernsey Press Co Ltd, Guernsey, Channel Islands

CONTENTS

Introduction   vii
Acknowledgements   viii
Disclaimer   viii

THE GUIDE PART 1   1

Chapter 1   Background   3

Chapter 2   Planning and Preparations   11

Chapter 3   In Albania   17

THE GUIDE PART 2 — Cities and Regions   37

Tirana   39
Five Excursions from Tirana   47
Along the Via Egnatia to the Southeast   56
The Southern Highlands   66
The Southern Coast   72
The South-Central Interior   82
The North   87
The Northern Interior   98

THE JOURNALS   101

Foreword to the Journals   102
Notes   102
The Tirana Journals   103
The Southern Journals   127
The Northern Journals   161
Driving Through the Heart of the Country   189
Backtracking: Elbasani and Vlora   198
Goodbye Tirana   201

APPENDIX

Language   205

Further reading   210

Index   212

AURON EXPEDITIONS

Albania, a shore unknown...

The pioneers of adventure and cultural travel in Albania.
Our friendly Albanian staff with Dutch management welcomes inquiries from individual travellers and groups to explore Albania. Travelling with us is about discovering the nature, culture and the secrets of this mysterious and forgotten land.
Special interests: trekking, culture tours, diving, archaeology, caving, and one and two day tours from Corfu.

Rr Bajram Curri N-408   c/o Albanian Lines
Tirana, Albania   Spiro Mouriki St 1, Corfu 491000, Greece
Tel/fax: +355 42 33050   Tel: +30 661 21833, Fax: +30 661 27123
                              Mobile: +30 94 348921

PREFACE TO NEW EDITION

In the penultimate paragraph to our 1989 journal, we wondered whether Albania would follow the example of the other Communist countries who were busy reshaping their political structures—Albania had been described as 'the last domino'. The changes came faster than we, or others, could have expected. Whilst preparing for our visit, and whilst writing our journal, to find a Western press reference to Albania was a rarity; 12 months later, the press cuttings made an impressive pile as Albanians demolished the statues of Enver Hoxha, and Western news broadcasts showed the 'last domino', in Europe at least, falling with a fairly convincing thump. It was a poignant sight to see the frantic news footage of Albanian refugees clinging to the sides of freighters or making spectacular jumps from these vast ships into the waters of Brindisi harbour.

The writing of the journal was a curious challenge, since at that time only officially approved group travel was permitted. We therefore had six days to gain some sort of impression of the country, taking account of what our guides would allow us to see, and were rather grandiosely prepared to compile a travel guide and commit our impressions to publication. As journalists and writers were not permitted to visit the country, we could not call upon official help to guide our writing, nor could we tell other members of our group, or the British group leader, what we were up to, for fear of putting them in a compromising position (although we discovered, towards the end of our visit, that one of our party, 'Richard', was in fact a holidaying TV reporter, using a second passport which listed his profession as 'electrical engineer' or similar, and so we did confide in him. This gave him great satisfaction, and was a great help to us, as thenceforward he asked official guides the sort of risky journalistic questions that we, as rank amateurs in the investigative business, wouldn't have dared to ask). The writing in Albania, therefore, whilst hardly a dangerous business, was necessarily furtive, consisting of note-taking on the back seats of coaches, or less furtive writing-up in hotel rooms. Whatever it might be, however, the journal never pretended to be anything other than a record of six days in Albania; an encyclopaedic coverage of the country it could not be.

There was one further slight complication in the writing of the journal. In 1989 there were only two English language guides to Albania published in the West, neither of which was allowed to be taken into the country. We had agreed with Hilary Bradt, our publisher, that we would try to write our guide and journal so that it would be acceptable, to the Albanian authorities, for visitors to Albania to take in with them. This meant that whilst, for both Hilary and us, it would have been unacceptable to tell lies or to indulge in any whitewashing of facts, we might have to be in some ways restrained with the truth, or to tread carefully in our descriptions. We hoped that 'between the lines' reading might encourage readers to get our meaning.

However, there are a few things that we maybe weren't as precise about as we could have been. We mentioned the pillboxes and concrete bunkers being much in evidence: in fact, around 700,000 of them were spread across the country to allay Hoxha's fear of invasion following the USSR's occupation of Czechoslovakia in 1968. We mentioned the alleged suicide, in 1981, of Prime Minister Mehmet Shehu, Hoxha's former Partisan comrade: the 'suicide' has always been suspect, and there are long-standing rumours that Hoxha himself shot Shehu at a Politburo meeting. The disparaging accounts, given by our Albanian guides and by the Hoxha-inspired histories, of lack of support from the Allied Forces during World War II are not borne out either by official sources or by, for example, David Smiley's account of his experiences with the partisans. Indeed, one of the ironies of this is that Hoxha's National Liberation Movement forces were, rightly, identified by the Allies as those most likely to carry on the anti-Nazi struggle, rather than other more right-wing groups such as National Union (Balli Kombtar). We assumed, probably wrongly, a knowledge of the life of Enver Hoxha on the part of our readers. No doubt there will be a full biography one day, but for the present one has a picture of a leader who liberated his country, but with a ruthless disregard for human rights. We had read about, but did not refer to, the planned invasion of Albania in 1950 by anti-Hoxha elements, together with its debacle of an ending resulting from Kim Philby's betrayal, and, as David Smiley notes, 'the deaths of many brave and patriotic Albanians'.

The brevity of our experience in Albania may have been open to criticism, but our sense of delight and excitement at being among the first groups of tourists to visit a gradually unfolding country cannot be denied, and neither can the warmth and hospitality extended to us. We did not get the impression that we were merely presented with a deliberate façade of delusion, sham or party line, though there was, without doubt, propaganda perpetuated 'for the good of the country'. The land we encountered was partly that of the donkey cart, the flared trouser, the shop selling prams with cracked plastic hoods, the common cause of groups of seed sowers and ditch diggers, but also the bared teeth of the pillboxes, which ultimately could not repel an invasion of a movement which in Albania's recent history was scarcely thought possible. It is hard to imagine the effects of such political and social upheaval on a people previously caught in a 1950s' timewarp: the Albanians must still be bewildered and disorientated by the events which overtook the 'Land of the Eagle'.

Peter and Andrea Dawson, 1995

INTRODUCTION

Albania's breathtaking beauty is matched only by its amazing resilience. Jagged peaks contrast with silver sand, torrential rivers with pristine mountain lakes; stone houses cling to the hillsides and ancient ruins bask under a southern sun.

Occupied by outsiders throughout most of its history, Albania nevertheless has managed to hold onto its unique culture. The people are proud that their Illyrian heritage survived the Greeks and Romans, Slavs and Crusaders, Venetians and Turks.

Of all the subjugations, however, the iron rule of one of its own—Enver Hoxha—had the most devastating effect. Isolated for nearly half a century by a madman who brooked no opposition, who stayed in power by means of wholesale torture and regular purges of his deputies, Albania became, as author Ismail Kadare writes, Europe's biggest prison.

But the collapse of Communism in Eastern Europe sparked rebellion at last. In December 1989 the students of Shkodra rallied in an attempt to overturn the statues of Stalin and Hoxha. In March 1990 the students of Kavaja took to the streets. The demonstrations were savagely ended by the Sampistët (riot troops) and Sigurimi (secret police) but nothing could stop the cry for freedom.

The world was shocked by the desperation of those first shiploads of refugees who fled to Italy. It was shocked by the pent-up rage that manifested itself in the destruction of public property: factories and collective farms were plundered, museums were looted.

Now Albania is coming to terms with its past and is once more knocking at Europe's door. For the next decade tourists, too, will be faced with the ravages of the Hoxha regime. It will take time to build the infrastructure—hotels, restaurants, roads, communications—that will attract mass tourism. But for the tourist who visits Albania now with an open mind and an open heart, the rewards will be greater.

The beauty of the landscape is enhanced by the friendliness of the people. Visitors are welcomed with inborn hospitality and a fair measure of curiosity. The people have almost nothing, but share everything with their guests. To be a tourist now carries a great responsibility—to the Albanians who offer their unquestioning friendship, and to future tourists who will be treated according to the way we act.

Linda White, 1995

Acknowledgements

I would like to thank Ani Tare for setting off the spark that renewed my interest in Albania; Aleksandra and Isa Tare for providing me with a home in Tirana; and all the people who welcomed me during my travels around the country. Special thanks go to Isa, whose faultless stewardship, extensive network of friends, reliable information and outstanding organizational abilities made the greater part of this book possible.

I am deeply indebted to Gazmend Goci for expertly guiding me through the labyrinth of the language. Thanks to Ari Vruzhi for translating beyond the point of exhaustion; to Ylli Bulku and his friends for shepherding me over the worst road I have ever driven, at night, in a thunderstorm; to the Estref Bega family for their hospitality and books; to Ismail Hoxha and his Albturist staff, Adriana Janina of the Ministry of Tourism and Sulejman Dashi of the Institute of Cultural Monuments for answering my endless questions; to Anke Halfter for her patience in booking and re-booking my tickets; to Kent and Faye Prince and Renate and Pepe Stecay for critiquing the manuscript, to Mary Neth and Manfred Blaszczak for holding down the fort while I was away, and to Neil Taylor of Regent Holidays for reading and updating the text.

I would also like to thank Hilary Bradt for her enthusiasm in publishing this book and my editor Tricia Hayne for her patience. It would not have been possible without Peter and Andrea Dawson, whose book it was first and who kindly allowed me to update their *Albania: A Guide and Illustrated Journal* published in 1989. Their collaboration and advice were indispensable. Extracts from their journey have been inserted in italics in this book.

Disclaimer

I have striven for accuracy in both fact and spelling. When sources disagreed, I tried to judge which was most reliable. This has been made more difficult by the fact that the Hoxha regime pursued a policy of non-information that is still in force simply through inertia.

Changes are taking place so swiftly in Albania that it is hazardous to comment on restaurants, hotels and entertainment, and even to say with certainty what can be seen at historic sites: looting is still going on and even the stones of ancient ruins are being carted away. Telephone numbers seem to change with great regularity.

Albanian is a language of inflection that is particularly difficult for foreigners to comprehend; the variations in spelling seem unlimited. The spelling of Albanian place names varies not only according to the grammatical endings of gender, number and case, but also with definite and indefinite forms. For the most part, I have used the definite forms (for example, Tirana, Gjirokastra, Berati) rather than the indefinite forms (Tiranë, Gjirokastër, Berat) in an attempt to be consistent. In the case of Ohrid and Skopje, however, I have used the more commonly recognised form rather than the Albanian Ohri and Shkup.

I appreciate the help and advice of those who read this manuscript, and any mistakes in it are my own.

Safety
It is reported from the north of the country that a number of Albanian nationals are caught up in blood feuds. Travellers to the country should be aware of this, but are unlikely to be affected.

The Guide
Part 1

A perverted young bard in Albania
Had a quite irresistible mania
For using, in verse,
Words which got worse and worse —
Nothing sacred, and each time
                    profania.....

Chapter One

Background

The land

Albania forms part of the western seaboard of the Balkan Peninsula, bordered on the north and northeast by Montenegro and Kosova (both part of 'rump Yugoslavia'), on the east by Macedonia, on the south by Greece and on the west by the Adriatic and Ionian Seas.

It is a small country, about the size of Wales or the state of Maryland, with an area of 28,748km². Its greatest length is 340km from north to south and its greatest width is 148km from east to west.

A rugged country lying at the bottom of the Alpine fold, Albania is more than 75% mountains or hills. The Albanian Alps in the north are for the most part over 2,000m with Jezerca (2,693m) being their highest peak. Albania's highest mountain is Mount Korabi (2,751m), northeast of Peshkopia in the Korabi range near the borders with Kosova and Macedonia.

The lowlands along the west coast from Shkodra to Vlora and a small area around Saranda are the most densely populated and the most important for agriculture. The indented coastline stretches 472km, with good beaches at Velipoja and Shëngjini in the north, Durrësi in the centre, Divjaka, Semani and Vlora farther south, and Borshi, Saranda and Ksamili near the Greek border. The 100km Ionian coast is called the Albanian Riviera and it is here that the mountains dip their toes into the sea.

Much of the Adriatic coast was swampland before World War II; during the Communist era the swamps were drained (using forced labour) for agriculture. The only remaining swamp of any importance is Kuna near Lezha which is now a nature park.

Albania is rich in lakes and rivers springing from the mountains. Of its 136 rivers, the largest is the 285km Drini, formed by the Black Drini, which flows through Lake Ohrid, and the White Drini, which rises in the Zhleb highlands of Kosova. It discharges into the Buna (44km, Albania's only navigable river) in the north, which rises from Lake Shkodra. The 115km Mati rises in the Martaneshi Mountains and is noted for the torrential flow of its upper reaches.

The Semani (281km) and Shkumbini (180km) converge in Berati and meander to the coast. The Vjosa (272km) in the south rises in the Pindus Mountains of Greece, its loveliest stretch running through the narrow Këlcyra Gorge. The Bistrica in the south drains into the Ionian Sea.

The rivers are an important source of electric power, which Albania exported during the Communist regime. There are three major hydroelectric plants on the Drini alone and damming the river created the country's largest artificial lake, Fierza. In the process of total electrification of the country, a number of other artificial lakes were created, including the Ulza, Vau i Dejës, Komani, Thana and Shkopeti.

Among Albania's major natural lakes is Lake Shkodra, largest on the Balkan Peninsula and shared with Montenegro. Ancient Lake Ohrid (Ohri in Albanian), shared with Macedonia, is almost as large and is among the oldest and deepest lakes in the world. Some of its unique fish are 'living fossils'. Nearby is the relatively shallow Lake Prespa, shared with both Macedonia and Greece.

Groups of glacial lakes in the mountains, especially the Lura Lakes, are noted for their clarity and beauty. Among the salt lakes are Narta (near Vlora) and Karavastas (near Divjaka) on the Adriatic coast and Butrinti (near Saranda) in the far south. These lakes are actually lagoons connected to the sea by natural channels and are used extensively for mussel and oyster cultivation. Mineral springs are found throughout the country.

Once Albania was the most forested country in Europe, with about 40% of its land trees. Since 1991, however, much of the landscape has been denuded as the people cut down trees for fuel. There are still some beech and conifer forests in the north, oaks and pines in the south, and the occasional avenue of plane trees, but to a large extent even the scrub is struggling to survive the axe.

Most of those trees that have been protected are in the national parks. Among the most beautiful are Divjaka National Park on the shores of the Adriatic with forests of umbrella and wild pine, Thethi National Park in the Albanian Alps made up mostly of beech, Lura National Park with black pine, fir and beech, Dajti National Park near Tirana with varied vegetation, and Llogara National Park at a mountain pass above the sea with black pine and fir.

Albania's climate can be divided into two distinct zones—Mediterranean along the coast and Continental inland. In winter, mild sea air keeps temperatures along the west coast above freezing, while in the eastern highlands temperatures have been known to fall to -25°C. In summer the entire country is hot, with temperatures reaching into the 40°s C. Winter is the rainy season; in summer, cloudless skies are the rule.

The people

The 1990 census recorded a population of around 3.25 million. More recent figures show that the capital, Tirana, has grown to some 290,000 because of the influx from poorer regions over the past two years. Ethnic Albanians make up about 95% of the population; a Greek minority of some 60,000 (Greece claims 400,000) lives in the south, and there are a few Vlachs, Slavs, Armenians and Gypsies. The Albanians themselves are divided into Ghegs in the north and Tosks in the south.

About 5 million ethnic Albanians live outside the country; almost 2 million in surrounding Kosova, Montenegro and Macedonia, some 80,000 in the United States, and others in Greece, Italy, Egypt, Turkey, Romania, Bulgaria and the Ukraine.

The population within Albania is very young, the average age being 26. Families are large and the tradition of the nuclear family is maintained. Often one child and his/her family remain with the parents as long as they live.

In spite of the fact that Albania was declared an atheist state in 1967, its religious profile has remained intact. Some 70% of the population is Muslim, 20% Orthodox and 10% Roman Catholic, the last concentrated in the north. The Orthodox church derives from the Byzantine Empire, acknowledging the rite and primacy of the Patriarch of Constantinople. The Albanian Orthodox Church today has the same rites as the Greek, and the primate is Greek; however, some of the churches hold services in the Albanian language.

The Albanian language is difficult, full of Qs, Xs and umlauted Es. An isolated descendant of ancient Illyrian, it is unlike any present-day European language, though it derives from Indo-European. Modern written Albanian is young; the Latin alphabet was officially adopted only in the 1880s. Legend says that a long-lost alphabet was given to the people from the mouth of a dragon.

In addition to Albanian, many people speak Italian, Greek and French. The older generation may speak Russian, while many young people are learning English. German is seldom spoken, but undoubtedly will become more common as many Albanians are working temporarily in Germany, Switzerland and Austria.

The name Albania comes from *Albanoi*, a 2nd century BC Illyrian tribe. Since the 17th century, the Albanians have called their country *Shqipëria,* their language *Shqipe* and themselves *Shqiptar.*

The official name of the country is *Republika e Shqipërisë*—The Republic of Albania.

'Gather like steel around the Party.' (PPSH is the Labour Party of Albania.) Faded political posters from the Communist regime remain on many walls.

A chronological history

BC

to 10,000	Middle and Late Palaeolithic dwellings at Kamniki and Maliqi in the southeast.
5000	Neolithic settlements such as Maliqi and Cakrani on the south coast.
2700-1200	Bronze Age settlement at Maliqi near Korça.
2000	Pelasgians, ancestors of the Illyrians, migrate to the Balkans.
627	Greeks, mainly from Corfu and Corinth, colonize the coast at Epidamnos (Durrësi).
500	Illyrian power increases, with centres at Butrinti, Apollonia, Durrësi, Lezha and Shkodra.
385	Dionysius of Syracuse rules from Lezha.
232	Illyrian leader Glaukias seizes Epidamnos, then allies himself with Rome.
229-168	Province of Illyria established after Roman invasions; Illyrians become known as *Arbers*. Major development of roads, bridges, aqueducts.

AD

395	Division of Roman Empire: Arbëria becomes part of the Eastern (Byzantine) Empire. Barbarian invasions begin with the Visigoths, followed by the Huns.
461	Invasion by the Ostrogoths.
529-640	Invasions by the Antes, Huns, Lombards and Gepides. Northern Illyria overrun by Slavs and Avars, who eradicate Illyrian influence. Southern Illyrians (in the area of modern-day Albania) stand firm, emerging in the Middle Ages as the Albanoi.
840	Byzantine rule re-established.
851	Bulgarian invasions.
1014	Byzantine rule re-established under Basil II.
1081-1109	Normans invade Durrësi from Italy.
1096	Invasion by armies of the First Crusade.
1190-1198	Progon establishes feudal state of Arbania with Kruja as its capital.
1272-1286	Charles of Anjou introduces Roman Catholicism to northern Albania. Domination by Angevins.
1331-1355	Serbian domination under Stefan Dušan. Feudal Albanian states controlled by three noble families: the Dukagjinis in the north, the Kastriotis in central Albania and the Arianitas in the south.
1385-1417	Ottoman invasion under Sultan Murad I. Venetian occupation of coastal towns of Shkodra, Lezha and Durrësi. Series of uprisings protest against military and financial obligations and the abolition of rights to own land.
1405?-1468	Emergence of Gjergj Kastrioti, known as Skënderbeg, who leads resistance against Ottoman forces from the capital Kruja. Decline in status of towns: the only buildings of importance are mosques at Berati, Vlora, Korça and Elbasani.

1444	At Skënderbeg's initiative, the Albanian League is formed at Lezha to unify resistance against the Turks.
1506-1912	Domination by the Ottoman Empire. Scattered resistance in the mountain areas. Thousands of Albanians emigrate, especially to southern Italy.
1741-1822	Gradual decline of the Ottoman Empire and subsequent development of *pashalics*—estates ruled by the semi-autonomous feudal class. Ali Pashë Tepelena rules over the *pashalics* of Shkodra and Janina (now part of Greece). Civic and military building flourishes until the suppression of the *pashalics* during the early 19th century. Development of a national awareness evolves into the National Resistance, spearheaded by the poet Jeronim de Rada and writers Andon Zako Çajupi and the brothers Naim and Sami Frashëri.
1878	Albanian League founded at the Congress of Prizrën (now in Yugoslavia) to establish unity and independence.
1881	Provisional government proclaimed despite Turkish occupation; Albanian League dissolved.
1899	League of Peja aims to establish complete autonomy. Turkish forces control north and central Albania.
1912	Widespread mass uprisings result in Proclamation of Independence on 28 November and formation of a national government at Vlora, headed by Ismail Qemali (1844-1919). The end of 500 years of Ottoman occupation.
1913	London Conference of Ambassadors endorses the Proclamation, but creates new boundaries effectively excluding territory occupied by nearly half the Albanian people. The German aristocrat Prince Wilhelm von Wied is appointed Head of State; uprisings soon force his and his government's departure.
1914	At the outbreak of World War I, Greek and Italian forces occupy southern Albania. Austro-Hungarian forces invade northern Albania.
1915	Montenegro occupies Shkodra. Secret Treaty of London. Allied Powers agree on redistribution of Albanian territory after war.
1916-1918	French military protection helps Albania govern the new 'autonomous province' of Korça.
1918	Peace Treaty of Versailles: the problem of partition remains.
1920	January: Albanian patriots convene the Congress of Lushnja to form their own government and successfully demand the withdrawal of all foreign troops. Capital transferred to Tirana. December: Albania admitted to League of Nations.

1920-1924	Two factions now hold power and resist reform: semi-feudal landowners in the lowlands and tribal chieftains in the highlands. Chieftain Ahmet Zogu (1895-1961) consolidates his power.
1924	June: Zogu regime overthrown by a group of Liberal-Democrats. The Albanian-American writer and historian Bishop Fan Noli (1882-1965) heads the new government. His inability to cater to both landowners and peasants leads to the Yugoslav- and Italian-backed return of Zogu to Tirana.
1925-1929	Zogu proclaimed president with Italian support. In 1928 he becomes King Zogu.
1939	April: Fascist Italy overruns Albania, incorporating it into the Italian Empire. King Zogu immediately flees the country.
1941	November: Local communist groups formed in the 1930s begin holding secret meetings in occupied Tirana. The Communist Party of Albania is born, electing Enver Hoxha as Head of the Central Committee.
1942	September: The National Liberation Movement is formed to free Albania from occupying forces.
1943	September: Nazi Germany replaces the capitulating Italians. National Liberation Army uprisings increase.
1944	Democratic Government of Albania formed in liberated Berati. Following the liberation of Shkodra and Tirana, the new government enters the capital, finally securing Albania's independence.
1945	December: Democratic Front (National Liberation Front) wins first general election.
1946	January: People's Republic of Albania formed; banks, mines and trades are nationalized.
1948	End of four-year alignment with Tito's Yugoslavia. Influence of Soviet Russia begins.
1957	University of Tirana founded.
1961	End of aid from and diplomatic relations with the Soviet Union as Albania accuses the Soviets of 'revisionism'—departing from Marxist-Leninist doctrine. Alignment with the People's Republic of China.
1967	Albania becomes an atheist state; all religious institutions closed.
1976	Change of constitution. The official name of the country becomes the People's Socialist Republic of Albania.
1978	Break with China; beginning of Albania's isolationism.

1981	'Suicide' of Mehmet Shehu, former Prime Minister accused of plotting to assassinate Enver Hoxha.
1982	In a major reshuffle, Ramiz Alia becomes nominal Head of State.
1985	Enver Hoxha dies of diabetes, sclerosis and Parkinson's disease. Ramiz Alia assumes position as First Secretary of the Central Committee of the Party of Labour of Albania.
1989-90	Seemingly unshaken by the collapse of communism in Eastern Europe, Albania remains the 'last domino'.
1991	The domino falls. A multi-party system is established in March. The Communists win the first elections, but a strike and street demonstrations force the cabinet to resign. In June the Communist Party of Labour is renamed the Socialist Party. The year is marked by unrest, destruction of public property and looting of museums.
1992	The Democrats win a landslide victory in the March elections, capturing 92 of the 140 seats in parliament. Sali Berisha, a doctor from the northern district Tropoja, is elected president.
1993	Albania's economy chalks up the fastest growth rate (GDP up 11%) on the Continent as it begins to recover from the collapse of the communist system. Some 900 small and medium-sized enterprises are privatized, with preference given to former owners, former political prisoners and employees.
1994	Criticism is levelled at the Berisha government for its tight rein on the press and continued high unemployment; three cabinet shake-ups occur within a six-month period. Relations with Greece are severely strained, resulting in several border incidents. Albania calls international attention to the plight of Kosova Albanians as Serbia pursues its policy of 'ethnic cleansing'.

It says 'Please don't spit on the ground'. [I was sure it was a memorial to someone killed in riots. LW]

Chapter Two

Planning and Preparations

Tour operators
International
Regent Holidays, 15 John Street, Bristol BS1 2HR, England. Tel: 0117 921 1711; fax: 0117 925 4866. Flights, individual travel and group tours.
Exodus, 9 Weir Road, London SW12 0LT, England. Tel: 0181 675 5550. Trekking groups.
Skanderbeg Reisen, Wittener Strasse 71, 44789 Bochum, Germany. Tel: 0234 308686; fax: 0234 308505.
Hauser Exkursionen international, Marienstrasse 17, 80331 Munich, Germany. Tel: 089 2350060; fax: 089 2913714.
Antonia Young, c/o Research Unit in South East European Studies, Bradford University, Bradford, West Yorkshire BD7 1DP, England; or, c/o Sociology-Anthropology Dept, Colgate University, Hamilton, NY 13346, USA. Contact for information on academically oriented travel in northern Albania.

In Albania
Travel agencies within Albania are opening at a great rate. The largest and most experienced is Albturist, still state run but in the process of being privatized. Some established agencies include:

Albania Travel & Tours, Rr Durrësit 102. Tel: 042 32983; fax: 33981.
Albturist, Shëtitorja Dëshmorët e Kombit (in the Dajti Hotel). Tel: 042 34572; fax: 34359.

A note about addresses
Street addresses are not very useful in Albania, as some street names have been changed. Streets are not regularly signposted and most buildings do not show numbers. Spelling may vary startlingly on street signs. Rather than name a street, people give vague directions—'behind the theatre', 'across from the maternity hospital'. Even taxi drivers prefer references to landmarks.

Atlas Tirana, Rr Dedë Gjon Luli, 168/8. Tel: 042 23141; fax: 32229.
Auron Expeditions, Rr Bajram Curri N-408, Tirana, Albania. Tel/fax: +355 42 33050. Nature and cultural tours for individuals and groups.
Skanderbeg Travel, Rr Durrësit 5/11. Tel/fax: 042 23946.
Tirana Travel & Tours, Rr Kongresi i Lushnjës 2. Tel/fax: 042 33519.

Other organizations

The Albania Society, c/o 7 Nelson Road, London SW19 1HS, England. Publishes a journal three times a year entitled *Albanian Life*.
Anglo-Albanian Association, Hon Secretary-Treasurer Denys Salt, Flat 6, 38 Holland Park, London W11 3RP, England. Tel: 0171 727 0287. The organization was founded in 1912 to support Albania in its attempt to break away from Turkey. During the Communist era it assisted exiles; today it is branching out into cultural activities.
Friends of Albania, PO Box 155, Taunton, Somerset TA2 8YW, England. Publishers of a quarterly journal and an information service to subscribers only. An sae should accompany enquiries.
Albania Report, Jack Shulman, PO Box 912, New York, NY 10008, USA. Although publication of the report has ceased, current books about Albania can be ordered from this address.
Deutsch-Albanische Freundschaftsgesellschaft eV (German-Albanian Friendship Society), Bilser Strasse 9, 22297 Hamburg, Germany. Tel/fax: 040 5111320. The group publishes a quarterly magazine, *Albanische Hefte*.

Overseas embassies and consulates

UK: British Embassy, Rr Vaso Pasha 7/1. Tel/fax: 042 34973/4/5. The embassy may move at the end of 1996.
USA: Embassy of the United States of America, Rr Elbasanit 103, Tirana. Tel: 042 32875 or 33520. Fax: 32222.

Embassy of the Republic of Albania

UK: 38 Grosvenor Gardens, London SW1W OEB. Tel: 0171 730 5709; fax: 0171 730 5747.
USA: The Investment Building, 1511 K Street NW, Suite 1010, Washington, DC 20005 USA. Tel: 202 223 8187; fax: 202 628 7342.

Passports and visas

Visas are issued at the border to holders of valid British (and European Union), US and Canadian passports. Photographs are not required for these visas. Visa fee varies between US$5 (£3.25) and $25 (£16) according to country of citizenship. A tax of $10 (£6.50) is collected upon departure from the airport.

   Sometimes, but not always, passports must be handed in at hotels.

Customs and immigration

Formalities are simple and relatively fast. Only spot checks of luggage are made. Special export permits are required for precious metals, antique coins and scrolls, antiques, books and works of art that form part of the national culture and heritage. The import and export of Albanian currency is prohibited.

Personal safety

Travellers should use the same 'street-wise' precautions in Albania that are necessary when travelling anywhere in the world. Don't wear expensive jewellery, don't flash large rolls of cash and be especially careful if you attempt to change money on the black market—do so in the daytime in a busy place, check each bill for authenticity and count the money to make sure the amount is correct.

It is a good idea to keep money in several different compartments of a handbag or in various pockets of clothing, preferably using inside jacket pockets with zips—hip pockets are good targets for thieves. The popular 'belly bags' are recommended for holding money for shopping, meals and other immediate needs; plenty of money belts, shoulder holsters and other means of stashing cash are available in travel shops. Keep money separate from credit cards and important documents such as passports and driving licences.

Streetlighting is inadequate in most places in Albania, electricity is subject to frequent failure and sidewalks and streets are full of holes; therefore a powerful flashlight is necessary for walking at night even in the centre of town. As everywhere, avoid dark, lonely streets. Know where you are going before you start out and write down directions if necessary.

Anyone planning to travel away from the major cities would be well advised to have an Albanian guide or friend along; this applies especially to women. Language is a major problem for travellers in some of the farther reaches of the country, and the poverty that still prevails sometimes makes foreigners travelling alone or in small groups a tempting target for theft or robbery. Although most Albanians are honest, friendly and helpful, there is a criminal element here as in the rest of the world.

Health and immunization

Immunization is not required, but the traveller should consult a doctor for current advice, especially considering the cholera outbreak in 1994. Tetanus, typhoid and hepatitis A immunization—and rabies protection for those planning to hike in the mountains—are suggested. Useful information can be provided by the Medical Advisory Service for Travellers Abroad (MASTA); application forms are available at Boots Pharmacies or by phoning 0171 631 4408 in Great Britain. A list of English-speaking physicians in more than 140 countries (Albania may be included in the near future) is available from the International Association of Medical Assistance for Travellers (IAMAT), Dept TH, 736 Center Street, Lewiston, NY 14092, USA. Tel: 716 754 4883.

Medicine is in short supply in Albania, so bring ample dosages of any you anticipate needing. Medical care is free to visitors in emergency situations; however, services such as hospitalization and medical consultations must be paid for unless a reciprocal health agreement exists with the visitor's country. There is no such agreement as yet with the UK or the US; travel health and accident insurance including coverage for emergency evacuation should be purchased before leaving home.

Medical facilities are extremely basic. Syringes and needles are reused so you may wish to bring disposable syringes and needles and a packet of disposable rubber gloves in case of emergency (please donate them to a hospital when you leave).

Currency

The unit of currency is the lek (plural lekë), divided into 100 qindarka. Notes are in denominations of 1, 3, 5, 10, 50, 100, 200, 500 and 1,000 lekë. Coins are extremely rare but may be found in 1 and 2 lekë and 5, 10, 20 and 50 qindarka. Three different types of 500 lek bills were in circulation at press time. Counterfeit 500 and 1,000 lek notes have recently appeared. If a note is genuine, a line can be seen when holding it to the light. Bills of 100 lekë and smaller are often frazzled but accepted.

Plans are being made to mint 1, 2, 5, 10, 20 and 50 lek coins to replace the 1, 3, 5, and 50 lek notes.

Many Albanians still speak in terms of 'old lekë' and shops may even mark their prices according to the old value. To change 'old' to 'new' lekë, drop the last zero.

Black-market money dealers congregate at the back side of Skënderbeg Square in Tirana and near the exchange offices beside the buses in Shkodra; those around the hotels usually give a lower rate. Visitors should be aware that the black market is officially illegal, even though it is quite open and is regularly policed for counterfeit bills.

The US dollar is the currency of choice for many Albanians, although its value dropped sharply against the lek in 1994. The convertible currencies most widely accepted in addition to the dollar are the German mark, the Swiss franc, the Italian lira and the Greek drachma. Many black-market dealers will not change British pounds, though pounds can be changed at banks. Shops and street vendors often quote prices in dollars, though they are marked in lekë. Some will accept either lekë or convertible currencies, others accept lekë only, and a few want only convertible currencies. It is advisable to bring small denomination bills, in good condition but not brand new, and not to change too much money at one time.

Only a handful of businesses accept credit cards, Eurocheques or travellers cheques. American Express is located on Rr Durrësit and provides a full range of services including emergency cash for card holders. Clients issued travellers cheques here are advised to cash them at the Savings Bank; they are issued in dollars and can be cashed in dollars. Cash in Western currency is issued against EuroCard, MasterCard and Eurocheques at the Banka e Kursimeve, Rr Skënderbeg (Embassy Row).

Banking hours are Monday-Friday 8.00-14.00.

What to bring

Useful items include a powerful flashlight and a supply of batteries, a universal sink plug, an alarm clock, an international electric plug adaptor (electricity is 220V AC, plugs take round Continental poles), toilet paper, moist tissues, monthly hygiene necessities, a basic first-aid kit including treatment for stomach upsets, mosquito repellent, sunscreen, sunglasses and film. It is also useful to have a supply of small souvenirs for people you may visit (suggestions: handcream or perfume for women, flashlights or basic household tool-kits for men, T-shirts, sweatshirts or small reflectors to attach to clothing for children; pocket calculators and English language textbooks; aspirin, antibiotic cream for cuts and scrapes, cough drops, vitamins).

Clothing

Life is informal; ties are not required for men but are becoming more common in business circles. Wear comfortable clothing—especially sturdy shoes—for sightseeing. There is almost no air conditioning although many buildings have ceiling fans, so dress coolly in summer (linen is recommended). A sunhat is indispensable; a sweater or jacket may be needed in the evenings, especially in the mountains. In winter, bring watertight boots and other rain gear, as well as a coat and clothing that can be layered; a warm robe and slippers will be welcome in unheated rooms. Women will find skirts more practical than trousers in view of the toilet situation.

The latest Western garb, including miniskirts and leggings, is popular with young Albanians. However, in the more conservative reaches of the country people still frown upon women in shorts or other revealing clothes. Nudist bathing has not yet been accepted in Albania.

MASTER LIST

Loo roll	List of numbers	universal sink plug
clothes (see clothes list)	Towel	Pens
	Guidebooks	Pencils
Film: slide	Passports	Eraser
: print	Tickets	Drawing books
Pentax	travel guff	quids:
" lens	wallet	sterling?
" flash	chequebook	dollars?
camera bag	chequecards	T'cheques?
Pentax zoom	creditcards	gifts: Brit stamps?
camera cleaning stuff	anti-mosquito stuff?	p'cards?
Addresses list	Imodium	soap?
Washing stuff etc (see clothes list)	Stugeron?	Books
	Water Tablets?	Travelwash?
alarm clock	needle/thread	Plasters
sunspecs	Bite cream	other 1st Aid stuff
Swiss Army Knife	Torch	Sun tan stuff?
Spare batteries for cameras etc	Throat lozenges	Fags
Brolly	Plastic straws	Lighter
Hardware list	This list	Sun hats?
		Nose squirter

Luggage

Porters are available in some hotels, but it is best to travel light. Hotel lifts seldom function, so you may have to carry your suitcase up several flights of stairs

Chapter Three

In Albania

Customs and manners

In Albania, a shake of the head means *yes* and a nod means *no*. Sometimes in negation the Albanians perform a curious rocking of their heads, clicking their tongues and wagging their forefingers at the same time.

It is polite to remove your shoes when you enter an Albanian home, although the hosts usually insist that guests keep them on. Shoes must always be removed when entering a mosque.

Shake hands all around both as greeting and goodbye. If you shake hands outside someone's home, the host and hostess will repeat the procedure inside because guests are traditionally greeted inside the home.

Albanians never go visiting empty handed. Usually they take fruit or cookies as a hostess gift. If you want to plan ahead and bring souvenirs from home, see suggestions under *What to bring* (page 15). It is also acceptable for guests to leave 100-200 lekë tucked under a coffee cup.

Many museums are now closed, having either been plundered during the 1991 chaos or their buildings reclaimed by former owners and their exhibits stored for safekeeping. Those that still function have varied opening hours. It is not unusual for the ticket fee to be collected as you leave. Little written material is available about the exhibits but guides are on hand and many of them speak English. References to dates in most cases remain *para erës sone* (before our era) instead of BC.

Accommodation

Arrangements can be made through travel agencies, directly with a hotel or with a private person for a room in a home. Telephoning ahead to a hotel outside the major cities can be difficult; a telegram may be more effective. Hotel space in Tirana and on the coast is limited and may be booked up, especially in summer. A few private hotels have already opened; some state hotels are in the process of privatization. In Tirana, the Hotel Tirana is being renovated and is scheduled to reopen in late 1995; a four-star hotel is under construction by an Austrian firm, and a five-star hotel is being built by Kuwait.

While some hotels are quite comfortable, most rooms are simply furnished. Twin beds are the rule, and single rooms are limited. Heat often is not available in winter and the hot water heater may function only in one room in a hotel, with the key being passed around to those who wish to shower. Water usually comes on for about an hour once or twice a day. Some rooms have private bath and toilet, and sometimes a telephone, radio and television (though they may not work).

A scheme is being organized to help individual Albanians upgrade their homes as bed and breakfast accommodation. At present, outside Tirana toilets are usually a porcelain square with two footprints and a hole in the floor, without running water and often outdoors. Showers may be non-existent, though some families rig an effective shower by means of a wooden platform that fits over the toilet square. Heating is usually limited to the living room, but quilts and blankets are in good supply and beds are comfortable. Private accommodation can be arranged through some travel agencies.

Hotels

Hotel prices in Albania are decreasing. However, as facilities improve and tourism increases, prices may well rise again. At present a room costs the equivalent of US$8-$45 (£5-£29) per person per night, depending on the location and facilities.

Bajram Curri
Shkëlzen Hotel, above the sports stadium.

Berati
Tomori, city centre, tel: Tirana Central 042 10 and ask for ext. 462 or 602.

Durrësi
Adriatik, at the beach, tel: 052 23051; fax: 23612.
Apollonia, at the beach (rather run down), tel: 052 23051; fax: 23612.
Durrësi, at the beach (rather run down), tel: 052 23051; fax: 23612.
Pameba, new hotel, city centre, tel/fax: 052 24149.

Elbasani
Skampa, opposite the fortress walls; tel: 0545 2651; fax: 2093.

Gjirokastra
Çajupi, Sheshi Çerçiz Topulli; tel: 0726 3621; fax: 0726 3626.

Korça
Iliria, city centre; tel: 0824 2473; fax: 2855.

Kruja
Skenderbeu, town centre; tel: Tirana Central 042 10 and ask for ext. 467 or 529.

Kukësi
Kukësi, on the promontory above the lake; tel: Tirana Central 042 10 and ask for ext. 699, 251 or 269.

Lezha
Hunting Lodge, about 5km outside town; tel: Tirana Central 042 10 and ask for ext. 483.

Lushnja
Ardenica Inn, in the monastery.

Pogradeci
Guri i Kuq, on the lake front; tel: Tirana Central 042 10 and ask for ext. 269 or 259.

Saranda
Butrinti, on the water front at the edge of town; tel: Tirana Central 042 10 ext. 538 or 417.
House of Relaxation of Saranda, on the water front at the edge of town; tel: Tirana Central 042 10 ext. 448.

Shkodra
Rozafa, city centre; tel: 0224 2354; fax: 3590.
Park Hotel, at the Kafja e Madhe (Grand Cafe), Rr Çlirimi.

Tirana
Arbana, Bd Shqipëria e Re; tel: 042 34549.

Arbëria, Shëtitorja Dëshmorët e Kombit; tel/fax: 042 42813.
Dajti, Shëtitorja Dëshmorët e Kombit; tel: 042 33326; fax: 32012.
Diplomat, Rr Muhamet Gjollesha prane Shkolles Vasil Shanto; tel/fax: 042 42457.
Drini, Rr Seremedin Seid Toptani; tel/fax: 22741.
Europark, Bd Deshmoret e Kombit; tel: 042 35035; fax: 35050.
Tirana, Sheshi Skënderbeg (Skënderbeg Square); tel: 042 34185; fax: 34188.

Vlora

Adriatik, city centre; tel: Tirana Central 042 10 and ask for ext. 2415.
Asim Zeneli, House of Vacations of the Workers, on a hill above the beach.
Llogara Tourist Camp (located just off the highway at Llogara Pass, a tourist village of 11 furnished cabins and a restaurant); tel: Tirana Central 042 10 and ask for Vlora ext. 2181.

There was a young fellow from Durres
Whose stomach was giving him wurres:
'Twas his own fault, his meals
Were pies of stewed eels,
Punctuated by vindaloo curres.....

Restaurants

New restaurants, cafés and snack bars spring up daily. It would be impossible to present even a fair survey, so only a few are listed here— with the advice to choose a restaurant not from its façade but by going inside and taking a look around. Sometimes you will be allowed a peek into the kitchen. If you stay in a private home, you may have meals there.

The price of food seems cheap to Westerners but it is expensive for Albanians. A meal with wine in a tourist-oriented restaurant costs a minimum of 700 lekë per person, while a 'local' restaurant might charge 200 lekë for the same meal. (Keep in mind that the monthly salary in Albania is about 3,000 lekë.) Prices are rising and those quoted are given only as a thumbnail guide.

Bajram Curri
Logu, on the main street.
Jezerca, at the foot of steps off the main street.

Himara
Goro, on the sea front.

Kruja
Tourist restaurant, on the fortress grounds.

Pogradeci
Poradeci, Rr Naim Frashëri.

Shkodra
Bar Antik, in the Turkish baths, Rr Banja e Vogel.

Tirana
Agoli, Rr Durrësit.
Alba, Rr Durrësit.
Arilda, Rr Bajram Curri 178; tel/fax: 042 32207.
Bemano, Rr Emin Duraku 8; tel/fax: 042 42859.
Berlini (German), Rr Vaso Pasha 7 (corner Pjëter Bogdani); tel/fax: 042 33337.
Chez Laurent, (French), Rr Kavajës 17; tel: 042 42529.
China, Sheshi Mustafa Ataturk.
Güden (Turkish) Rr Durrësit; tel: 042 32096.
Kalaja, Rr Myslym Shyri 11; tel: 042 42662.
L'Aigle Noir (French), Vildan Luarasi 24.
La Perla (Italian), Rr Konstandin Kristoforidhi 84; tel: 042 42951; fax: 32516.
Lausanne, Rr Vaso Pasha 5.
Made in Italy, Rr Budi 61.
1 Maji, Rr Punëtoret e Rilindjes; tel/fax: 042 33337.
Mondial, Rr Muhamet Gjollesha; tel: 042 27322.
Petrela (Albanian specialities), Rr Hamit Shijaku 26 (just off Dëshmorët e Kombit); tel: 042 42516.
Pelikani, Rr Barrikadave 3.
Schatzi (Austrian), Bd Zhan d'Ark.
Shang Hai (Chinese), Rr Dëshmorët, E 4 Shkurtit Pall 16.
Shiponja e Zezë, Rr Vildan Luarasi 24.
Tafaj, Rr Mine Peza.
Union (Turkish), Rr Durrësit.

Food and drink

Albanian dishes show a definite Turkish and Balkan influence; try the regional specialities at every opportunity.

The thimbleful of coffee that Edith Durham complained of in 1908 is still the rule of the day. Usually it is Turkish, although some new cafés serve only *espresso* and *capuccino.* Where Turkish is served, you will be asked how much sugar you want—*pak* is 'a little' and *shumë* is 'a lot'. A glass of plain water usually is served with coffee.

Albanian tea is very good. A few restaurants serve it and it is available in the markets—a yellow-green dried plant. To brew, break up one or two of the whole stems with leaves and flowerets, bring to the boil and steep a few minutes to reach the desired strength. A refreshing drink in Kukësi, *thana,* is made from the cornel berry; a similar one in Tropoja, *boronica,* is made from the bilberry. Kruja is known for *boza,* a thick drink made from cornmeal, sugar and water that is said to lower the blood pressure and that is actually quite tasty when served chilled.

Breakfast may or may not materialize. Even in hotels, you may have to go in search of it unless you are with a group. It consists of some or all of the following: bread, butter, cheese, honey, jam, eggs, yogurt (Albanian yogurt, *kos,* is very good). However, in non-tourist restaurants it is more usual to eat *pilaf, fricassee* or *biftek* for breakfast.

Lunch is the big meal of the day, served 13.00-15.00. It usually starts with soup and includes salads, vegetables and meat. Dessert may not be served but there are almost always oranges, apples and nuts. Dinner is a smaller version of lunch and is served from about 20.30 to as late as 22.00.

Albanian cooks have a heavy hand with both sugar and salt. For a Muslim country, pork appears surprisingly often and lamb surprisingly seldom; beef is on all menus. Goat should be eaten with caution, if at all; it has a well-deserved reputation for causing Hoxha's Revenge in foreigners. Chicken may be domestic or imported. Fish is expensive, but on the coast and at Lake Ohrid it is fresh and tasty. Leeks, spinach, okra, aubergines, carrots, onions, lettuce, tomatoes, cucumbers and olives appear often on home menus, but any vegetable other than a tomato, cucumber and onion salad and sometimes grilled pepper is rare in a restaurant, though fried potatoes seldom fail to appear. *Pilaf,* a rice and cheese dish, is available throughout the country. Spaghetti without sauce (one seldom sees sauces of any kind) is served occasionally. *Salc kosi,* a thick yogurt and garlic dressing similar to Greek *tsatsiki,* often accompanies meals. White bread made from imported flour is most common now, though the brown bread made of Albanian flour is tastier. Cornbread is a speciality of Kruja.

Kruja is also a good place to try *fërgëse,* a hot pot made of *gjizë* (a cross between sour cream and cottage cheese), eggs, liver, tomatoes and red pepper. *Tavë kosi* or *tavë Elbasani* is a savoury mutton and yogurt dish.

Byrek, layers of pastry filled with any number of things—cheese, meat, pumpkin or leeks—can be bought at street stands. In Korça, it is called *lakror* and is made with a very thin pastry. The best Turkish delight, *llokume,* is made in Pogradeci; it is full of nuts for extra flavour. Pogradeci is also the place to eat *koran,* a type of trout unique to Lake Ohrid.

Glina bottled water is not so readily available as in the past, but there are new brands of Albanian sparkling water including Joe's, Jultina and Cola 1, as well as Italian water. However, bottled water is not available everywhere. Pitchers of plain ice water are often placed on the table in restaurants. Outside the major towns, the water comes directly from wells or rivers. When travelling into the interior, take bottled water or use purification tablets.

Soft drinks (Greek and American brands) and most beer (Macedonian, French, Belgian and German brands) are imported, though Albanian beer (unnamed and unlabelled) can be found. Coca-Cola opened a bottling plant in Tirana in 1994.

Raki, a clear brandy usually distilled from grapes after they have been pressed for wine, is the traditional drink. If you order raki at meal time, you'll probably get a tumbler full. Raki comes in varying strengths (that from Leskoviku is smoothest) and is a good digestive.

Albanian Skënderbeg brandy is quite good; Përmeti and Korça have the reputation for producing the best brandy. Many foreign whiskies and liqueurs are available but are relatively expensive.

Italian, Hungarian, Bulgarian and Albanian wine is plentiful. The Albanian red is definitely better than the white; red is sometimes served chilled and drunk with fish.

Entertainment
Major towns have theatres, movie houses (though most movies now are pornographic films from Greece), night clubs and discos. Ask for information at your hotel. Here are some suggestions for Tirana:

Theatre *Teatri Kombëtar*, Shëtitorja Dëshmorët e Kombit; tel: 042 22395 or 23022.
Puppet Theatre *Teatri i Kukullave*, Sheshi Skënderbeg; tel: 042 22446.

There was a young man from Tiranë
Who kept a quite evil piranhë:
To keep it calm he would holler
Songs from Leiber and Stoller,
Marie Lloyd, and 'Carmina Buranë'.......

Opera and Ballet *Teatri i Operas, Beletit dhe i Ansamblit,* Sheshi Skënderbeg (Palace of Culture); tel: 042 25856; fax: 27495.
Folk Music *Te Këngëve dhe Valleve Popullore,* Sheshi Skënderbeg (Palace of Culture); tel: 042 26747.
Circus *Cirku,* Shëtitorja Dëshmorët e Kombit; tel: 042 27330.
Variety Theatre *Teatri i Estradës,* Shëtitorja Dëshmorët e Kombit; tel: 042 23476.
Discos *Albania,* Rr Bajram Curri; *Lux,* Sheshi Skënderbeg (behind the Palace of Culture); *Cafe 'des Artistes,* Sheshi Skënderbeg (terrace of the Palace of Culture); *Rilindja,* Rr Bajram Curri; tel: 042 32134; *Heavy Metal,* Rr Luigj Gurakuqi.
Night clubs In the major hotels. Requests are played in clubs and restaurants that have live music, usually a mix of modern and traditional songs. A cover charge for live music may be added to bills at restaurants.

Sports

Sports facilities for tourists are still in the planning stage. The swimming season runs from the end of May until mid-October. Most beaches are open to the public, although a 'private beach' with restaurant and parking has opened between Durrësi and Golem. Divers, surfers and windsurfers should bring their own gear. Rowing boats can be rented privately at Durrësi beach; there is a tennis court at the Adriatik Hotel there. Horseback riding may be developed in the future. Travel agencies can book guides for mountain trekking; independent guides are also available.

Radio and television

Radio/Televizioni Shqiptar—TVSH (Albanian Radio-Television) is state run. It transmits for 12 hours a day on one channel, though it hopes to increase air time to 16 hours and to add a second channel for entertainment. TVSH broadcasts brief news in English, French and German each day at 13.30 and shows many American films and soap operas, as well as Italian films, with Albanian subtitles. TVSH broadcasts via satellite daily 18.30-20.30 for the diaspora, especially for Kosova Albanians.

Three Italian television channels (RAI 1, 2, 3) can be picked up and in some places Greek and Turkish programmes can be received. Satellite dishes (and there are many) pick up a large range of programmes.

Tirana has installed its own satellite station receiving CNN, France 2, NBC Super Channel and Italia 1, in addition to the RAI stations. Durrësi is planning to install its own satellite station, as well.

Both the BBC World Service and the Voice of America broadcast to Albania. In early 1994, the BBC's medium-wave sender was shut down by the Albanian government, probably because the BBC provided coverage of the opposition as well as the Democrats. The BBC can be picked up on shortwave and FM.

Radio Tirana International has powerful transmitters, thanks to Enver Hoxha, to broadcast shortwave worldwide; it broadcasts in English, French, Spanish, German, Italian, Serbo-Croatian, Greek and Turkish. For current shortwave broadcast schedules, see the *World Radio TV Handbook* or contact Radio Tirana International, Rr Lekë Dukagjini, Tirana. Tel 042 22481; fax: 23775.

Telephoning

Private telephones are rare in Albania but the network is nevertheless overloaded. Telephoning from a hotel costs about three times as much as phoning from the public telephone offices in Tirana. Two offices with direct-dial phones have been set up by Italian Telecom in truck beds in Skënderbeg and Sulejman Pasha Squares. Telecomi Shqiptar (Albanian Telecom) has eight direct-dial phones as well as telefax on Shëtitorja Dëshmorët e Kombit a couple of blocks behind the Hotel Tirana (look for the queues). Phone calls can be put through by switchboard operators at local post offices (PTT).

To telephone *from* most locations within the country, phone the Telephone Central in Tirana 042 10 and ask the operator to place the call. To call *to* many locations outside Tirana, call the local PTT and ask for the individual extension.

To phone internationally *from* Albania where direct-dial is available, first dial 00, then the code of the country you are calling, then the city prefix and individual number.

To telephone *to* Albania, use the country code 355. The city prefixes are Tirana 042, Elbasani 0545, Durrësi 052, Korça 0824, Shkodra 0224, Gjirokastra 0726, Vlora 063. Drop the 0 when calling from outside the country.

Post

The main post office in Tirana is located one block off Skënderbeg Square behind the bank. Post offices in other cities are centrally located.

They are open 24 hours in major cities.

When using the post office, be sure to get in the queue for mailing letters, not for other transactions. Stamps may be available at hotel desks. Letters take two to eight weeks to and from Albania. Letters and packages sometimes do not arrive intact, but EMS is reliable.

Transportation

If you travel on a group tour, you will be on board a comfortable bus unless you have chosen a mountain trek.

It is now possible to travel on your own in Albania, and this gives you a choice of transportation. If you really want to explore, you will need a car, either your own or (preferably) rented, with or without a driver. To get deep into the countryside, a four-wheel-drive vehicle is needed. A road toll of US$1 (64p) per day is collected upon departure from persons bringing their own cars. Note that only liability insurance (not theft or collision) is currently applicable in Albania.

Driving in Albania is an adventure. Despite short distances, travel is time consuming because of poor road conditions. Of the 18,000km of roads in the country, less than half are considered main arteries. All are in need of repair. (The first construction work has begun on a 32km stretch between Tirana and Durrësi in an Albanian-Italian joint venture.) Traffic is often heavy; drivers are generally inexperienced. Pedestrians, bicycles, donkeys, horse carts, sheep and goats crowd the roads.

One of the busiest roads follows the ancient east-west Via Egnatia across the country from Durrësi. Its southern branch starts at Fieri and the two branches converge at Rrogozhina. In ancient times, it was an important link between Rome and Constantinople; today it is a major artery to Macedonia, Bulgaria and Turkey.

Police roadblocks are frequent; be sure to have a current international driving licence and a valid green card, showing that you have liability insurance applicable in Albania. Both diesel and regular fuel—*not* unleaded—are available at state-owned and private stations, as well as

on the black market. Diesel is considerably cheaper than petrol. Stations are at wide intervals, so carry *at least* 10 litres of fuel along in a canister. Some problems with watered fuel have been reported, so use caution when buying. The API brand, an Albanian-Italian joint venture, is reliable.

Fast driving would not be advisable even if it were possible. Roads are narrow, crooked and rough. Guard rails are lacking in the mountains.

During rainy periods roads become slick and are often flooded. Drivers do not turn on their lights until it is black dark, making dawn and dusk especially hazardous as this is the time when herds of sheep, goats and cows are most often in the roads. Many vehicles have only one functioning light; some drivers keep their high beams on, while others switch their lights off when meeting oncoming traffic. Wagons and bicycles seldom have reflectors, much less lights.

Breakdowns are common, the cars stopping in the roads without hazard lights or warning triangles, though around the vehicles the drivers lay out a ring of stones extending about a foot farther into the road, thereby increasing the hazard instead of providing warning.

People often stop in the road simply to chat. Drivers may use signal lights when they have no intention of turning and not signal when they do turn or stop. If they do signal, it may be for the direction opposite to the one they actually turn.

Roundabouts are as popular in Albania as they are in the UK; right of way seems to belong to whoever takes it.

Direction signs to major towns are most plentiful along the west coast but may be lacking completely to villages. Streets in the centre of towns may be closed to vehicles 17.00-22.00 for the *passeggiata*. One-way streets may be poorly marked.

In spite of this, by using caution driving can be one of the most rewarding ways of seeing the country because of the places that can be reached only by car (sometimes only with a four-wheel drive) or by a very long hike.

'Aged red wine'

Guarded parking is recommended; it costs about 100-300 lekë per day. In addition to car parks at the Hotels Dajti, Diplomat and Arbëria, here are some others in Tirana: Bemano, Rr Emin Duraku 8, tel: 042 4285; Kalaja, Rr Myslym Shyri; Kozeli, Rr Muhamet Gjollesha, tel: 042 22393; Shoqeria "KS-Tirana", Rr Kavajës; Larje, Rr Irfan Tomini.

Garages in Tirana include the following: Bua, Rr Muhamet Gjollesha (at the Dinamo Sports Stadium); Dajti, Rr Luigj Gurakuqi; Ferlut, Rr Muhamet Gjollesha; Gan/Has, Rr Mine Peza 78; Arani, Rr Bajram Curri; Lavanteri Auto, Rr Elbasanit.

Border crossings: *With Yugoslavia*—Hani i Hotit/Podgorica, Qafa e Prushit/Kosova, Morina/Prizrën. *With Macedonia*—Bllata/Diber, Qafa e Thana/Struga, Tushemishti/Ohrid, Gorica/Resnja. *With Greece*— Kapshtica/Florina, Kakavija/Ioanina, Konispoli/Sagiada, Pera/ Melissopetra.

Car rental

Chauffeured cars are available through travel agencies at a minimum cost of US$40 (£25) per day plus 40 cents (25p) per km (with prices increasing rapidly). Kompas Hertz offers self-drive and chauffeur-driven cars at its Rinas Airport office. Reservations can be made through the Hertz international reservation system.

Taxis (*Taksi*)

Taxis can be found near hotels and in Tirana on Skënderbeg Square. Some taxis bear the yellow-and-black *taksi* or *taxi* sign atop the cars. They don't have meters. Shared taxis (minivans holding up to 10 passengers) travel regularly between neighbouring cities. They cost more than buses but are considerably cheaper than normal taxis. Many private individuals are willing to drive for a fee. Negotiation is the most common way of establishing the fare. Always agree on the price first, *including* expected waiting time. Taxis may be ordered from Albtransport, tel: 042 23026.

Buses

Urban buses are state-run with fixed fares. Tirana has six routes and is planning to add a seventh; funding has been set aside to buy 21 new buses.

An excellent long-distance bus network, now private, operates in Albania. Fares on those buses are not fixed but a maximum is set so that the price remains affordable. Tickets are sold on board the bus once it gets under way. (Note: I travelled by bus from Tirana to Shkodra, more than 100km, with an Albanian friend for the equivalent of US$1 (64p). He said that the price could have been US$10 (£6.45) if I had travelled alone as a foreigner.)

In Tirana, buses depart from the Dinamo Stadium on Rr Gjin Shpata for Elbasani, Fieri, Gramshi, Berati, Librazhd, Vlora, Pogradeci, Tepelena, Korça, Gjirokastra, Erseka, Saranda, Bilisht, Përmeti and Lushnja. Buses depart from the Asllan Rusi Sports Palace on Rr Durrësit for Bajram Curri, Puka, Shkodra, Rrësheni, Burreli, Peshkopia, Lezha and Kukësi. Buses for Durrësi depart from beside the railway station.

Some buses have scheduled departures, others go when the bus fills up. The buses themselves vary considerably in age and degree of decrepitude, most having been bought secondhand in Greece or Italy. The destination is given on a hand-lettered sign propped in the right front windscreen. There are no official timetables.

An international bus service connects Tirana with Sofia, Bulgaria (from Pastiçeri Flora); Athens, Greece (from Sulejman Pasha Square); Istanbul, Turkey (from Pastiçeri Flora), and several towns in Macedonia (near Hotel Tirana). The bus agents can be found in kiosks on the streets around Skënderbeg and Sulejman Pasha Squares.

Road distances from Tirana
Figures in brackets () indicate approximate driving time in hours.

Berati	(3)	122	Lushnja	(1¾)	83
Durrësi	(1)	39	Përmeti	(5)	217
Elbasani	(1½)	54	Peshkopia	(4)	182
Fieri	(2½)	113	Pogradeci	(3)	140
Gjirokastra	(6)	232	Puka	(5)	146
Korça	(4)	181	Saranda	(8)	284
Kruja	(¾)	32	Shkodra	(2½)	116
Kukësi	(7)	208	Tepelena	(5)	200
Lezha	(1½)	69	Vlora	(3)	147

Trains
Albania has about 700km of railways with both passenger and freight service. The engines are diesel. The carriages are in good condition, having been brought from Italy to replace those that were destroyed (pieces were carted away for fuel) in 1991. Daily connections are as follows:

Tirana-Elbasani-Pogradeci via Durrësi
Tirana-Durrësi
Tirana-Fieri-Vlora
Tirana-Fieri-Ballshi
Tirana-Shkodra
Ballshi-Fieri
Ballshi-Vlora

There is a timetable posted on the wall of the railway station in Tirana.

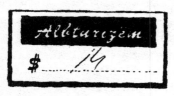

Airlines

Rinas Airport is 24km from Tirana; a bus operates between the city and the airport at flight times only. At press time, the taxi fare to Tirana was US$15-20 (£9.75-£13) (driving time about 30 minutes). The airport has a duty free shop, which accepts most foreign currencies.

Airlines serving Albania include Adria Airways (Slovenian), Alitalia, Austrian Airlines, Hemus (Bulgarian), Lufthansa (German), with four flights a week, Malev Hungarian Airlines, Olympic (Greek) and Swissair.

There are no inland flights. Plans are being made to convert military airports and landing strips to civilian use in Gjirokastra, Korça, Peshkopia, Saranda and Vlora.

Ferries

Albania's main ports are Durrësi, Vlora and Saranda. Ferry connections (times approximate, provided by the ferry companies) include Durrësi-Bari (Italy) 9 hrs; Durrësi-Trieste (Italy) 23 hrs; Durrësi-Ancona (Italy) 20 hours; Durrësi-Kopor (Slovenia) 22 hrs; Vlora-Bari (Italy) 9½ hrs; Vlora-Brindisi (Italy) 8 hrs; Vlora-Otranto (Italy) 8 hrs; Saranda-Corfu (Greece) 1½ hrs. A new ferry service is being planned between Durrësi and Vasto (Italy). A passenger service Durrësi-Vlora-Saranda is envisioned for the future.

Hydrofoil

La Vikinga Lines, Rr Durrësit; tel: 042 28417; fax: 27665, runs hydrofoils (no vehicles) Durrësi-Bari 3½ hrs. Tel in Italy (+39) 80 523 2429.

Shopping

Shopping hours vary; regular hours are 9.00-12.00 and 16.00-19.00, but sidewalk stands and many shops open earlier and remain open into the evening. Prices are given in lekë; shopkeepers rarely ask for dollars or other convertible currencies.

Souvenir shops in hotels and tourist areas sell carpets, silver filigree, brass Turkish coffee mills, copper, straw-inlaid wooden boxes, costume dolls, embroidered bed and table linens, Albanian flags, wood carvings, traditional music instruments, cassettes of folk music and Albanian wine and brandy. Traditional dress such as wide embroidered belts, knitted socks and entire costumes are excellent souvenirs. Traditional costumes can be made to order by two firms in Tirana: Firma Lleshi, Rr Durrësit, tel/fax: 042 33030. Qëndistari Erebara, Rr Dedë Gjon Luli, corner Rr Durrësit. Traditional dress, cutwork tablecloths, embroidery and crochet are available at Qëndistari Florence Reçi on Rr Kavajës.

The National History Museum on Skënderbeg Square has a good shop for old textiles, copies of ancient pottery, jewellery, books, etc. The art gallery *Salloni i Artit* on Rr Dedë Gjon Luli behind the History Museum carries an excellent selection of works by Albanian painters. A private art gallery, Ti+Ge, Rr Durrësit 144A, has changing exhibitions by young Albanian artists.

Music cassettes are sold on the street and in kiosks. Bookstores and sidewalk stands in the centre of Tirana carry books about Albania in English, French, German and Italian. Not all shops carry all books, so if you don't find the English version in one shop, persevere. Some excellent books on folk dress, music and historic sites are written in Albanian but include synopses in other languages.

Carpets can be purchased directly from the Avakian Carpet Factory in Korça (Rr 1 Maj, open 7.00-14.00 Monday-Saturday), a newly privatized company making high-quality hand-knotted rugs as well as traditional *qilima* (kelims). The state-owned carpet factories in Kavaja and Kukësi have closed, but carpets are made at home.

In Kavaja, they are displayed along the road and in shops on the main street. Hand-loomed Gjirokastra carpets are sometimes available at the Ethnographic Museum, and Kruja carpets are sold in the local bazaar. Many cottage weavers throughout the country sell their own work.

Last-minute shoppers can find a reasonable selection of goods (carpets, Albanian wine, raki and brandy, silver filigree, music cassettes), albeit at higher prices than in town, at the Duty Free Shop in Rinas Airport. At flight times, vendors sell handicrafts in front of the terminal.

Photography
Take plenty of film with you. It is available in Albania, but supplies are limited and you may not find exactly what you want. Visitors are free to photograph what they wish. However, it is polite to ask permission before photographing people. They seldom refuse and usually ask for a copy of the picture.

Time
Albanian time is one hour ahead of Greenwich Mean Time, six hours ahead of New York time. Summer Time (Daylight Saving Time) is in effect from the end of March until the end of September.

People's estimates of the time needed to drive or walk from point to point may be far removed from reality.

Public holidays
1 and 2 January, New Year; 1 May, Labour Day; 28 November, Independence Day and Liberation Day; 25 December, Christmas. Easter and Bairam are movable holidays.

Maps
Maps are available at bookstores, sidewalk stands and hotels. The best road map of Albania is published by Bartholomew. Others include those published by Ravenstein Verlag (Bad Soden, Germany) and Cartographia (Budapest, Hungary). Maps are best purchased before leaving home: all maybe obtained from Stanfords, 12-14 Long Acre, London WC2E 9LP, England; tel: 0171 836 1321.

Tipping and showing appreciation

Tipping either in lekë or convertible currency is appreciated by service personnel. If you are invited to stay in a private home that is not a formal bed and breakfast with set charges, you should give an appropriate sum to the woman of the house when you leave. If you are visiting friends, an item for the house will be appreciated.

Children seldom ask for gum or pens now, though some street children beg for money.

Visitors' books on display in places of interest are there to invite your impressions. Don't hesitate to write in them.

Toilets (*Nevojtore*)

International symbols may denote toilets, but if not, G is women (*Gra*) and B is men (*Burra*). Sit-down toilets are found primarily in hotels, in a few restaurants in major towns and in some homes in major towns. Cleanliness usually leaves a lot to be desired in public toilets.

Laundry

Laundry service is available in some hotels. Give plenty of notice to the service staff if you want laundry done. Dry cleaning is not available. It is a good idea to bring along a small quantity of detergent and do your own washing.

Smoking

The move toward no smoking in public places has not yet caught on in Albania. The few no-smoking signs that do appear say *Ndalohet pirja e duhanit*.

Religious services

Many religious organizations are now represented in Albania. Ask at your hotel for details about when and where services are held.

Holidays for thinking people

EXPERTS IN TRAVEL TO ALBANIA SINCE 1970

- Special air fares to Tirana available from London and Manchester
- Tailor-made itineraries throughout Albania
- Flexible arrangements
- Experienced and knowledgeable staff

15 John Street, Bristol BS1 2HR
Tel: (0117) 921 1711 (24 hrs)
Fax: (0117) 925 4866

Suggested Itineraries

Those who have limited time in Albania may wish to concentrate their sightseeing on specific interests. Here are some suggestions:

Beaches

The most accessible beaches with the better hotels are at **Saranda, Durrësi/Golem** and **Vlora**. Beaches a bit more difficult to reach and with fewer creature-comforts but just as lovely and sometimes less crowded are **Dhërmi, Divjaka** and **Velipoja**. As of this writing, there are no 'foreign-tourist' hotels at the last three; visitors should contact a travel agent for up-to-date advice about accommodation or look for rooms in a private home.

It is to be hoped that free-roaming livestock will be removed from Shëngjini and other beaches, and that pollution problems will be solved.

Hiking

The best Alpine route is **Thethi-Valbona.** A bus runs between Thethi and Shkodra, but be prepared to cover the 36km between Valbona and Bajram Curri (the nearest public transportation) on foot, to hitch a ride or to hire a car. Less accessible but even more beautiful are the **Lura Lakes.** Both of these areas are suitable for campers who bring their own gear, food and water.

Art

Visit **Voskopoja** for the frescos in the Shën Kollit church; **Berati** for the Onufri Museum containing works of Albania's most important medieval artist.

Archaeology

Albania is a treasure trove of Illyrian, Greek and Roman ruins. **Apollonia, Butrinti** and **Durrësi** are the major sites. Visiting some of the other areas requires much time and either long hikes or a four-wheel-drive vehicle. The **Archaeology Museum** in **Tirana** contains finds from throughout the country.

Fortresses

Shkodra, Lezha and **Kruja** have the most interesting fortresses—Shkodra and Kruja restored, Lezha less developed for tourists but beautiful.

Albania's 'Museum Towns'

Gjirokastra and **Berati.** Each forms a cohesive picture of traditional-style houses, well worth the time-consuming journeys to them. Gjirokastra is brown, Berati is white.

Around Lake Ohrid

Those who want to see eastern Albania but demand good hotels can stay on the Macedonian side of the border and make a round tour of Lake Ohrid, covering both Albania and Macedonia. Ohrid town has long been developed for tourism and has excellent facilities.

On Skënderbeg's trail

Kruja and **Lezha** are required visits for history buffs interested in Skënderbeg. Traces of the national hero can be found throughout the country; most accessible from Tirana are the ruins of the small **Petrela** and **Preza** fortresses.

The capital

Tirana, a city of museums, art galleries, restaurants and entertainment, also offers the liveliness of an oriental market.

The Guide
Part 2

Cities and Regions

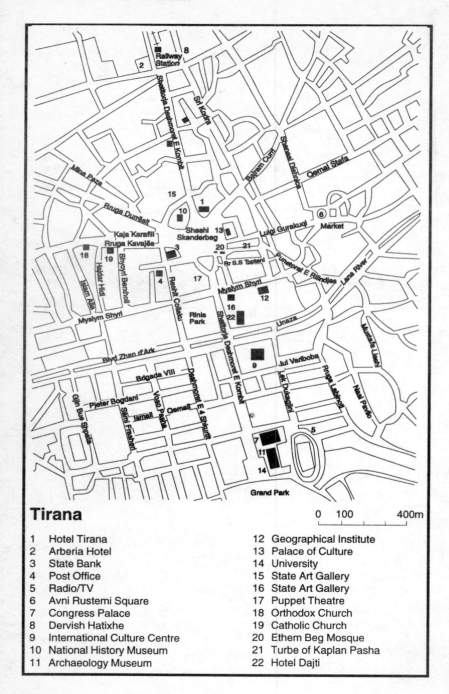

Tirana

0   100   400m

1	Hotel Tirana	12 Geographical Institute
2	Arberia Hotel	13 Palace of Culture
3	State Bank	14 University
4	Post Office	15 State Art Gallery
5	Radio/TV	16 State Art Gallery
6	Avni Rustemi Square	17 Puppet Theatre
7	Congress Palace	18 Orthodox Church
8	Dervish Hatixhe	19 Catholic Church
9	International Culture Centre	20 Ethem Beg Mosque
10	National History Museum	21 Turbe of Kaplan Pasha
11	Archaeology Museum	22 Hotel Dajti

TIRANA

Now that Rinas Airport, 24km from the capital, is served daily by international flights, most British and US tourists will arrive in Albania via Tirana. While it is not the most picturesque city in Albania, it is one of the liveliest and most diverse, thanks to the university, the artistic and intellectual communities, the embassies and consulates, foreign and domestic businesses and the headquarters of international organizations.

Tirana is a young city, made the capital in 1920 by the Congress of Lushnja to put the seat of government in the centre of the country. The decision signalled a fresh start for Albania, turning neither to the historical capital Kruja nor to the feudal centres Shkodra, Berati or Gjirokastra.

Tirana sits on a plain on the site of a Byzantine fortress built by Justinian in 520 BC. A Roman map marks the spot as Theranda, and by the 15th century it was known as the Plain of Tirana. The modern town sprang up in 1614 when Sulejman Pashë Mulleti built a bakery at the crossroads of a trade route to cater for the caravans. Soon a *hammam* was added, then a mosque and finally a bazaar.

In the 18th century Tirana began to thrive because of i silk, cotton and leather industries. In the 19th century the To lords took control of the city. It was occupied by the Ser 1913, then briefly by Esat Pashë Toptani who plotted to of Albania but was assassinated on 13 June 1920 by Av young Albanian revolutionary.

When Tirana became the capital it had a population of less than 20,000. Today, it is Albania's largest city with a population of 290,000. Its streets radiate from Skënderbeg Square (Sheshi Skënderbeg), the best point for taking bearings to explore the city.

The bronze equestrian statue of Gjergj Kastrioti Skënderbeg, Albania's beloved hero, was set up in the square in 1968 to mark the 500th anniversary of his death. The goat's head on his helmet has become a national symbol. Legend says that when the Turks besieged the Albanian forces at Kruja Citadel, Skënderbeg tricked them into an ambush. He put candles on the horns of a flock of goats and drove them into a secret passage. When the Turks followed the flickering lights, Skënderbeg attacked and routed them ... and the goat's head became his insignia.

The statue of dictator Enver Hoxha that once stood on the square—and the others of him in town—were pulled down by students in the unrest of 1991. Tirana's statues of Lenin and Stalin were quietly dismantled at night by the government of Ramiz Alia, Hoxha's Communist successor.

Moving counterclockwise around the square from Skënderbeg's statue, one comes first to a classic Albanian mosque, the **Haxhi Et'hem Beg Mosque**, begun in 1792, completed in 1820 and restored in 1985. The burial place of the Beg, it is elaborately decorated with floral frescos inside and out because the Beg's son wanted it to be as beautiful as St Sofia in Istanbul. The *muezzin's* call to prayer resounds from a loudspeaker atop the ribbed minaret typical of the late Ottoman period. The square clocktower behind it dates from 1830 when personal clocks were almost unheard of in the Balkans. The complex of a mosque and clocktower became quite popular in Albania. Many of the towers originally contained acoustic clocks—the faces and mechanisms were added later.

Across the street is the **Palace of Culture** built by the Soviet Union, some of its windowpanes still shattered from the wrath of 1991. Concerts are sometimes held here; a coffee shop occupies the ground floor and the **National Library** is housed at the rear.

Continuing around the square, the nearest thing to a skyscraper in the city is the Hotel Tirana, being renovated in a joint-venture with Italy and scheduled to reopen in late 1995. The large building with the mosaic depicting *Partizanis* holding their weapons aloft in defiant Communist Realism (though the red star has been removed) is the **National History Museum**, opened in 1981. The museum is well worth a visit for a brief lesson in Albanian history.

It begins with a map of Albania made of stone; the variou~~   ~~ the rooms demarcate one epoch of Albanian history from The fine 6th century mosaic called the Belle of Durrës is with objects from Illyrian tombs and the 4th century BC B~~u~~ a sculpture unearthed in Butrinti early this century and recen to Albania by Italy.

However, the priceless 14th century Epitaph from Gllavenica (near Berati), a heavy tapestry worked in gold, the symbolic burial cloth of Christ used in Orthodox Good Friday processions, was stolen early in 1994.

Maps and photos describe the mass emigrations to Italy and Greece during Turkish rule. The top floor of the museum treats the Albanian Renaissance (1831-1912) with portraits of patriots who resisted the Turks. The last section open to view is Independence (1912-1939), showing how the Western powers arbitrarily redrew the boundaries of Albania, reducing its territory by about two thirds, from about 94,000km² to about 28,000km².

The remaining sections (King Zogu, 1925-1939, Italian Occupation, 1939-1943, German Occupation, 1943-1944 and Communism, 1944-1992) are being reorganized.

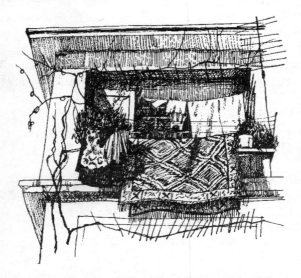

Back on Skënderbeg Square, the **State Bank** stands on the corner of Rr Kavajës. The main post office is one block away from the square, behind the bank. The area behind Skënderbeg's statue is taken up with deep yellow Italianate government buildings. The Puppet Theatre (*Teatri i Kukullave*) is squeezed in among the ministries, and the National Theatre (*Teatri Kombëtar*) is one block away, behind the mosque.

Remains of a 16th century castle wall can be seen on Rr Myslym ri two blocks from the National Theatre. Behind the wall is one of the lovely old Toptani family homes which now houses the **Geographical Institute**. One street over and parallel—on Rr Seremedin Seid Toptani—a similar Toptani house is now the **Institute for Cultural Monuments**.

Skënderbeg Square is bisected by Shëtitorja Dëshmorët e Kombit, a spacious avenue that runs from the railway station in the north to the university on the south side of town.

Near the railway station just off the avenue (on Rr Asim Vokshi) is

an unimposing villa, a Turkish-style house known as **Dervish Hatixhe**, a sacred place that survived the atheist state. Hatixhe lived there in the time of cholera in the 18th century, caring for the sick and burying the dead. She survived the epidemic and was given the name *Dervish* by the Muslims— a title never before bestowed upon a woman.

When Hatixhe died in 1798, the *turbe* that marked her grave became a shrine for Albanians of all religions. Even during the era of official atheism, her descendants welcomed those who came to pray and light candles. They disguised the room around the grave by furnishing it as a normal house and hid the most precious relic, Hatixhe's woollen hat, but the authorities remained suspicious of the many visitors. Now the family has replaced the hat on the *turbe* and visitors come openly to pray and bring gifts.

Back on Shëtitorja Dëshmorët e Kombit, the middle-class Arberia Hotel is not far from the railway station; on the avenue on the south side of Skënderbeg Square, the **Hotel Dajti**—the country's best hotel— sits back among trees next door to a state art gallery (*Galeria e Arteve*). The large Rinia Park across the street is filled with cafés and fast-food restaurants.

Continuing from the Hotel Dajti in the direction of the university, the avenue crosses the canalized Lana River and passes the pyramidal International Culture Centre, opened in 1988 as the **Enver** **Museum**. The centre is used for receptions and special exhib coffee shop frequented by university students is situated in or the basement and the United States Information Service Libr

Streetside snack bars are springing up everywhere

other. A couple of blocks farther along the avenue a hotel and office complex is being built by an Austrian firm.

Then come more ministry buildings, the president's office and the **Palace of Congress**—a sumptuous official showplace—before the street ends at the **University of Tirana** with its Science Academy, Academy of Arts and Polytechnic University. Its buildings date from the Italian occupation of the early 1940s, when they served as army headquarters.

The **Archaeology Museum** is in the university grounds. Most of the museum's collection is intact, although some Arberian items—the medieval culture that links pre-Christian Illyria and present-day Albania—have been stolen.

The exhibits are labelled in Albanian only. They cover the period from the Stone Age to the Middle Ages, starting with flint tools from 8000 BC. There are many neolithic ceramics dated 6000-2800 BC, and good finds from the Bronze Age include ceramics, knives, axes and swords. Among the best Illyrian items are a helmet and a number of gravestones with inscriptions in Greek letters. Ceramics imported from Athens and Corinth show that trade flourished; there are many examples from the Roman era as well, including lamps, jewellery and small marble figures. Items from Apollonia, one of the most important archaeological sites in Albania, include Ionic capitals and fragments of friezes from the Doric temple of the Acropolis. There are also capitals from Ballshi and from the basilica at Arapaj and a 2nd century altar (with a Latin inscription) found near Elbasani. Among the medieval articles are ceramics, belt buckles, fibula, earrings (some of gold) and rings.

Behind the university, the city's largest park, the **Grand Park**, contains a minute zoo, a lovely man-made lake and outdoor swimming pools.

The large but prosaic home of Enver Hoxha on Rr Ismail Qemali, in the villa area behind the ministries, is presently being used as a government guesthouse, although its original owners are demanding its return. The buildings in this section of town, once the enclave of favoured officials, are being taken over by foreign residents and international organizations such as the World Bank and the European Union.

Bulevardi Shqipëria e Re and Bulevardi Zhan d'Ark run along either side of the Lana River; to the west, Russian-built apartment houses give way to newer constructions. To the east are the **Parliament** and the lonely 19th century Tabakeve Bridge over nothing amid a lively area of apartment blocks, parks and street markets.

To visit the **Cemetery of Martyrs**, drive along Rr Lekë Dukagjini past the Radio-Televizioni Shqiptar studios, turn left at the Qemal Stafa football stadium to reach the Elbasani road and follow it into the terraced hills on the southeast edge of town.

Mother Albania, a 40-foot tall statue holding a star and a laurel wreath, towers over the graves of 900 men and women who died in the War of National Liberation in the 1940s. Across the road from the cemetery is the palace of former King Zogu, still used for official functions.

Back at Skënderbeg Square, the business section of town fans out to the northeast and northwest. A **state art gallery** (*Salloni i Artit*) and a souvenir shop are on Rr Dedë Gjon Luli behind the National History Museum.

Rr Kavajës and Rr Durrësit are lined with travel agencies, airline offices, western boutiques, shops selling made to order traditional dress, electronics stores and street vendors. The startling Caribbean rococo confection decorated with pink pineapples is the former Cuban embassy, now taken over by the Vatican.

Down Rr Kavajës one comes first to the **Xhamia e Re** mosque built in 1933 and newly renovated, then to the Catholic Church (with superb new stained-glass windows from Italy) and finally, down a small lane, to the **Orthodox Church of the Annunciation**, built in 1964, turned into a gymnasium in 1967 and reopened as a church in March 1991.

In the opposite direction from Skënderbeg Square, behind the Palace of Culture, a definitely Turkish atmosphere pervades the vicinity of the big food market which begins at Avni Rustemi Square. The market spills out of the vegetable stands, out of the butter and cheese and meat halls, and into streets and alleys where farmers display live turkeys, hens and sheep, among leaf and cut tobacco, shoes, bathroom fixtures, water containers and sewing machines. At the end is the bicycle market.

In this area, a lovely old *teqe* of the Halveti sect sits on Rr Barrikadave behind a vacant lot across the street from the Pelikan Restorant.

Nearby in Sulejman Pasha Square several cafés and ice-cream parlours offer excellent spots for a break. The remains of the **Pasha Kapllan tomb** from 1810 stand beside a children's playground. At the site of the **Pazari** *teqe* (1609), a gigantic hole surrounded by a wooden fence is a reminder of one of the first and biggest scams pulled on the Albanian people since the country opened up in 1991. A Kosova Albanian from Switzerland arrived in town and collected 3 million lekë 'to build the biggest Sheraton in the Balkans'. He left with the greater part of the cash and the city was left with the hole.

FIVE EXCURSIONS FROM TIRANA

Kruja (32km northwest of Tirana, full day)

The small town of Kruja has been called the 'Balcony of the Adriatic', its mountain citadel affording a magnificent view across the coastal plain to the sea. Legend has it that the hill where the citadel stands was once part of Kruja Mountain behind it, but that the hill—citadel intact—broke away in a landslide. From behind, it looks almost as if this could be true.

The name Kruja means 'spring' and springs are plentiful on the site. It has been inhabited since the 3rd century BC. The Byzantines maintained control over the city until the end of the 12th century. In 1190, when it was already known for its handicrafts, Kruja became the capital of the large feudal state of Arbania, considered the first Albanian state. By the 14th century the town had passed to the Topias family of feudal lords and in 1415 the Turks established a garrison there.

The finest hour of the town's history came when the forces within the citadel, which was seized by Skënderbeg in 1443, repulsed the Ottoman forces three times in spite of being greatly outnumbered. And therein lies the tale that makes Kruja a place of pilgrimage for all Albanians.

As the Turks swept relentlessly toward Europe, two men stood in their way—Janos Hunyadi of Hungary and Gjergj Kastrioti of Albania. Historians disagree about Gjergj's early life. It is popularly believed that he and his three brothers were sent by their father as hostages to the Sultan in 1415 when Gjergj was nine years old, that he grew up in the Turkish court, distinguished himself in the Turkish army and was awarded the title *beg*.

However, other theories hold that he would hardly have become a rebel in such a case; they say he was sent as a hostage for short periods of time on several different occasions, that he took the name Skënder, and in 1438 was appointed overlord of his father's lands, receiving the title *beg*. It was then that he began to make overtures to Venice, Ragusa (now Dubrovnik), Naples and Hungary for support in freeing Albania from the Turks.

The Hungarian rout of the Turks at Niš on 3 November 1443 was the signal Skënderbeg needed. He seized Kruja citadel and on 28 November raised the Kastrioti flag—the black double-headed eagle that became Albania's national symbol.

Skënderbeg was an excellent organizer, a man with charisma it would be said today, who personally recruited much of his army. His military victories strengthened his political influence, and he was able to consolidate his authority to the extent of forming a centralized state. This did not sit well with the feudal lords, however, and after Skënderbeg's death the bickering of the powerful families led to Albania's fragmentation once more.

Meanwhile, the Turks attacked Kruja citadel in 1450, 1466 and 1467, each time being driven back by Skënderbeg's forces. They finally took the fortress in 1478, ten years after Skënderbeg's death. Skënderbeg died on 17 January 1468 of malaria and was buried in Lezha. Within 40 years the Turks dominated most of Albania. Kruja became almost a

ghost town as its citizens fled to Italy, founding the Arbëresh towns in Calabria and Sicily that even today retain their language and customs.

War, time and earthquakes have taken their toll on **Kruja fortress**: it was built originally in the 5th and 6th centuries, rebuilt in the 13th century by Charles I of Anjou, torn down and rebuilt by the Turks, shattered by the earthquake of 1617 and almost totally destroyed in World War II. Quite a bit has been restored.

The remains of the wall follow the contour of the hill on which the fortress perches. The grounds are dominated by the **Skënderbeg Museum** opened in 1982, itself built as a fortress to tell the story of the man and his struggle against the Turks. What should be its most precious objects, Skënderbeg's helmet and sword, are copies—the originals are in the *Hof-, Jagd- und Rustkammer* (Weapons Museum) of the Hofburg in Vienna.

At the highest point of the hill to the northeast stands the clocktower, and nearby is the spot where signal fires were lit as warning that the Turks were approaching.

To the west near the wall lie a brick **16th century** *hammam*, possibly the oldest Turkish bath in Albania (restored in 1967), and the **Dollma Teqe**, a lovely shrine of the Bektashi sect, built in 1789.

Founded by Haxhi Bektashi Veli in the 13th century, Bektashism took firm hold as Albania converted to Islam under Turkish pressure. The Albanian version encompasses elements of both paganism and Christianity, as well as mysticism. Women are not veiled, alcohol and pork are not forbidden, prayers are not formal, God lives in nature. When the sect was suppressed in Turkey in 1925, its world headquarters transferred to Albania where it remained until 1949. Kruja was a holy site of the Bektashis from the 16th to 19th centuries.

A small community of about 20 houses (in its heyday there were 80) remains within the walls of Kruja Citadel. The houses are spacious two- or three-storey whitewashed buildings with carved wooden ceilings and covered verandahs called *çardhaks*. The ground floor was used for livestock and storage, while the family lived above.

Kruja's **Ethnographic Museum**, housed in one of these buildings, is among the richest museums in the country; for security reasons, it is often closed. Telephone Kruja central and ask for extension 425 to find out when it will be open.

Its ground floor includes a smithy, a potter's wheel and a tannery, along with a sheep stall and a collection of iron and bronze sheep's bells on wooden or chain-link collars. There are a raki still and wine barrels, an olive press and beating-boards and forms for making felt fezzes.

Upstairs in the Women's Room are looms, a bride's dowry chest and a crib. Good original frescos dating from 1764, in gold and green, remain on the upper walls of this room.

The rich gold-and-pearl ornamental costumes for both men and women are typical of the Kruja area, as are the leather slippers called *opinga*.

The most unusual feature of the house is the bath, a circular domed room heated by the fireplace in the adjoining bedroom. Its origins are believed to be Indian rather than Turkish.

Among the kitchen items on display are graduated sizes of flasks made of juniper wood: milk, butter and jam could be stored for months in them because the wood killed bacteria.

The 'tourist restaurant' on the citadel grounds is at the top of the steep incline to the north, worth lunch or at least a coffee break. At the far end of the bazaar, another restaurant with elaborate wood carving and low seats also serves Kruja specialities.

Among Kruja's springs is a covered late 14th century one (restored in 1813) bubbling beside the path that leads from the citadel down to the bazaar. The bazaar was rebuilt in 1965-67 in its 18th century form. Its wooden buildings line a straight, cobbled street; the tops of the Dutch doors can be opened allowing the bottoms to serve as counters. The roofs of the buildings overhang the street as shelter from the weather. Most of the shops are devoted to souvenirs—carpets, silver filigree, traditional costume. A tiny mosque nestles among the shops.

Petrela (12km southeast of Tirana, half day)

Little but a tumble of walls and towers remains of **Petrela Castle**, an 11th century fortress that once defended the road to Elbasani. It made up the southern corner of a triangle of fortresses—Kruja, Preza, Petrela—in Skënderbeg's defence system. He sent his sister Mamica there during Turkish attacks.

The castle is a steep climb up from the village, with a fine view across the Erzeni River to the distant mountains that swallow up the road to Elbasani. On clear days, Kruja Citadel is visible.

Nexhmedin Kyqi has the key to the gate and collects the entry fee.

Preza (22km northwest of Tirana, half day)

The squarish 15th century citadel on 11th century foundations that stands on a hilltop at Preza village not far from Rinas airport was a lookout post facing Kruja. This is where Skënderbeg's troops waited for the Turks to retreat from Kruja, then attacked and decimated the exhausted army.

It was a small fortress used mainly to alarm Kruja and Petrela of the approaching Turks. Guardtowers remain at its four corners, one having been made a clocktower, though the clock is now gone. The Austrians turned the fortress into a prison. Today, a café has been opened in one of the towers; above it an iron compass can be seen embedded in the tower floor.

Durrësi (39km west of Tirana, full day)

Durrësi, the main harbour and second-largest city in Albania, is also one of its oldest. The Greek king Epidamnos founded the city in 627 BC, naming it for himself and the port for his grandson Dyrrah. Gradually the name Dyrrachion prevailed. In the 4th century BC it became an independent city-state. The Illyrians under Glaukias seized it in 232 BC and allied themselves with Rome three years later. The Romans renamed it Dyrrachium and used it as a springboard for their Balkan invasions. It was the starting point of the Via Egnatia that linked Rome with Constantinople.

In the divided Roman Empire, Durrësi became the chief port for Byzantium. Subsequent invaders included the Bulgarians, Normans, Crusaders, Venetians, Angevins and Serbs. It was retaken, refortified and renamed Durazzo by the Venetians in 1392 and captured by the Turks, who called it Dratsch, in 1501.

Esat Pashë Toptani set up a separatist government, the so-called Senate of Central Albania, here in 1913 in opposition to the Vlora administration which had declared Albanian independence the previous year. It was occupied briefly by the Serbs in 1916; during World War II it was held by the Italians and Germans.

Much of ancient Durrësi has not been excavated because the city has been built and rebuilt on the same spot over the centuries. Albanian archaeologists are hoping for new digs in cooperation with their foreign colleagues but the problem of shifting the residents who live on top of layers of history is a major drawback. Durrësi 'underground' has been declared a cultural monument and new construction is allowed only by special permit.

The main square (formerly Sheshi Stalin) is dominated by the **Xhamia e Madhe** (Grand Mosque) of 1414, totally renovated in 1994. It was used as a culture centre during the Hoxha regime.

The **Roman Amphitheatre**, just off the main square and reached by steps near the Grand Mosque, is believed to date from the 2nd century; it could seat 15-20,000 spectators. Dank underground tunnels speak of caged lions and gladiators; the animal chamber has a rounded brickwork corner (looking surprisingly art deco) so the lions would not be injured as they hurled themselves into the arena.

A **Byzantine Chapel** with a panel of mural mosaics from the 10th century and tombs of a king and queen perches incongruously on the seating at the west side of the arena. Fourteen other graves have been found there. A second chapel underground contains faded remnants of frescos. Farther along is the entrance to a tunnel that led about 2km to Currila beach.

The amphitheatre was abandoned in the Middle Ages, when the limestone facings were removed following an earthquake and used for building in the town. It was uncovered only in 1966.

Houses typical of the Turkish period stand above the amphitheatre on the site of the acropolis destroyed by the earthquake of 1273.

The remains of the fortress walls behind the amphitheatre are 6th century, with additions from the 13th and 14th centuries. Anna Comnena, Byzantine emperor's daughter and tireless chronicler, noted that the walls were wide enough for horsemen to ride four abreast atop them. The city walls, a montage of marble fragments, gravestones and rock are an excellent spot from which to view Durrësi and its harbour.

Roman baths were uncovered in 1962 when construction began for the Alexander Moissi Theatre on the main square. (Moissi was an actor born near Durrësi who won critical acclaim on the German stage early in this century.) They were left uncovered and reveal a black-and-white checkerboard paved hall, a hypocaust and a large pool underneath the theatre, which sits on concrete pilings. The baths unfortunately are used as a toilet

The **Alexander Moissi Museum** on Rr Naim Frashëri is a fine example of a 19th century merchant's home in the style of the open-stair house. It served as a prison toward the end of World War II, then as an apartment house, and was restored as a museum in 1983.

About a block away on the same street, the **Fet'hije Mosque**, used for storage during the old regime, is being restored and is once more in use. It incorporates fragments of walls of a Paleo-Christian church.

The Belle of Durrës, a superb polychrome mosaic of a woman's head surrounded by flowers—possibly the goddess Flora—was discovered in Durrësi but removed to the National History Museum in Tirana. Nevertheless, Durrësi's **Archaeological Museum** on the seaside promenade, Rr Qemal Stafa, is one of the richest in the country.

The Illyrian tombstones, local ceramics and the 2nd century marbles are especially good, and there are many terracotta Aphrodites. The museum garden is filled with Turkish tombstones and a set of lovely columns from the 18th century mosque in Kavaja: once Albania's largest and most beautiful mosque, it was torn down in the 1967 crackdown on religion.

At the entrance to the modern harbour, a 13th century Venetian bastion stands as reminder of the days when the city was named Durazzo. A magnificent **Villa of King Zogu** overlooks the sea from a hill above.

Durrësi *plazh* (beach), one of the most beautiful beaches on the entire Adriatic, is situated 6km south of the city proper. Once the playground of royalty, then of workers, it appears ideal for bathing and many local people do swim here. However, the water may be polluted from harbour effluent and untreated sewage, a problem that has arisen at other beaches as well.

Three hotels, the Adriatik, Apollonia and Durrësi make up a complex for tourists. Programmes of folk music and dance are organized at intervals during the season on the hotel terraces. Durrësi is a starting point for excursions throughout the country during the summer.

Buses run between Durrësi *plazh* and Durrësi city, leaving from the post office in town. The bus is marked either *Urban* or *Plazh*, depending on the direction it is heading.

Plans call for a tourist village to be built south of Durrësi at Golem Beach, where 300 hectares have been set aside as a 'tourist zone'.

For the intrepid seeker of historical sites, Durrësi's beach area also has something to offer. Across the highway and railway tracks at the village of Arapaj lies a battleground of the war between Caesar and Pompey and later in the war between the Byzantine Comnenus and the Norman Guiscard. Digs here in 1980 brought to light the ruins of the 6th century Byzantine **St Michael's Basilica** with one of the largest floor mosaics known in Albania. It is easy to find in Arapaj but, like others, the 166m² mosaic is covered with plastic and a thick layer of sand for protection.

Dajti Mountain (25km northeast of Tirana, half day)

Dajti Mountain lies within sight of Tirana, its 1,613m peak promising cool, clear air in contrast to the sultry smog of the capital. Its national park is a place to picnic or simply to get out of town and look back over the saucer where Tirana sits under a haze.

Enver Hoxha had a house here and now the Scientology sect is restoring a hotel in one of the most picturesque spots as their base for expansion into the Balkans. The heights beyond the hotel are a closed military zone.

ALONG THE VIA EGNATIA TO THE SOUTHEAST

Elbasani

The road to Elbasani from Tirana passes the Cemetery of Martyrs, follows the Erzeni River to Petrela Castle and climbs into the Krraba mountains. Winding through Ibe village with its cold springs and the mining village Krraba, it reaches the Krraba Pass (933m) where the view stretches east to the Çermenika range and south to the sandstone Tomori Mountains.

The mountain road snakes over a pass, then descends to the plain of the Shkumbini River and Elbasani. The area is known for its olives, oranges, persimmons and figs, and in season the roadsides are lined with fruit sellers.

Alternatively, Elbasani can be reached by both road and railway from Durrësi, following the less picturesque Via Egnatia from its beginning and passing through Peqini, a post station on the ancient highway. The remains of the **Baths of Bradashesh** can be seen on the site of a *caravanserai* about 6km outside Elbasani.

Elbasani once boasted the most beautiful of settings, nestled in the deep green of its cypresses, but now from either approach the first view of the city is its gigantic steel mill, still working fitfully though most of its chimneys stand bleak and smokeless. The pollution from the steel mill, trapped in the valley, has done considerable damage to the health of the local populace.

The area was settled by the Illyrians; finds, especially ceramics, in nearby Pazhok date from the 11th to the 5th century BC. Elbasani is built on the site of the 1st century Roman Skampa that grew up during the construction of the Via Egnatia. The first documentation is the tombstone of a soldier who served in the Roman 11th Legion and who died in AD 168, 'in Skampa, where he was born'. The 2nd century city walls boasted 26 towers and three gates and—unusual for Albania—were surrounded by a moat.

The Byzantine Emperor Justinian I constructed a fortress in the 6th century when the city, the seat of a bishopric, was called Neon Kastron (New Citadel). The Bulgarians razed it in 1230, but in 1466 Sultan Mehmet II rebuilt the fortress as a base from which to launch his attacks on Kruja, naming it El-basan (Fortress). Later, Ali Pashë Tepelena used it in his campaigns. An engraving of the city in 1609 shows a skyline of minarets.

In the 16th and 17th centuries, Elbasani became a trading centre. Some 80 sorts of handicraft were practised, but the city was noted especially for its silver, woodwork, leather and silk. The houses within the old fortress walls date from the 19th century. After an uprising by the local feudal lords in 1832, the Turks destroyed most of the walls; only a section to the south with eight towers and one gate remains.

The fortress gate, flanked by fountains (now dry) on either side, stands opposite the Hotel Skampa. Inside, above the gate, is a marble inscription in old Turkish script. The old town within the walls occupies an area roughly 350m²—a jumble of low whitewashed stone houses in the Turkish style and a few two-storey villas, all with carefully tended courtyards. The cobbled streets are original. A couple of copper and silver workshops remain in the old stone buildings.

Not far from the gate stands the **Xhamia Mbret**, the King's Mosque of the Castle. Many Kosovans settled in Elbasani during the rule of King Zogu, who gave them land which they called Mbret, Field of the King; the mosque was also named in his honour. During the Communist regime its minaret was torn down, its windows bricked up and it was used as party offices. The mosque is once more in use, both for worship and as a religious school, but is in poor repair. Its *mafil* (balcony) was removed, so now women worship on a straw mat in an outer room.

The Orthodox **Shën Mëri** (St Mary) Church within the walls is being totally renovated. The lovely old building is temporarily closed, but there are two gargoyles and inscriptions on its outer walls and a fresco over the door. Just outside the walls, **Shën Pjëtri** (St Peter's) Catholic Church is also being renovated. The huge new painting in its dome depicts Christ holding an open Bible, its words in Albanian. The church was built when the Italians occupied the city in the 1930s and attempted to convert the population.

The Orthodox Church is the burial place of Konstandin Kristoforidhi (1827-1895), a lexicographer who championed Albanian as the country's official language. He wrote in both Tosk and Gheg dialects (the Shkumbini River is the dividing line between Gheg and Tosk). A bronze plaque on one of the towers commemorates the triumph of the Albanian language over Turkish with Kristoforidhi's words '... Albania cannot be taught, neither can it be illuminated, nor become civilized by foreign languages, but only by its mother tongue, which is Albanian ...'

Elbasani is the birthplace of the *Partizani* hero Qemal Stafa (1912-1942) and the site of Albania's first teachers' college opened in 1909.

The **Ethnographic Museum** is located across a spacious park from the Hotel Skampa in a typical 18th century house. Its wooden floors are covered with carpets bearing the eagle motif and it contains a good collection of gold- and silver-embroidered Albanian dress. The ornate belts worked in threads of precious metal show that Illyrian motifs have survived through the ages.

The Silk Room of the museum is devoted to one of the city's most important crafts of years past, when high-quality Elbasani silk was exported as far away as India. A room of costumes includes forms for making fezzes and the model of a felt-making *destila,* a sort of water mill where wool was treated and beaten before being made into fezzes and stout waterproof coats. Shaggy Elbasani carpets are also on display; the white ones are called *velenxe,* the coloured ones, *thekie.*

A low table on the open veranda is set for serving a special Elbasani dessert called *ballakume,* eaten on 14 March in observance of *Dita e veres* (Summer Day). The **Men's Room** still has original wall paintings and an ornate carved wood ceiling. It contains the violin and fez that belonged to Isuf Myzyri, who wrote more than 80 songs and whose portrait hangs in the hall.

Although Elbasani is staunchly Muslim, minorities of Orthodox, Vlachs and Gypsies live here. Shën Kollit (St Nicholas), the parish church of the Vlachs, was razed during the crackdown on religion in 1967; it is said that the stones were taken to Korça for the church there; the elaborate woodcarved 17th century iconostasis is in Tirana being restored. The Vlachs themselves have been to a great extent assimilated into the population.

Outside the fortress wall, just beside the Hotel Skampa, the restored *hammam,* probably 16th century, has been turned into a disco. However, Turkish baths are not the only baths in the Elbasani district, which is known for its thermal waters. Llixhat, 14km south of the city, whose hot sulphur springs reach 60°C, was once King Zogu's royal spa with a park and casino.

To the southeast of Elbasani are **four churches** decorated with frescos by Onufri, Albania's greatest medieval artist: Shën Kollit (St Nicholas) at Shelcani (14km), one of Albania's richest churches from the standpoint of painting; two churches in Shpati, and Shën Premtja (St Paraskevi) in Valeshi, a village in the mountains that can be reached only by a three-hour hike.

From Elbasani to Lake Ohrid

From Elbasani, the Via Egnatia follows the Shkumbini River eastward past the skeletons of collective farms and soon leaves the plain behind. It passes through the mining town of Librazhd—the area is rich in nickel and iron, as can be seen in the red of the stones—and under Albania's tallest railway bridge. The names of many towns in this area have a Slavic ring, reminders of early occupations.

These days the road is heavily travelled by trucks from Turkey and Bulgaria. In the past, it was the route of Roman legions, Normans and Crusaders, and from the east, Goths and Bulgarians.

Just before the Thana Pass (893m), a small road turns off to the right toward Kotodeshi. At the bridge, the left-hand turning leads to **Selca e Poshtëme** where four monumental Illyrian graves of the 3rd century BC have been unearthed. The site is a short climb up from Selca village.

Digging began in 1969-70 and the tombs were opened in 1973-74. Some of the finds are in the National History Museum in Tirana. Among the most beautiful objects are golden earrings, badges and an ornamental Eros. The most impressive find still on site is a cenotaph decorated with an Ionic colonnade. The grave chambers, hewn in the rock of a flat-topped mountain, have been stripped of all but their façades and two ornate sarcophagi inside one tomb. Several niches are carved into the rock face and trenches in the floors of the tombs.

From the mountain top, the view stretches out over the **Domosdova Plain** where Skënderbeg won his first major encounter against the Turks in 1444. The Turks named the plain 'cursed land' because of their heavy losses.

Back on the main highway, the road forks at the top of Thana Pass, the left hand leading to Macedonia 4km away, the right hand continuing toward Pogradeci. As the descent begins, Lake Ohrid and Mount Galicija (snowcapped in winter) make a picturesque backdrop for the red roofs of the fishing village Lini.

Detour to the hilltop in **Lini** to visit the remains of a 6th century Byzantine basilica whose eight floor mosaics are some of the largest and best preserved in the country. The ruins are partially fenced. As protection, the mosaics are covered with a heavy layer of plastic and sand; they can be seen properly only by previous arrangement (for groups only) with the Institute of Cultural Monuments. They are well worth the effort for the multicoloured vines, fish, fruit, birds, water plants and a bee.

Pogradeci (the name means 'Under the Castle') sits below the site of the Illyrian fortress Encheleana that was reconstructed in the Middle Ages by the Bulgarians. The Turks turned the town into an administrative centre. Little remains following the destruction of two World Wars, but a few characteristic houses that have been protected as cultural monuments are to be found in the Old Town.

Pogradeci is an ideal spot to spend a lazy vacation. The lake front has a lovely beach and the Drilon Park nature area—once Enver Hoxha's private retreat—is a perfect picnic setting. For night life, the Disco Diamond, a block off the lake front, provides lively entertainment.

Lake Ohrid, shared by Albania and Macedonia, is beautifully translucent—on clear days visibility reaches a depth of 22m—and is one of the oldest and deepest lakes in the world, along with Baikal in Siberia and Tanganyika in Africa. Some scientists estimate it to be 4 million years old. It is 30km long, up to 15km wide, and its depth recently was sounded at 312m.

Among the unique species of life that thrive in the lake is the *koran* (Albanian) or *plašica* (Macedonian), a tasty trout served in restaurants on both sides of the border. In summer its meat is white, in winter, red.

A round tour of the lake, its shores dotted with Byzantine churches, is possible now that the border crossings with Macedonia are open. The crossing at Tushemishti is just a few kilometres from the impressive Monastery of St Naum in Macedonia, where neighbouring Lake Prespa empties into Lake Ohrid through an underground river. An excursion into **Macedonia** can start at Sveti Naum Monastery, perched on a bluff above the lake and giving a wonderful view across to Pogradeci. Originally dedicated to the Archangel Michael, the monastery was built in 900 by Naum of Ohrid, a leading Slav scholar who was buried here in 910. The original church was destroyed by the Turks.

The present church was built between the 14th and 17th centuries. The frescos were done in 1806 by the Albanian master Trpko of Korça and some of the figures wear clothes of that period. The baroque iconostasis dates from 1711. The chapel above Naum's tomb contains paintings portraying his miracles. His death scene shows his teachers, the brothers Cyril and Methodius, and his contemporary, Kliment of Ohrid. Together, these four men created a thriving centre of Slav literary and cultural activity at Ohrid.

About a dozen churches were built in and around **Ohrid** town (Macedonia) in the early days of Christianity, and several of these remain to bear witness to their influence. The Cathedral of Sveta Sofija (Holy Wisdom) is the oldest in town, rebuilt between 1036 and 1056. It was once seat of the archbishopric and contains a unique and valuable gallery of paintings from the 11th to the 14th centuries, among them the first known portraits of Cyril and Kliment. Among the best are *The Communion of the Apostles, The 40 Martyrs* and *St Sofia.*

Nestled among the houses of the old town are the 14th century Sveta Bogorodica Bolnička (Virgin Mary) where three layers of frescos have been discovered, the unornamented Sveti Nikola Bolnički (St Nicholas) and the little Mali Sveti Kliment (St Clement Minor).

Other churches in Ohrid include the 13th century Stari Sveti Kliment (originally Sveta Bogorodica Perivlepta or St Mary Perivleptos); the 14th century Sveti Dimitrije, the mausoleum church Sveti Konstantin & Jelena (SS Constantine and Helena); the 14th century Sveti Kuzman & Damjan (better known as Mali Sveti Vraci or the Little Holy Magi); Sveta Bogorodica Čelnica (Virgin Mary); the small Sveti Nikola Čudotvorac (St Nicholas the Miracle Worker) and Sveta Bogorodica Kamensko (Virgin Mary).

Just on the edge of Ohrid, the 13th century Sveti Jovan Bogoslov (St John the Divine) stands on a lovely promontory overlooking the fishing village Kaneo and its beach. Its icon *The Virgin with Christ* is one of the best works of the 19th century Debar workshop. From here a path through the woods leads to the restored Imaret Mosque which contains remnants of the oldest Slav monastery, Sveti Pantelejmon, built by Kliment in 893 as his own burial place. It was here that the first Slav university was established. Beside it is the 15th century *turbe* of Yusuf Chelebi, who built the mosque, and nearby are the remains of an early Christian church with lavish floor mosaics.

The old town of Ohrid is charming, its narrow streets shaded by the overhanging upper floors of the houses. The buildings are constructed of wood on stone foundations, designed to fit small odd-shaped plots of ground so only the upper storeys could be expansive. The Samuel Fortress (almost a total ruin) above the town was the twin of that across the lake in Pogradeci.

The *Čarsija*—Ohrid's old-fashioned shopping centre—still has the feel of a bazaar. It is here that one can buy Ohrid pearls made from the scales of the *plašica* fish that lives in Lake Ohrid. The Filevo and Talevi families make some of the world's best simulated pearls and have shops attached to their homes.

The Ohrid Festival of music and theatre is held each July-August.

Still in Macedonia, near the town of Struga with its picturesque Saturday market where women wear traditional dress, the Black Drini River (really a deep bottle green) flows out of Lake Ohrid, beginning a journey that takes it across Albania to the Adriatic Sea.

US and European community visitors can get Macedonian visas at the border; whether another Albanian visa is required upon return seems to depend on the mood of the border guard.

Korça

Back in Albania, the road from Pogradeci to Korça—one of the widest and smoothest in the country—soon leaves Lake Ohrid behind to follow orchards and wheat fields. Apples, pears, quinces and walnuts are for sale by the roadside in season. The wide Korça Plain, flanked by terraced hills, stretches toward the Morava Mountains.

A bypass has been built around the town of **Maliqi**, founded in 1951 to house workers in for a new sugar refinery. Pilings that once supported Bronze Age huts were discovered as the swamp was being drained, but have since rotted away. The more portable finds were taken to museums in Tirana and Korça.

The atmosphere in downtown Korça is reminiscent of the days when it was called 'Little Paris', though the city is heralded by belching smokestacks and bleak factories on its outskirts. The architecture of the houses varies, with hints of baroque here and there, and many villas—badly in need of carpentry and paint—sit back from the streets. Theatres and art galleries were once plentiful; parks and fountains still lend an air of leisure.

The name Korça derives from the Slavic Gorica; in Roman times it was called Peliom. It grew as a commercial and carpet-making centre during Turkish rule, though it was staunchly Orthodox. It was here on 7 March 1887 that the first school teaching in the Albanian language was founded. A Museum of Education is in the original school building.

Korça fell on hard times in the 19th century and many people emigrated to Romania, Egypt and the United States. Early in this century, the city was occupied first by the Greeks, then by the French who established the short-lived Republic of Koritza (1915-20), then again by the Greeks in 1940.

Hops are grown on the nearby Buçimas Plain and Korça is the home of Albania's first brewery, which has been reopened. The city is also known for the high quality of its brandy. The local carpet factory has been privatized and can be visited.

The **Museum of Medieval Arts** has a wide-ranging exhibition covering the 5th to the 19th centuries. The best examples are the 10th century Dhimiter iconostasis and the works by the icon painter Onufri. The **Mirahori Mosque** built 1484-96 is lead-roofed and has no minaret.

Inquiries about the house on the Rr Republika where Enver Hoxha lived when he taught here in 1937 are not well received. His rented room was once a museum, complete with desk, books, pipe and coffee cup.

Grave beside highway near Korça: Jetmor Potka 1968-1991

Excursions from Korça

Several excursions can be made from Korça; the trip to **Voskopoja** is highly recommended for the frescos in Kisha e Shën Kollit (Church of St Nicholas). The road leading from the factory area at the north end of Korça is not marked and the 24km drive into the mountains takes about an hour.

Voskopoja, dating at least from the 14th century, was once a flourishing commercial centre with an art academy, a university and a printing press. In the 17th and 18th centuries it was Albania's largest and most cosmopolitan city with about 40,000 inhabitants and 24 Orthodox churches. As an Orthodox stronghold and a city of intellectuals, it ran foul of both the Turks and the conservative feudal families who controlled the country. It was invaded and plundered in 1769, 1772 and 1780, and the people fled to Korça. Finally only a few shepherds remained. Fierce fighting there during the two World Wars almost finished its destruction.

It was rejuvenated somewhat as a ski resort during the Communist era as the site of the country's Alpine ski championships. Today it numbers about 200 houses.

Of Voskopoja's five remaining churches, Shën Kollit (St Nicholas) is the most impressive. Constructed 1721-26, almost every inch of walls—inside and out—is covered with frescos. More than a thousand figures have been counted in the paintings. Because the church was built under Turkish rule, its outer appearance from a distance is unimpressive but the seven-arched porch is covered with rows of brilliantly coloured saints. The inside is dim, and weather and the army once stationed there have taken their toll, but the rich colours and flamboyant figures are breathtaking, nonetheless.

The interior is primarily the work of David of Selenica, who took six years to complete it. The paintings of SS Michael and Gabriel are in reasonably good condition; others must be studied closely to pick out a Christmas scene of Vlach herdsmen in traditional dress or the portrait of a leading citizen, Haxhi Jorgji. The narthex paintings are by the brothers Constandine and Thanas Zografu.

The frescos decorating Shën Thanas (St Athanasius) on the south side of town, are in better condition but are not so impressive, nor are those in Shën Mëhillit (St Michael). Kisha Shën Mëri (the Cathedral of St Mary) is large but almost bare of surviving art. The Monastery of Shën Prodan was burned in World War II.

Other churches in the Korça vicinity interesting for their frescos can be found at **Boboshtica**, 15km to the south: Shën Jovan (St John) whose 15th century works are mostly hidden under 18th century paintings and Shën Dimiter (St Dimitrius) with 17th century frescos. Boboshtica is known for its black mulberries which produce a strong, high-quality raki.

The 14th century Kisha e Shëndëllisë (Church of the Ascension) in **Mborje** on the outskirts of Korça has both external and internal frescos.

Vithkuq, 26km southwest of Korça, once had 14 churches. Two remain in relatively good condition: the 17th-19th century Shën Mëhillit (St Michael) and the 17th to 18th century Shën Mëri (St Mary). Shën Pjëtri dhe Pavli (Monastery of SS Peter and Paul) built in 1709 lies east of the village.

Another excursion from Korça goes to **Lake Prespa**. There are actually two Prespa lakes, e Madhe (large) and e Vogël (small), connected by a natural channel and lying partially within Macedonia and Greece.

Lake Prespa is higher and colder than Lake Ohrid and its scenery is starker. Mountains rise steeply from the water's edge, but marsh land lies between the large and small lakes. Prespa is fed by many streams and has no above-ground outflow, but its level seldom fluctuates because it flows into Lake Ohrid by an underground stream.

Tren Cave and **Spile Rock**, where rock paintings have been discovered, lie near the village of Tren near Prespa on the road to Bilisht. The paintings depicting armed horsemen hunting deer with dogs were believed for a long time to be Iron Age, but the recent discovery of a painted cross has led some archaeologists to say they more likely date from the Middle Ages. Tren Cave is known to have been inhabited from neolithic to medieval times.

Dardha village to the far south, almost on the Greek border, is a promising site for a winter sports centre.

An aesthetic young man in Albania
Has a Pre-Raphaelite kind of mania:
For a girl by Burne-Jones
He yearns and he moans —
Now tell me, just what could be zanier?

THE SOUTHERN HIGHLANDS

Leskoviku

The stark white mountains of southeastern Albania are wild and lonely, their bareness broken only by an extensive pine forest at the Barmash Pass (1,759m). This is ideal terrain for guerrilla warfare and indeed the area saw fierce fighting by the *Partizanis* in World War II.

In 1943, the Germans razed the village of **Borova** just past Erseka, executing 107 men, women and children. A spiral monument on the hilltop commemorates the deed; the top circle made of 107 stones represents the victims.

The road of narrow hairpin curves runs through the Barmash Gorge, through Germenj village and on to Leskoviku. A spa in the vicinity has fallen into disuse but in the town itself there is a spring, a holy place for both Muslim and Orthodox. It sits at the top of a small hill, covered with a brick-and-stone arched construction built about 180 years ago and containing an Orthodox shrine. A monastery is believed to have stood on the site; the local people say they found graves when the present houses were being built and that once a mosque stood there, too.

Përmeti

At Leskoviku the road veers northwest up into the wild mountains once more, following the Vjosa River to Përmeti. Vineyards appear; Përmeti wine and raki are regarded as some of the best in the country. The landmark of the town is a huge rock towering over the river.

Albania's first National Liberation Congress was held in Përmeti. The small one-storey rectangular building (opposite an army post) where it took place is locked now, but the plaque remains: 'Here on 24-28 May 1944 the First Anti-Fascist National Liberation Congress was held that unanimously decided to set up a new democratic Albania for the people.'

Some 200 delegates took part in the congress. Enver Hoxha was named chairman of the Anti-Fascist Liberation Committee that served as a provisional government and nullified all international agreements King Zogu had made, effectively cutting Albania's links with the West. Hoxha also was made commander-in-chief of the army and promptly ordered an offensive to liberate the country.

The **Frashëri Teqe** here, used as a hospital, was once the most famous Bektashi *teqe* in Albania.

A short detour south to **Leusha** is worthwhile for a superb woodcarved iconostasis in the church, the product of three generations of work. On the main road north, the 15th century church at **Kosina** is notable for its brickwork exterior.

Then the Vjosa River makes a slight bend and enters the **Këlcyra Gorge**. The ruins of a seraglio can barely be distinguished from the grey mountainside where it sits; the ruins of a 4th century BC Illyrian fortress lie hidden from sight on Mount Trebeshinës.

The road runs through the gorge, and a cascade and small falls plunging down the mountainside suddenly appear. Pools have been arranged to catch some of the falls, others are allowed to run wild, and picnic tables are set all around—a miniature Plitvice among old plane trees. A wooden bridge leads to the restaurant on the river's edge.

Tepelena

The road continues along the path of the Vjosa to Tepelena, where the river joins the Drinos. Tepelena's main street—named Ali Pasha, of course—leads to the fortress erected in the 5th century, restored in the 11th century, captured by Ali Pasha in 1789 and completely rebuilt in 1819.

Ali Pashë Tepelena (1740-1822) was born in nearby **Dragot**. A power unto himself for a long while, he built fortresses throughout southern Albania but in the end failed to achieve an autonomous *pashalic* and was beheaded by the Turks.

Lord Byron visited him in 1809, writing delightful accounts of the pasha and his palace in his letters and describing the glittering minarets of Tepelena in *Childe Harold's Pilgrimage*. A plaque on the fortress wall commemorates his visit.

The fortress suffered in the earthquake of 1920, but it is possible to wander through the grounds and clamber on to the partially restored walls for a view of the river. Houses, chickens, children and garbage heaps prove that life continues within the walls.

Turn back south from Tepelena, following the Drinos, and stop for refreshment at the picturesque **Uji i Ftohtë** springs (the name means Cold Water—there are many such places in Albania).

The site of ancient **Antigonea** is generally considered to be **Lëkeli** near Tepelena, but some archaeologists put it nearer Gjirokastra, where an Illyrian-Greek city was unearthed in the 1960s.

At the Lëkeli site, ruins of a 3rd-2nd century BC peristyle house have been unearthed and its colonnades re-erected. A 3rd century BC bronze Poseidon figure was among the finds. A four-wheel drive vehicle is needed to visit the ruins.

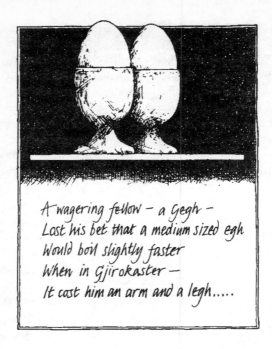

A wagering fellow — a Gegh —
Lost his bet that a medium sized egh
Would boil slightly faster
When in Gjirokaster —
It cost him an arm and a legh.....

Gjirokastra

Gjirokastra, clinging to Gjërë Mountain (Mali i Gjërë) above the Drinos, crowned by its imposing fortress, is one of the most beautiful cities in Albania. It is the birthplace of Enver Hoxha and of author Ismail Kadare whose *Chronicle in Stone* paints a colourful picture of growing up there during World War II.

The Byzantine chronicler Kontakuzeni in 1336 wrote of Gjirokastra as both a town and a fort. It became the seat of the Zenevia feudal lords, then fell to the Turks in 1419. In 1908 Çerçiz Topulli led the Albanians against the Turks; his guerrillas killed the Turkish police chief of Gjirokastra, and the fighting that ensued inflamed the entire country. In 1940 fierce battles raged here between Greece and Italy; the Greeks managed to drive the Italians out of Gjirokastra but could not mitigate the greater threat of the Germans.

Gjirokastra's **fortress** was built in the 6th century on a site occupied as early as the 4th century BC by the Illyrians. Ali Pashë Tepelena rebuilt it in 1811-12 and stationed 5,000 soldiers there. It was never occupied by force and therefore remains in good condition.

It has three main gates; the east entry is open for visitors, leading through a tall arched hallway where water drips from the ceiling as in a cave.

Until the 12th century, the town of about 200 families was entirely enclosed within the castle walls; then houses began to spill down the hillside as the town grew. A bakery and prison were built within the fortress during the Turkish occupation. Ali Pasha's construction project added a 12km aqueduct to bring around 100,000 litres of drinking water per day from Mount Sopot. King Zogu had the aqueduct destroyed and used the material to build a prison. The last time the fortress was used for protection was during the German and British bombings in 1943-44.

The tiny American spy plane forced down in 1957 still sits rusting behind a few elderly cannon, but the superb collection of gold- and silver-inlaid rifles in the National Museum of Weapons has been stolen. An open air theatre on the grounds was the site of Albania's national folk festival held every five years. The last was held in 1989, but there has been no money to stage it again. A UNESCO study has recommended Gjirokastra as the site for a Balkan-wide folklore festival to be held every two years.

Below the fortress walls the roofs of the town extend like stair steps down the slope. The house where Hoxha was born in 1908—enlarged and refurbished, if not totally rebuilt, to exalt its scion—is locked, a few windows broken; it is impossible to tell what remains inside.

However, just up the street around a corner is the **Ethnographic Museum**, another characteristic Gjirokastra house that is still open to the public and intact. The large three-storey house built in 1820 is almost entirely original.

The ground floor was used exclusively for storage, one room reserved for wine and cheese because the floor was built higher and remained cooler. Firewood was also stored there. The first floor contains the winter rooms with small double-paned windows; the top floor with larger windows—some of stained glass—was used in summer and contains the lavish guestrooms.

The main rooms have conical fireplaces with niches in the walls on each side where old people could set their coffee cups as they warmed their hands by the blaze. In summer, cloth skirts cover the fireplaces. Built-in wooden cabinets hold dishes and ornaments, and at one end of the rooms are wooden balconies with cubbyholes underneath—some for storing blankets, some extending to bath and toilet. The wooden ceilings are elaborately carved.

The women's rooms are not so decorative, though in many cases carved latticework screens give a view into other rooms so the women could keep an eye on the man of the house and his guests and see to their needs.

Rich carpets in the traditional Gjirokastra colours of red, black and beige (the brown dye made from walnuts, the red from boxwood) cover the floors and divans. The seat cushions are stuffed with cornshucks but only wool is used for the bedding.

Cisterns filled by means of roof guttering are typical of Gjirokastra; some 300 houses still have them, though not all are in use.

The entire city centre was declared a protected 'museum town' in 1961, when a great deal of restoration work was begun. Some 70 houses were placed in the 'first category', 15 of them being 'very beautiful'. A second category is made up of about 150 houses and a third of around 400. The overall architectural conformity that makes Gjirokastra such a lovely picture from a distance is belied by the diversity in detail that the houses show at close range.

Gjirokastra houses are notable for their spaciousness; this was after all a governmental seat and the officials built houses in accordance with their positions.

Their defensive characteristic—the high stone walls, some with loopholes instead of windows for viewing the surroundings, no doubt influenced by the strife among the feudal lords—is immediately evident. Many of the structures lean into the mountain for support. There are three variations: the perpendicular house which is the basis for the other two, the one-wing (the most common type) and the two-wing house. Most are two or three storeys high. The style probably dates from the beginning of the 18th century, though 1800-1830 was the major building period.

The differentiation of the floor levels is evident from the outside as well as in. The ground floor is quite plain, but the façade near the roof is often decoratively painted or adorned with baroque friezes that are repeated in the guestrooms inside. Stone and wood were the building materials, expertly handled by master craftsmen who came from Kolonja and Dangëllia in the southeast.

Gjirokastra is divided into quarters that developed as distinct communities according to the terrain. Five streets leading to the most interesting houses converge at the **Bazaar Pass** in the centre of town. The most beautiful houses with the most varied façades are in the **Pllake** and **Hazmurat** quarters. They vary markedly from the large buildings in **Palorto** and **Manalat** that create a more unified picture. The **Dunavat** and **Teqe** quarters show more individuality, but the green quarter **Cfake** is more artistic.

The **Old Market** quarter climbs the hill from the main square, Sheshi Çerçiz Topulli, in front of the Hotel A Z Çajupi (named for a poet). The hotel bar has a lovely carved wooden ceiling. The **New Market** was built in the early 17th century and rebuilt toward the end of the 19th century following a devastating fire. It remains today much as it was then, the commercial district.

A number of **mosques** are scattered throughout Gjirokastra, the most important being the one at the market built in 1757 and the 16th century one in the Mecite quarter with a lovely fountain at the foot of its minaret. Two **basilicas** date from the end of the 18th century, one at the Old Market and the other in the Varosh quarter. The 17th century Turkish **baths** are near the Mecite mosque.

Gjirokastra is all narrow up-and-down cobblestone streets and steps. Although some streets are open to vehicles, the best way to see the town is on foot.

Excursions from Gjirokastra

Worthwhile excursions from Gjirokastra include:

Libohova—14km to the southeast for its four clocktowers (the clocks were stolen in 1912), three 800-year-old trees and the cruciform-domed Shen Meri (St Mary's) church believed to be 13th century.

Peshkëpi—30km to the southeast, nearly on the Greek border, for its three-aisled Shen Meri church from the 12th century.

Labova e Vogel—30km to the northeast for its 10th century Shen Meri church built by Justinian for his mother, the most important example of Byzantine architecture in Albania.

Sofratika—28km southeast, a Greek minority village near Glina where Albania's best mineral water is bottled, for its ancient burial mounds. The Illyrian theatre with seating for 4,000 has been destroyed.

A scattering of **Greek minority villages** can be found in the southern corner of Albania around Gjirokastra in the Dropulli Plain. About 60,000 Greeks live here; they retain their language, have their own schools and newspaper and hold a few seats in parliament. This area is a bone of contention between Albania and Greece, which considers the region 'Northern Epirus'. Several border incidents, some fatal, occurred here in 1994.

THE SOUTHERN COAST

Albania's intricate coastline is one of the most beautiful parts of the country. Along the southern shore, spectacular mountains reach down to the Ionian Sea, leaving space here and there for quiet slivers of beach. Along the Adriatic Coast, wide expanses of sand stretch temptingly toward a calmer sea.

Saranda

Saranda is Albania's southernmost port and its most popular honeymoon town. The palm- and oleander-fringed promenade around its bay looks across the channel to Corfu, about 10km away, and is the setting for the evening *passeggiata*. Long hours of sunshine in summer and mild winters—Saranda is sheltered by mountains—make it attractive year round. A marina with berths for more than 300 yachts is projected.

In the 1st century BC the Illyrian port Onchesmos lay near the present town. During the Byzantine era, the city walls were fortified and churches built. At the end of the 1980s, the remains of a 6th century basilica were found, revealing a lovely floor mosaic of fish and animals—now sand-covered for protection.

The town declined during the Turkish occupation but was revived briefly as a port by Ali Pashë Tepelena. Greeks from Corfu burned it in 1878, and in 1940 Greek forces used it as a base for the invasion of Albania.

Within the ruins of the old city walls are the remains of Ajii Saranda, the **Monastery of the 40 Saints**, from which derived the name of the of the town (used only from the beginning of this century). The festival of these 40 Martyrs of Sebaste (in Armenia) takes place on 9 March.

The ruins of the Fortress of Lekurës, built at the end of the 16th and beginning of the 17th centuries, stand on a hill to the southeast of town. The History Museum in town contains local finds.

Between Saranda and Delvina is the 17th century village **Kamenica**, abandoned during the plague, with seven churches and chapels still standing.

The ruins of **Finiqi**, the 4th century BC Phoinike, spread over a flat-topped hill about 10km from Saranda. Bits of wall, the foundation of a basilica and parts of a theatre are visible.

The delightful 11th century **Church of Mesopotam** (Shën Kollit—St Nicholas), built by Constantine XI, stands tantalizingly off the road about 5km farther on. The name literally means 'Between the Rivers' and the church looks almost like a moated castle in its swampland between the Kalasa and Bistrica. As a fortified church of unusual architecture, it protected the bishops of Finiqi during various invasions. Inside the church is a superb fresco of Dimitrios of Thessaloniki, and on the walls outside are animal figures.

The most famous site in the area is Butrinti, 15km south of Saranda at the tip of the Ksamili Peninsula. Ancient Buthrot provides a comprehensive portrait of the epochs from the 6th century BC to the 18th century. Huge Illyrian stone walls stand cheek by jowl with a Greek theatre and Roman dwellings—and above it all towers the medieval **Vivari Fortress**, finally abandoned by Venice in 1796.

Virgil credits the Trojans with having founded Butrinti, but archaeologists say it was settled by the Kaonian tribe of Illyrians, who were joined by Greek traders from Corfu in the 6th century BC. The Illyrians fortified it in the 5th century BC; it expanded on to the plain in the 3rd and 2nd centuries BC and in 167 BC fell to Rome, which made it a colony with its own coins by 44 BC.

Under Byzantine rule Butrinti was the centre of a diocese. The Normans conquered it in the 11th century, the Venetians in 1690 and Ali Pashë Tepelena in 1797. The Turks ruled from 1822 until Albanian independence in 1913.

The winding road from Saranda to Butrinti is spectacular, passing wheat fields of the Bistrica River Valley, then crossing a narrow ridge with Butrinti Lake (ancient Lake Pelos) shining silver on one side and the deep blue sea on the other. Mussel farms protrude from the lake; water fowl skim the surface. The terraced land is thick with olive and citrus plantations.

Just at the start of the isthmus near **Çuka** stands a concrete guard house and military post. On the hilltop are the ruins of a fortified monastery. From here, Corfu seems within touching distance.

A bit farther along, **Ksamili State Farm** is still in operation and there is talk of making it a joint venture. The state-run restaurant on the hilltop of the town offers a superb view of the sea daubed with four small forested islands.

The road passes high above Ali Pasha's watchtower and customs house, then comes to an end at the ferry landing on Vivari Channel that connects the lake and the sea. On the other side sits a small triangular 14th-17th century fortress (restored) and used by Ali Pasha. Beyond it the Vrina Plain stretches toward Greece.

Butrinti

A shady path leads from the gate beside the ferry landing to the excavations. Butrinti was excavated first by Italian archaeologists (1927-1940) and later by Albanians.

The complex, built around the hillside, begins at the large city baths paved with black-and-white mosaics near the 2nd century **Temple of**

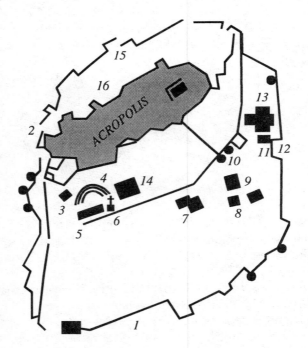

1	Landing stage	9	Thermal baths
2	West entrance	10	Main gate
3	Apollo's temple	11	Nymphaeum
4	Theatre	12	East entrance
5	Aesculapius's temple	13	Basilica
6	Early Christian church	14	House with hall
7	Storehouse	15	Lion gate
8	Baptistry	16	Citadel and museum

Asklepios (Roman Aesculapius), the Greek god of medicine. The temple's covered portico and inner chamber stand on earlier foundations and are connected to a 3rd century theatre.

The theatre is compact and steep, just 19 tiers of seats to accommodate about 1,500 people, its unusual quadrangle shape dictated by the terrain. An altar to Dionysos is in the orchestra pit and inscriptions on the corridor wall are said to commemorate the freeing of slaves. The 'Goddess of Butrint' (a 4th century BC head of Aphrodite or Apollo, depending on which camp you follow) found in one of its niches was recently returned to Albania by Italy and is now in the National History Museum in Tirana.

This area contains traces of Roman dwellings and shops and the **Brides' Well**, its white marble rim deeply trenched by ropes drawn up over the centuries. There are also two-storeyed warehouses and a Roman temple cum medieval church.

The 1st-2nd century **gymnasium** is floored with mosaics and contains a nymphaeum with three circular niches. It was built as a rectangular courtyard surrounded by separate rooms for exercise and for relaxing after a bath.

The path breaks out of the undergrowth again at the 5th century circular **Baptistry**, one of the best examples of early Christian architecture in the country. Two rings of 15 granite columns surround the font, all enclosed by a brick and stone wall. The floor is decorated with 67 coloured mosaic medallions laid out in seven concentric circles. Geometric figures and plant motifs dominate five of the circles, while the other two represent bird and animal life. Like other important mosaics throughout the country, these are covered with a heavy layer of plastic and sand for protection.

The imposing walls of a 6th century **basilica** reveal its T-shaped construction; arched pilasters divide it into three sections, the highest with windows above the arches.

A 2nd century brick **nymphaeum** is tucked into the undergrowth not far away. It contains a well and a chamber with walls niched for statues.

Then comes a fragment of 4th century BC **walls** made of huge rectangular stones. Dates of sections of Butrinti's walls vary, as reinforcement continued into the Middle Ages. Some of the early walls reached about 9m and were built with many bays and buttresses, making towers unnecessary at the time, although two towers reinforce the 3rd century BC Tower Gate on the south.

Once six gates led into the city. Surviving gates include the 4th century BC **Main Gate** (5 : high), the **Lake Gate** and the most beautiful, the

low 4th century BC *Porta e Luanit* (Lion Gate), named for the lintel relief of a lion attacking a bull. Behind the Lion Gate semicircular steps lead to a 3rd century well.

The path climbs a steep incline with a view of the lake to the site of the **Acropolis**, now occupied by the medieval castle. Behind its wall is a peaceful garden of palms and cannon. A museum is located in the castle, but the best items from its collection have been sent to Tirana for safekeeping.

The top of the wall gives a good view of the layout of Butrinti. Beyond the ruins, the delta land is cut by the Vivari Channel and guarded by the triangular fortress. The small **Church of Vrina** sits on a knoll in the distance.

From Butrinti to Vlora

The road north from Saranda passes near the sea at Lukova, then climbs quickly into barren mountains; it is narrow, curving and much patched, but now and then gives glimpses of the sea below. A pause at **Borshi** with its many springs is well deserved. The village **Qeparo** nestles in a cypress grove at the top of a rocky gorge.

Then the road begins to twist like a sidewinder on the run, giving dizzy views of the sea and its coves: now beaches, now waves licking the mountainsides, the kaleidoscope colours even more stunning at sunset.

On a peninsula in a deep bay, called **Porto Palermo** since Venetian days, stands another of Ali Pashë Tepelena's fortresses. It is in a military zone, once a top-secret submarine base.

Over the Piluri Pass is **Himara**, a twin town—its modern quarter on the seashore, the stony-brown old town on the mountainside. Known as Chimarra in pre-Christian times when it was settled by Greeks from Corfu, Himara developed into a stronghold of the Orthodox Church. It was the seat of a bishopric in the 9th century and became strong enough to spend very little time under Turkish domination. It once boasted 62 churches, and today is the site of Albania's oldest preserved church, Shën Sergjit (St Sergius) built in 1018, and in the process of being renovated. Ruins of an Illyrian fortress are on the top of the hill.

At the edge of the beach town is the Cave of Himara (Shpella e Himarës), site of a prehistoric settlement.

Continuing north the road passes through picturesque **Vuno** and descends to **Dhërmi**. This lovely cove, a workers' vacation colony, is certainly destined to become one of the best tourist developments on the coast. The well-bunkered beach is of pure white sand, the sea azure; pines, cedars and olives are interspersed with orange groves and honeysuckle on the shore. Shën Mëri (St Mary's Church), damaged in World War I but containing 13th and 14th century frescos, is a 20-minute walk up the mountain from town.

Palasa village perches at the foot of the Çika Mountains that shield the riviera from north winds. Caesar landed here in 48 BC to wage war against Pompey, and from here the road starts its steepest and roughest climb through a national park to the Llogara Pass (1,027m). All manner of vegetation thrives here, from pine trees to Mediterranean shrubs, parting now and then to give glimpses of the Ionian Sea shining deep

blue below. At the top of the pass is the Flag Pine, designated a 'cultural monument', so named because the constant winds have bent it into the shape of a flag. Where the road begins to descend there are two restaurants and a new tourist village, an excellent base for hiking in the area.

On the plain below, **Dukati** lies level with the Gulf of Otranto where the Ionian and Adriatic Seas meet. Here, too, the vegetation loses its Mediterranean character, and the houses are built to withstand the winters, of stone instead of brick, with small windows and without balconies.

The road now widens and is in better repair. At **Orikumi**, an important settlement in the 4th century BC, the Gulf of Vlora opens out in a shining expanse, protected by the Karaburuni Peninsula (22km long, 6km wide). A military base keeps the peninsula inaccessible. The road follows the coast to Vlora, passing delightful coves, excellent beaches and another Uji i Ftohtë (Cold Water) with 40 springs.

Just at the mouth of the bay is **Sazani**, Albania's largest island, whose history is as checkered as that of the mainland. Known as Sason in the 4th century BC, it was controlled in turn by the Venetians, Turks, British, Greeks and Italians.

Vlora

Vlora has also been earmarked for early tourism development, not only because of its beautiful coast but also because it is easily accessible from Italy. Vlora was famous for salt, wine and olives even when it was known as Aulon and it succeeded Apollonia as Illyria's major port. The ancient site is a few kilometres to the north of the modern town on the road to Narta. Southeast of Vlora, the ruins of ancient **Amantia** can be seen near the village of Plloça.

Vlora was captured by the Normans in 1081 and by Charles of Anjou in 1266. It became a part of the Kingdom of Arberia in 1272. Byzantines and Serbs were here, and the Ballshajs feudal lords from northern Albania; the Turks seized Vlora in 1417 and built a seaside fortress in 1531. In 1812, Ali Pashë Tepelena took control. The city is best remembered for 28 November 1912, when Ismail Qemali declared Albania independent and Vlora its capital. The triumph was short lived; Italy occupied the city in 1914.

Today, Vlora is Albania's second-largest port and a naval base. The **Mosque of Muradie**, built by the architect Synon for Sultan Sulejman in 1538-42, graces the central square. Its architecture is similar to that of Byzantine churches, a style adopted often by the Ottomans in the 15th to 17th centuries. A lively market hall crowned by a clock tower is nearby and one block away is the small **Historic and Ethnographic Museum** devoted to regional exhibits.

On a hilltop at the edge of town, the Kus-baba restaurant gives an excellent view of the town and its bay. **Kanina fortress** above the town is still in use as a naval base. It is of Venetian construction on Illyrian foundations.

A detour off the main road goes to **Narta**, a town at the tip of a large lagoon of the same name. Two of the lagoons' three channels to the sea have silted up, leaving only the northernmost one. Salt has been collected at Narta since the Middle Ages. A lovely little 13th century church can be seen here.

Fieri/Apollonia

Fieri is the next sizeable city, a mere youth growing up beside one of Albania's oldest inhabited sites. It was founded by Omer Pashë Vrioni, a local landowner, as a marketplace for the surrounding fertile plains, and it quickly developed as both an agricultural and industrial centre.

Its wide straight streets and apartment blocks were built by the French architect Barthelemy in 1864-70 on a former Vlach pilgrimage site— the church of St George, where herdsmen assembled for festivals every 23 April and 26 October.

The attraction of Fieri lies 12km away at Apollonia, quite possibly Albania's most important archaeological site, though most of it has yet to be uncovered. Take the road toward the resort town Semani and turn left toward Pojan. The ruins of Apollonia are just outside the village.

Apollonia was founded by Greeks from Corinth and Corfu in 588 BC—one of many cities in the realm dedicated to the god Apollo. Its proximity to the Aoos River (now the Vjosa) and the sea promoted thriving trade with other Adriatic and Mediterranean cities. At one time it had around 55,000 inhabitants and was a centre of Greek art and philosophy.

In the 1st century BC Caesar used it as a base in his war with Pompey, granting it free city-state status in return for its support. Following an earthquake in the 3rd century the Aoos changed course and Apollonia declined, giving rise to Aulon (modern Vlora).

Extensive remains of the 4th century BC city wall, nearly 5km long and about 3.5m thick, flank the hillside on which Apollonia was built. Many drainage channels are still visible, spaced under the wall about every 60m.

The 2nd century Hall of Agonothetes, called the **Bouleterion**, in the centre of the city served as council chambers. Its six-columned portico was restored by French archaeologists in the 1920s. Nearby are an obelisk dedicated to Apollo dating from the 4th century BC, a library and the Odeon, a small theatre that could seat 200.

Further remains include a niched portico from the 4th century BC, some Roman houses and shops including the 3rd century House of Mosaics and a 3rd century BC nymphaeum that collected water from five canals. The necropolis contains graves dating from Illyrian times, the oldest from the 6th century BC. A few years ago a Bronze Age helmet and shield were found there.

Many of the finds from Apollonia are now in Austria and France, taken by the archaeologists who first dug in Apollonia early in this century. Other items are displayed in Tirana. The Apollonia Museum in the former monastery is locked and empty but the gallery still holds a row of 1st-3rd century BC statues (headless but wearing elegant draperies) and a few amphoras and sarcophagi.

The monastery's **Church of Shën Mëri** (St Mary) is open. Dating from 1350, it is an architectural jewel but only a fragment of a fresco remains and the icons are badly damaged.

A detour of about 30km to the south of Fieri, near Ballshi in the Mallakastra highlands, leads to a very good Illyrian find. The ruins are near the village of **Hekali** and consist of part of the wall of a 3rd century BC Illyrian fortress, a 5,500-seat amphitheatre, a hippodrome, an agora and the mosaic floor of a basilica.

About 15km north of Fieri on the main highway, the Orthodox **Monastery of Ardenica** stands on a hilltop in the midst of a cypress grove. It was in use until the end of the 1950s, Albania's last functioning monastery in the Communist era. It has been turned into a small but very good hotel with a cellar tavern and a restaurant.

Its 13th century Shën Mëri (St Mary) Church is built on 6th century foundations. One of the walls collapsed in 1959 but it was rebuilt and the icons and wall paintings restored in the late 1980s. The 18th century frescoes are the work of Konstandin and Athanas Shpataraku of Korça; the icons are by Thanas of Elbasani.

Continuing north past Lushjna, a road turns off the main highway in the direction of **Divjaka**, a pine-forested national park that reaches to the seashore. It sits at the tip of the Karavastas Lagoon, almost completely enclosed by crab claws of land. Another students' and workers' resort of spartan hotels, the beach is one of the loveliest in the country. The European Union has provided a grant to help set up an eco-tourist zone here.

The main road continues inland to Kavaja and Lushnja, returning to the coast at Durrësi (see description on page 54).

THE SOUTH CENTRAL INTERIOR

The 'museum city' of Berati is worth a journey, even though it is somewhat out of the way. To reach it from Tirana, set out once again on the Via Egnatia from Durrësi. The road runs parallel to the railway; the Durrësi-Kavaja line was the first in Albania, built in 1947.

Kavaja is known for its carpets; though the state factory is closed now, weaving remains an important cottage industry and kelims wave like flags from roadside stands.

Kavaja was mentioned for the first time in the 16th century as Kavalje, when it was a medieval trade and crafts centre noted for its pottery.

In the centre of town are a mosque and a square clocktower. Outside town are the ruins of the Bashtova citadel, one of Skënderbeg's fortifications. To the east in **Çeta** is a 13th century church with Gothic remnants.

At Rrogozhina, the two branches of the Via Egnatia—from Durrësi and from Apollonia—converge; the town is both road and rail junction. Take the southern branch of the road across the Shkumbini River and into the 70km-long **Myzeqe Plain**, named for the Muzakaj family who owned it. Wheat, sunflowers, cotton and vegetables were produced on the collective farms here. Now privatization is under way.

Lushnja (ancient Marusium, medieval Lusnie) is where the congress held on 21 January 1920 re-established Albania's independence and voted to make Tirana the capital. The congress resulted in the short-lived administration of Fan Noli.

Leave the Via Egnatia here and take the smaller road into the Osumi Valley toward Berati. It passes through **Ura Vajgurore**, named for its sulphur springs where women once bathed in hope of fertility. This is also an oil-producing area; the industry is centred at Kuçova, formerly Qyteti Stalin. A Shën Kollit (St Nicholas) church dating from the 10th to 13th centuries can be found in the village of **Perondi** just to its south.

Berati

Overlooking a gorge of the Osumi River in the shadow of Mounts Tomori (2,415m) and Shpiragu (1,213m), the white city of Berati spreads up the hillside to its fortress.

The large blocks of stone at the foundations of the fortress denote the town's Illyrian origins 2,400 years ago. The town was called Antipatrea after the Romans took the city as a part of their Macedonian campaign. The Byzantine emperor Theodosius II strengthened it in the 5th century, renaming it Pulcheriopolis after his sister Pulcheria.

The city surrendered to the Bulgars in the 9th century and was a diocesan centre until the 11th century.

In the 13th century, the Despot of Epirus, Michael Angelus Comnenus, seized power, followed in 1345 by the Serbs under Stefan Dušan who named it Belgrad (White City), from which it takes its present name. It was the capital of the feudal principality Muzakaj for a time in the 14th century.

The Turks captured the city in 1450, and in trying to get it back Skënderbeg suffered his only defeat. Kurt Pasha built the bridge over the Osumi in 1780, but modern parapets have destroyed its former beauty. Ali Pashë Tepelena took the town in 1809.

After an earthquake in 1851, Berati developed into a crafts centre noted for elaborate woodcarving. On 22 October 1944, the Communists formed a government here, making it the first capital of the 'new' Albania. The city was liberated on 29 November 1944.

The fortress was burned by the Romans in 200 BC, strengthened in the 5th century by the Byzantines and rebuilt by the Emperor Justinian in the 6th century. Michael Comnenus rebuilt it again in the 13th century; it was during this time that houses began to be built within the walls. There were once 300 houses, but no water supply; water had to be carried up the hill from the river.

The only mosque inside the walls is the 14th century **Red Mosque**, the oldest mosque in Albania. Its ruined minaret points bleakly

heavenwards, exposing the influence of churches on mosque architecture in Albania. The minaret is unique in its round shape, made of three layers of brick, whereas most minarets are octagonal. Berati was a bastion of Orthodoxy; a national congress held here in 1922 declared the Albanian church independent of the Constantinople patriarch and Berati remained the seat of a bishop until Albania became officially atheist in 1967.

One of the seven churches still standing within the fortress walls, **St Mary's Cathedral** with its annexes, has been turned into the **Onufri Museum**. Shën Mëri or Kisha e Madhe—the Big Church—is 18th century, a three-aisled basilica with two cupolas. The museum contains a collection of icons by Onufri and other artists, as well as a lovely carved wooden iconostasis dating from 1806 and a superb wrought metal icon depicting the life of Elijah.

Onufri, the 16th century master icon and fresco painter whose works were rediscovered only in the 1950s, came from Berati and established a school of painting there that spread his style as far as modern-day Greece and Yugoslavia. He introduced realism into the icon and a new colour called 'Onufri's red' that he used in combination with a brilliant palette of violet, orange and turquoise.

Of the six other churches within the fortress, **Shën Mëri Vllachernes** (the Church of St Mary Blacherna, so named because it once had a copy of the Mary icon in the Blacherna Palace in Constantinople) contains murals by Onufri's son Nikolla; **Shën Triallës** (the Church of the Holy Trinity) is one of the best-preserved cruciform churches in Albania; **Shën Todher** (the Church of St Theodore) and **Kisha Vangjelistra** (the Church of the Annunciation) have paintings by Onufri himself. **Shën Kollit** (St Nicholas Church) contains frescos dated 1591; those in **Shën Konstandin dhe Jelena** (SS Constantine and Helena) are dated 1644.

Down a steep path outside the fortress wall is the small **Shën Mëhillit** (Church of St Michael), also known as Ton Archangelon (Holy Archangel).

The panorama terrace of the café/restaurant just within the fortress wall gives an excellent view over the city.

Berati is divided into three distinct quarters—**Mangalem** on the fortress side of the river, **Gorica** on the opposite side and **Kalaja** within the fortress itself. The characteristic houses are white and have two storeys, the wide top ones with many windows slightly overhanging the lower floor.

The main square in Mangalem is surrounded by the restored **Xhamia e Plumbit** (Leaden Mosque) from 1555 (noted for its good acoustics), the Hotel Tomori and the Palace of Culture.

The most beautiful mosque is the **Xhamia e Beqareve** (Bachelors' Mosque—bachelors were unmarried shop clerks who served as a militia) built in 1827. It stands at the foot of the path leading to the fortress and its outer walls are decorated with lush frescos of flowers and landscapes. In addition to the mosques, there is a *teqe* of the Halveti sect built in 1790.

The **Berati History Museum** contains many local finds as well as a Turkish room with low divans around the walls and lovely carpets on the floor. The **Ethnographic Museum** is in a characteristic 19th century house with a balcony. It contains traditional dress, a row of medieval 'shops'—goldsmith, shoemaker, coppersmith—and rooms furnished in Turkish style. An olive press on the balcony is a reminder that the city is known for its olives; the olives of Berati are best for eating, those of Vlora are used for oil.

The **city park** stretches out in front of the Hotel Tomori along the riverbank, a pleasant stroll to the bridge and across to the Gorica quarter, formerly the quarter of Vlachs and Jews, an excellent place to wander for a view of the town and to stop for a coffee at one of the small cafés.

The 11th century St Athenas Church can be seen at **Poliçan**, about 20km southeast of Berati.

There was an old man in Berat
Had a quite unacceptable hat:
It sprouted carnations
And flags of the nations,
With a crown like a tall ziggurat.....

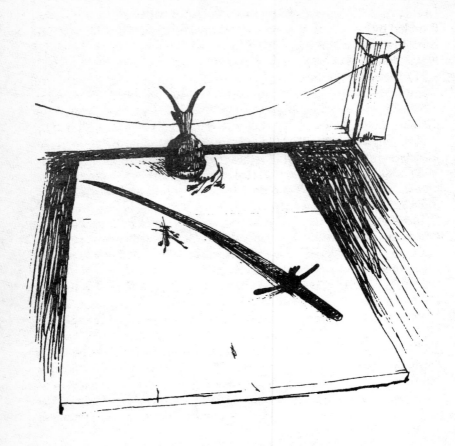

The Skënderbeg Memorial, a simple monument on the bank of the river, was built in 1968 on the ruins of the Cathedral of St Nicholas, where Skënderbeg was buried.

THE NORTH

Lezha

Lezha, called Lissus in ancient times, is one of Albania's oldest towns, founded by Dionysus of Syracuse. He erected the walls in 385 BC but soon lost the city to the Ardian Illyrians. It is situated on the Drini River about 70km northwest of Tirana.

Throughout its history, Lezha has been subjugated by foreign rulers. The Romans under Caesar conquered it in 68 BC, Byzantine domination followed, then Serbian. The Dukagjini feudal princes surrendered the town to Venice in hopes of protection but it fell to the Turks in 1478.

In March 1444, Skënderbeg convened the Albanian League in Lezha in an attempt to unite Albania against the Turks. He died on 17 January 1468 at the second meeting of the League and was buried there.

A memorial has been erected on the river bank on the site of **Skënderbeg's tomb**. He was buried at Shën Kollit (St Nicholas) Cathedral, but when the Turks overran the town they desecrated the grave. It is said that the soldiers used Skënderbeg's bones as amulets. A Bektashi dervish saved the empty tomb, however, and the church was turned into the Selimije Mosque.

The memorial hall has been built incorporating its ruins, roofed in steel and glass to let in half-light, with heavy bronze doors cast in 1981 bearing the reliefs of Skënderbeg's helmet, the double eagle and laurel wreaths. The walls of the hall are lined with the coats of arms of the 25 towns where Skënderbeg's battles took place. He won 23 of them, losing only one (Berati, 1455) and one ending in a draw (Sfetigrad, 1448). Copies of Skënderbeg's helmet and ceremonial sword have been placed on a marble slab beneath an altar which is graced by a bust of the hero sculpted by Odhise Paskali, who produced many of Albania's Skënderbeg statues.

St Nicholas Cathedral dating from 1459 was built on the site of a 13th century church. The remains of a second altar have been unearthed and a dim fresco of St Nicholas has been uncovered in the memorial hall. The windows are still bricked up, but from the outside it is possible to make out a rosette—a typical element of churches—over the door.

The earthquake of 1979 revealed a treasure trove for archaeologists around the tomb; houses were not rebuilt there to keep the area free for study. The low remains of an Illyrian wall run in front of the memorial.

On a steep hill above the present town lies the Illyrian, Byzantine and Medieval **fortress**. It was first built in the 6th century BC; some of the large polygonal stones at the base of the walls remain from Illyrian times. In the 4th century BC the city spread down to the river, and the entire area was enclosed within a wall that was 3-4m wide with a perimeter of 2,200m and had 54 towers and 12 gates.

By the Middle Ages, only the lower part of the city was inhabited, but in the 16th century the Turks under Sultan Sulejman built their own fortifications on the foundations of the old fortress above the town.

There are a few remains of a second, older fortress—possibly 4th century BC—on Shëlbumit Mountain southeast of town. The site was settled as early as the Iron Age. Two cities grew up—Lissus and Acrolissus—but the older Acrolissus was abandoned.

About 5km west of Lezha, the former hunting lodge of Mussolini's son-in-law, Galeazzo Ciano Conte di Cortellazo, has been turned into a hotel and restaurant. The nature reserve once used by government functionaries now provides hunting grounds for tourists.

About 8km northwest of Lezha lies **Shëngjini Beach**, a pleasant stretch of sand that ends at a naval base. Several waterfront restaurants have sprung up but as yet there is no hotel.

Shkodra

Shkodra, Albania's third-largest city after Tirana and Durrësi, is situated about 115km northeast of Tirana, 45km north of Lezha and 35km south of Hani i Hotit, the border crossing to Montenegro. It sits in a river delta—the Buna, Kiri and Drini converge on its outskirts—about 5km from Lake Shkodra.

Already inhabited in the 4th century BC, Shkodra became the capital of the Ardian Illyrians in the 3rd century BC and later was occupied by the Romans and Byzantines. In the Middle Ages it was ruled by the Ballshaj feudal lords who turned it over to Venice in 1396 in the face of the Turkish threat. Venice called it Scutari, a name sometimes still used.

The Turks besieged the city in 1474 with 80,000 troops but did not conquer Shkodra until 1479. This time Sultan Mehmet II led the campaign himself with 150,000 soldiers. The story is told by the priest Marlin Barleti who published the book *The Siege of Shkodra* in 1504.

The Turks named the town Iskenderia and built a huge bazaar that flourished until the mid-19th century. The Buna River, which flows 44km from Lake Shkodra to the Adriatic, gave Shkodra merchants access to the entire Mediterranean. The city itself was a handicrafts centre known especially for its silk and silver.

After the Ottoman decline in the 18th century, Shkodra became a *pashalic* of the Bushatllijtë family. In the early part of the 20th century it was occupied successively by Montenegro, Serbia, Austria, Italy and France.

Rozafa Citadel (881m perimeter) dominates the town from its steep hill (130m). The area was inhabited as early as the 2nd century BC and was the residence of the Illyrian king Genthius from 197 to 168 BC. A small castle stood here in Byzantine times and remains of 12th century houses have been found. The present fortress was constructed on Illyrian and Roman ruins; walls built in the mid-14th century by the Ballshaj lords were strengthened by the Venetians in the 15th century and by the Turks in the 16th century.

The citadel was strong enough to repulse the Turks in 1474; when the Ottomans finally prevailed, they made it the seat of a *pashalic*, moving to the lower city only in 1863.

Most of the remains today are Venetian. The fortress is made up of three systems of fortifications and seven towers, admirably illustrating military innovations through the years. One enters a small yard at the barbican; the Venetian lion presides over the gate and there is a tunnel under the tower. The second gate is 15th century and the passageway is L-shaped to slow down attacking armies if they breached the gate. Above the gate is a hole in the roof from which boiling oil could be poured on the invaders.

Inside the second yard, steps lead to the top of the walls from where there is an excellent view of Shkodra and a bridge over the Buna River. Here stand the ruins of the **Church of St Stephen**, enlarged and made a cathedral in 1319, then turned into a mosque in 1479 when the minaret was built. Near the mosque is a small building believed to have served as a prison and the ruins of what probably were houses. There are also two cisterns.

A third wall protects the large inner courtyard that contains the

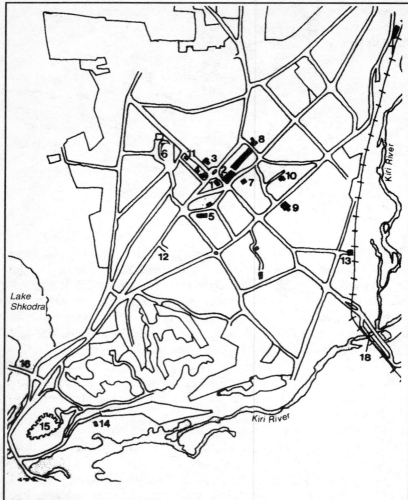

Shkodra

1   Rozafa Hotel
2   Museum
3   Theatre
4   Radio station
5   Government buildings
6   Stadium
7   Franciscan church
8   University
9   Cathedral
10 Luigj Gurakuqi Museum House

11 Osa Kuka Museum House
12 17th century Turkish baths–now
    restaurant
13 Railway station
14 Leaden Mosque
15 Rozafa Citadel
16 Buna Bridge
17 Bahçalleku Bridge
18 Kiri Bridge

restored arsenal, now housing a restaurant and museum. The fortress had seven secret tunnels leading to the Drini River; the entrances to two of them can be seen.

The top of the walls give excellent views of the three rivers that converge here, of Lake Shkodra and of Montenegro in the distance. The large **Xhamia e Plumbit** (Leaden Mosque) with its 14 cupolas sits isolated on a bank of the Drini below. Only the lower part of its minaret remains. Built in 1773 by Mehmet Bushati, it appears to have been influenced by Christian architecture, especially in relation to its large apse.

The modern city of Shkodra fans out from a central traffic circle, surrounded by the Rozafa Hotel, the round building of Radio Shkodra, the theatre and the Folk Museum.

Much of Shkodra was destroyed during World War II in the Hoxha regime's eradication of religious buildings and by the earthquake of 1979. The house containing the *Muzeu Popullor* of local history and ethnography may be reclaimed by its former owner. The typical 19th century house, built by an Englishman who attempted to start a

Protestant church in Shkodra, sits in a park across the street from the Rozafa Hotel. A mosque is under construction beside it.

In the museum, a relief map shows Shkodra's excellent geographical position 22km as the crow flies from the Adriatic Sea. Rich in forests and fish, with a good climate, it was settled in palaeolithic times. Axe heads used for trade and a sword from Mikene indicate that the Illyrians carried on commerce with Greece. There are spears, a fragment of a helmet and fibula from the Bronze Age and much jewellery decorated with the pagan symbols of sun and snake. During Illyrian times, Shkodra minted its own coins. Though the Illyrians had their own language, the coins are stamped with both Greek and Latin letters.

The museum shows that in the 2nd century BC Illyria lost its war with Rome because King Genthius fought on the open plain instead of trusting the strength of the fortress. Shkodra remained a Roman capital for 300 years; however, the Illyrian culture was not assimilated. Later, in the 4th-6th centuries when cities declined and most of the country became an agricultural backwater, Shkodra remained a progressive town. When the Roman Empire was divided, Shkodra became part of Byzantium but remained at Rome's side in terms of religion.

Exhibits depict the culture of the Arbers, descendants of Illyrians, ancestors of modern Albanians. A stone Latin cross with reliefs of palm leaves and the sun indicates that both Christianity and paganism were at work here at the same time.

There are catapults from the Turkish invasions, some of the stones weighing 650kg, the most modern weapons of the day. After the Turkish victory, many Shkodrans emigrated so as not to live under Muslim rule.

The upper floor of the museum is devoted to ethnography, with a photographic exhibition of Shkodra architecture, ornately carved ceilings, a decorative fireplace and a Turkish room. A large oil painting, *Two Roads,* was saved first from the cathedral when it was turned into a sports hall, then from the Museum of Atheism when it was closed. It uses Shkodra landscape and costume in a depiction of the paths to Heaven and Hell. The artist painted himself as a lute player on the road to Hell.

The museum in the **house of Luigj Gurakuqi** is intact but its future is uncertain as the house has been returned to its former owner. The gate at No 32 Rr Luigj Gurakuqi is imposing, in keeping with the family's political and social stature. The stone walls surrounding the house were once 5m tall.

A driveway of stone leads to the two-storey house built in the typical Albanian style of 200 years ago: the ground floor used for storage, the airy *çardhak* reached by wide stairs. For security reasons the entry is not at the front of the house. The *çardhak* here is on the corner of the house—typical of Shkodra—though in some houses it was situated in the middle. Several doors open off it and a 'women's corner' where textile work was done has been built at one side. In the 19th century, Shkodra was known particularly for silk garments worn on ceremonial occasions. Other sections of the *çardhak* are a platform over the stairs for musicians and a raised spot reserved for the mother of the house.

Two of the rooms treat the life of Gurakuqi and two others, the general ethnography of Shkodra. Gurakuqi was born in 1879 and began his career as a poet and translator. As the first Albanian Minister of Education in 1912, he opened 200 elementary schools. He participated in the Revolution of June 1924 and served as finance minister in the government of Fan Noli. He was assassinated on 2 March 1925. His bloodstained suit is displayed in a glass case, along with the red and black streamers from his funeral wreaths, his trunk, documents and photographs.

The ethnographic section of the museum is made up of a guestroom with an intricate balcony for the women and an ornately carved ceiling, and a kitchen whose unique fireplace creates a low stove. The house was heavily damaged in the war with Montenegro and restored as a museum only in 1963.

Another house from the same period—the birthplace and childhood home of both the popular hero Oso Kuka and Ramiz Alia, Albania's last communist leader—is being restored as the **Museum of Oso Kuka** on Rr Oso Kuka, leading from Radio Shkodra to the stadium. Kuka was a commander at the battle of Vranina at Lake Shkodra in the 1861-78 war against Montenegro. His elite troop of 24 holed up in a small tower at Vranina when Montenegro invaded. As the enemy clambered on to the tower, Kuka blew it up, killing 200 Montenegrins along with his own men. He has been revered since then as a hero of resistance.

From behind the Rozafa Hotel the tree-shaded Rr 13 Dhjetori 1990 leads to the large City Park with a school on one side and pink government buildings on the other. On a small side street, Rr Banja e Vogël, the Turkish baths have been turned into a restaurant. From the park, Rr Daud Borki leads to the huge statue of Isa Buletini who fought against Yugoslavia at the beginning of this century. He accompanied Ismail Qemali to the 1913 Assembly in Paris. A story is told about one of his diplomatic missions to London: the men were to leave their guns in an antechamber before going into the minister's office. Buletini placed his gun aside but when he faced the minister, he suddenly drew a small pistol to demonstrate that Albanians would not be disarmed.

Excursions from Shkodra

Shkodra is an excellent base for several excursions in the area and into the Albanian Alps.

Shiroka, about 5km away on the shore of Lake Shkodra, is a village presided over by a villa of King Zogu. There are several small beaches on the lake but the village has not been developed for tourists.

Velipoja beach lies 32km southwest of Shkodra on the Adriatic; its almost-untouched sand stretches 14km. The holiday flats here are popular with Albanians, but facilities for foreign tourists have not yet been developed.

The **Ura e Mesit**, the bridge over the Kiri River at Mesi about 8km northeast of Shkodra, is one of the most important and best-preserved Turkish bridges in Albania. Built in the 18th century by Mustafa Pashë Bushati, it is probably a reconstruction of a 15th century Venetian bridge. It has 11 arches and two niches graduated in size, is 112m long and reaches a height of 15m at the centre. It makes a slight turn just before the main arch. Its setting is marred by the modern bridge beside it and a quarry in the background.

Thethi, 76km to the northeast, is in the centre of the Albanian Alps. The road from Shkodra passes through picturesque scenery and the village of Boga. Along the road one sometimes sees people dressed in the traditional costume of the region. This is the country of the *kulla,* stone towers and tower-like houses built as protection during blood feuds. In Thethi, a tower *kulla* near the waterfalls on the Shala River can be visited.

The area is excellent for hiking in summer, surrounded as it is by 2,000m peaks. The tallest mountain here is Jezerca at 2,693m. In winter, there is usually 5-6m of snow, and winter sports facilities may be developed in the future. It is possible to hike around Jezerca from Thethi to Valbona, thus reaching the northeast side of the country in less time than it takes to travel by ferry or car.

Vermoshi, 95km to the northeast of Shkodra, is the northernmost town in Albania. Only the first 50km of road, which passes through seven villages of stone houses, are asphalted. Vermoshi spreads out in a wide valley along the Ceni River. This, too, is an excellent area for trekking, though one must be careful of the Yugoslav border which is just steps away from the village.

Komani to Fierza

The best alternative to hiking from northwest to northeast Albania is to travel by ferry across the lakes created when the Drini River was dammed in the 1970s. Dams separate the Vau i Dejës, Komani and

Fierza Lakes. Albania's biggest hydropower station, built 1971-75, is at the town of Komani and the second-largest is at Fierza.

The Vau i Dejës lake flooded the old city of **Sarda**, forming an island where seven churches remain above water. The city flourished in the 11th century. Shurdhahut Fortress here was the home of the Dukagjini feudal family; it fell to the Turks in 1491.

The car and passenger ferry from Komani to Fierza sails daily; Komani is a drive of about 1½ hours from Shkodra and a bus service connects with the ferry. At Fierza, buses to Bajram Curri meet the boat. The ferry trip takes about two hours and the bus to Bajram Curri about 40 minutes.

The ferry sails **Komani Lake** between wild mountains, running through narrow gorges of grey stone. The shores are much indented with quiet coves here and there.

Tropoja

Bajram Curri, called Kolgecaj until 1952, is the capital of Tropoja and the northernmost district capital in Albania. It is known for its chestnuts and plums and has major deposits of chromium, bauxite and copper. Its population is about 75% Muslim and 25% Catholic. The district is just across the border from Kosova and shares its culture and traditions.

Bujan, a small town about 6km south of Bajram Curri, was the site of the 1943 conference between Albania and Yugoslavia where it was agreed to unify Kosova territory and place it under Albania. However, the plan never materialized. Kosova was given to Serbia in 1913 at the London Conference, and so it remains.

Just to the northeast of Bujan are the ruins of an Illyrian wall from Rosnje fortress, dating from the 4th century BC.

The town **Bajram Curri** is named for the patriot who took part in the fight for independence against King Zogu and was executed by Zogu's troops in a cave at nearby Dragobi on 29 March 1925. His statue in front of the local museum dominates the town square.

The museum is devoted to local handicrafts and heroes; at the entrance is a fine example of the *sexhade*—a thick carpet unique to this part of Albania—with the motifs of an eagle, snowcapped mountains, electric power and guns (this place has been a battlefield many times). There are small collections of prehistoric pottery and Illyrian coins. The museum stresses that this land is ancient Dardania.

Four stained-glass windows depict Illyrian bards and warriors. A section about medieval times features the era of warrior-bards, particularly Gjergj Elez Alia—perhaps a mythical figure, though his tomb is said to be near Valbona. Among the songs he sang is the popular ballad of Ulkonja, a baby left in the mountains and raised by a wolf.

There is also a medieval room with a fireplace, furnished with low tables and stools, where the bards played the *lahuta,* the one-stringed lute, the string often made of horsehair.

A stone house typical of the region—home of Shpend Balia, compatriot of Bajram Curri—at the edge of town, on the road to Valbona, is a cultural monument that can be visited, though it is a private home. Farther along the road is another statue of Curri.

This is an excellent region for trekking and the best trek is into the mountains around Valbona 36km away. The road north from Bajram Curri follows the Valbona River. At **Shoshanit** the remnants of a Byzantine fortress have all but disappeared, but there is a picturesque and abundant spring here.

Dragobi village, a widespread grouping of *kulla* towers and houses, makes an excellent photo stop.

Valbona village sits at the entrance to a wide circular valley, surrounded by mountains that rise more than 2,500m. To one side is a group of mountains called Grykat e Hapëta and to the other is Kollata Mountain, the tallest here at 2,555m. Jezerca, the highest peak in the northern range, cannot be seen but there is a path leading to it that goes on to Thethi in the northwest of the country.

About 3km outside Valbona is the picturesque **Fushë e Gjehve** (Cattle Plain) where Albania won a battle against the Serbs and Montenegrins in 1913. A monument to this battle stands at the edge of the village.

The best hotel in Bajram Curri is the Shkëlzen, named for the mountain that towers over the town. The hotel in Valbona is closed.

Kukësi

The passenger ferry (no vehicles) on **Fierza Lake** from Bajram Curri to Kukësi sails daily except Sunday from Gropaj, a very simple landing stage below the dam and electric power station. There is no bus to Gropaj from Bajram Curri, a distance of about 30km. The ferry ride to Kukësi takes about four hours.

Kukësi can also be reached by a reasonably good road from Shkodra, via Puka and Fushë-Arrëza, going over the Malit Pass (740m). **Puka**, where the poet Migjeni taught, is known for its woodcarving. To the west of Puka the ruins of the medieval Dalmacia fortress can be seen at **Qerret i Epërm**.

Though the name Kukësi is shown on maps, the town is actually named Kukësi i Ri (New Kukësi). The old town, known as Gubuleum in classical times, was drowned in 1976 by Lake Fierza. The new town was once 'totally socialist' because it had never had private homes—only concrete blocks of flats. However, a few new private houses are now being built.

Chromium and copper mines bring in such income as there is. The carpet factory has closed, as has the local museum.

The town perches on a promontory of the lake; the highest mountain here is Gjalica (2,480m), an excellent place for hiking. One of the most picturesque spots is **Kroi i Bardhë** behind the mountain. Natural beauty and spaciousness are the great attractions here, though there are *kulla* villages and a scattering of ancient ruins, as well.

A good hotel sits above the ferry landing on the outskirts of town.

THE NORTHERN INTERIOR

The main road north from either Tirana or Durrësi leads through Laçi past an abandoned chemical factory. Shortly after Milot, the road forks: the left-hand turning goes to **Rubiku**, following the Mati and Fani Rivers.

On a hill above Rubiku is the little Shelbuemet Catholic Church, built in Byzantine style. The interior paintings also show Byzantine influence though they are Catholic in concept.

The road continues toward Rrësheni but shortly before reaching that town, a left-hand turn goes toward Shën Liezhri i Orosh, the Abbey of St Alexander of Orosh, perched at 1,300m just west of Rrëshen. The abbey was influential in Skënderbeg's time and in 1888 Pope Leo XIII made it the seat of a territorial prelate.

From here, double back and drive through **Rrësheni**; just outside Perlati, the high road of Mirdita leads to Kurbneshi and on to the **Lura Lakes**. The road is reasonably good, running along the Uraka River through rolling hills and pasture land.

Several villages sprawl under the Lura Mountains — Kroj-Lura, Fushë-Lura and Gur-Lura. The highest point here is Kunora e Lurës (Lura's Crown), a bare peak reaching 2,121m. The Lura Lakes can be reached from Gur-Lura by rough rock road (four-wheel drive needed for the height, if not for the pull). They are glacial cirques set in a forest of beech and conifers at about 1,200-1,500m.

Seven of the 11 lakes can be seen from the road; the other four are in the mountains, accessible only by hiking. The largest lakes along the road are Liqeni i Madhe (Big Lake), Liqeni i Zi (Black Lake), Liqeni i Lopeve (Cow Lake) and Liqeni i Luleve (Flower Lake). The three smaller lakes that can be seen from the road are Rasava, Kallabas and Prejkros Ligat. In summer, Luleve in particular is covered with waterlilies; in winter, the lakes freeze.

At present there is no hotel at the Lura Lakes though plans are being made to develop tourism here. This is an excellent spot for treks, less strenuous but just as beautiful as in the Alps.

From the Lura Lakes a very bad 75km road leads to Peshkopia, descending to the Murra Pass (950m) and running past the picturesque villages of **Murri** and **Selishta**. The **Bridge of Topojana** across the Black Drini near Peshkopia marks the spot of one of Skënderbeg's bloodiest successes, the Battle of Otonete in 1446.

About 35km from Peshkopia, but not visible from it, is **Korabi**, Albania's highest mountain at 2,751m.

Peshkopia itself is a backwater, though important strategically because of the proximity to the Macedonian and Yugoslav borders. It has a hotel and a health spa. The traditional-style house that was once the ethnographic museum has been turned into a bar and restaurant.

The shortest road from Peshkopia to Burreli cannot be recommended; however, the better road is just 72km, passing the picturesque village

Tobacco drying—house near Klos

of **Zerqan** and running through the new mining town of **Bulqiza**. The area is noted for its chrome, sulphur and marble. The road continues over the Buallit Pass (900m) to **Klosi**, once a market town for the entire Mati; from here it is possible to make an excursion to **Dars**, a village of *kullas*.

Burreli is the chief town of the Mati district; its hotel is closed, as is the regional history museum, but it is a good place to stop for lunch or refreshments. A new mosque is being built in the city park, and from here there is an excellent view across the rolling hills. Burreli is the birthplace of Pjëter Budi (1566-1622), bishop of Sada, who tried to convince the Pope to organize a crusade to free Albania from the Turks. Mustafa Xhani (1910-1947), known as Baba Faja of the Martanesh Teqe, made Burreli a centre of anti-Fascist resistance. The district was also the home of the feudal family that produced King Zogu.

The road from Burreli to Kruja cannot be recommended despite its beauty, especially around the Shtama Pass. Instead take the good road toward **Ulza** past the lovely artificial Ulza Lake and return to Tirana via Milot and Laçi.

The Journals

Foreword to the Journals

My assignment was to update the practical guide section of the 1989 edition of *Albania: A Guide and Illustrated Journal* by Peter and Andrea Dawson. However, the months I spent in Albania in 1993-94 were an experience that no foreigner could have dreamed of when the Dawsons were there, so I have written a parallel journal as well, more about people than places, telescoping time to make it more cohesive. I hope it will give an insight into a country of overwhelming hospitality and pride, a country that royally repays a visit in spite of the hardship it faces on the long road toward taking its place in the West.

Linda White, 1995

Notes

Time in Albania is divided into BEFORE and NOW. BEFORE refers to the 40-odd years of the Enver Hoxha regime. NOW begins with the sweeping changes of 1991. Time earlier than the Communist period is simply called 50 YEARS AGO.

Extracts from the Dawsons' journal are in *italics*. Place names may be spelled differently in the two journals (see note on spellings, page viii).

THE TIRANA JOURNALS

I entered Albania not through the infamous puddle of disinfectant (already long gone) but through an ankle-deep mud hole. I arrived in November in the middle of a rainstorm.

An acquaintance, Wilma, and I had taken the ferry from Trieste; we landed in Durrësi just as darkness fell. I paid US$5 for a visa. No one wanted to know what was in my luggage.

Our Albanian friend Ani climbed around a wall and came on board to meet us. His father, Isa, was waiting for us away from the dock.

It would have been impossible to fit four people into Wilma's car—it was packed to the gills—so Ani walked me across the dark, wet ground to the place where police were more or less holding back the crowd meeting the ferry. He whistled up his father (they must use a code like yodelling in the Swiss Alps) and handed me over.

Off we went into the wet darkness, slipping on loose stones, scrambling blindly over a railway track. I could not see to avoid the mud holes, but at least my boots were watertight. We reached the station just as the Tirana bus was revving up.

As we slow at the Yugoslav frontier, the previously extravagant lighting of farms and houses comes to an end, and the checkpoint stands in darkness, not a guard in sight.

We get off the coach and unload our luggage, in readiness for the walk across no-man's land. In Albania independent travel is not permitted, and our group of 40 people stands, chatting, eyeing the Yugoslav barrier, and, no doubt, eyeing each other in case any over-eccentric characters will need to be avoided during our enforced togetherness.

Sue, our English tour leader, and Stefan, the Yugoslavian coach driver, explore the darkened guard house in an attempt to find someone to sanction our crossing. We can see the Albanian checkpoint, illuminated behind their barrier, and in contrast it looks a lively spot. A coach is parked—waiting for us?—dark figures look back at us, and a guard stands in a low watchtower. Music from an Albanian radio drifts across. All very John le Carré.

At 11pm the Yugoslav guards emerge, after being roused by Sue and Stefan. Rumour has it that they were sleeping, having had a few drinks— a good job for them that the Albanians didn't choose tonight to launch an invasion.

Sue collects our passports, and goes with the guards to smooth the process of checking them off: Stefan lends them his torch to make this easier...

We collect our cases, say goodbye to Stefan and, like a works outing, stagger across the 200 metres of no-man's land to Albania.

A legend gone: there is a disinfectant tank in the road, but it appears to be for vehicles rather than pedestrians—certainly you would need to wear wellies rather than our fashionable trottercases to get through it.

We stand by the "People's Socialist Republic of Albania" sign, whilst the guard checks us off individually against the photos on the group visa list. This is not as easy as it sound: firstly, because of the traditional unrealism of photo-booth visa snaps; secondly, because the naughty French (who organize the group visas, having diplomatic relations with Albania) have shuffled the photos and split up husbands and wives, families and partners, trying no doubt to inject a little spice into our holiday.

The armed guards, in olive green with red star cap badges and red collar flashes, look on in a mildly bored and bemused way, whilst from the pink guard house (pink? for a guard house?) on our left, soldiers come out on to a balcony to give us a glance. The radio music comes from there: maybe there is a truce tonight, and they are having a party too. And do they have illicit games of football in no-man's land on May Day?

Checked off, we troop into the customs block on the right to sign our declaration forms: no pornography, Bibles or Korans. All this in a room with red plastic armchairs, Albturist ashtrays, a vase of plastic flowers and jade green colour-washed walls (Paint Magic comes to Albania). We are asked if we really *really don't have any porn or Bibles, and no one says, 'Oh, all right then, I have got a dozen copies of* Sexy Romps *in my case, sorry about that.'*

We line up for our luggage to be searched, by two amiable officials in chocolate brown suits with wide lapels. A glass-fronted cupboard has displays of books by Enver Hoxha, in brown covers with gold titles, and one photograph of Comrade Enver hangs on the far wall. My copy of Williams Bland's A Short Guide to Albania *is waved through (some guidebooks printed outside Albania are not permitted), along with our other two books: no blacklist for Robert Louis Stevenson or Chatterton. The three men with beards in our group are not ordered to shave: neat beards are acceptable, so another legend is laid to rest.*

Out of the customs house, and we load our cases on to a surprisingly modern Mercedes bus—we'd expected an ancient Russian or Chinese deathtrap—and climb aboard to the sound of a Dionne Warwick's Greatest Hits *tape, which the driver has helpfully put on.*

The hour-long ride into Tirana was uneventful. Isa spoke little English so my jumble of questions had to wait. We alighted somewhere among large blocks of flats where Isa bought loaves of bread at a hole-in-the-wall bakery. Clutching bread, luggage and umbrellas, Isa strode along and I struggled to keep up. The night was black and there were no streetlights. The last mud hole was deeper than the others.

Ani's family lives in a new block of flats, three floors up, no railing on the stairs. After the dizzy ascent, I was greeted with a glass of raki and was already settled in when Wilma and Ani arrived.

'With the Party at our head, we will strengthen our forces against the imperialists and revisionists'

We set off on a moonlit drive across the Shkodër plain, on what seems to be a reasonable road. It's too dark to see, despite the moonlight, much more than some irrigation ditches and concrete pillbox bunkers close to the road. However, even at 1.30am there are signs of activity: people going to or coming from the night shift, a tractor is harrowing by floodlight, and lights are on in many of the houses. Lights also in a factory or collective farm: the three shifts a day system is in operation, and the machines must be kept running.

Our Albanian guides introduce themselves: Rasim, who had helped us with the form-filling back at the border, and who speaks excellent English, and Pilo the driver. Pilo claims to know only 'Thank you very much'. As a welcome to Albania, he takes the microphone, drives one-handed, and sings an Albanian love song in a fine baritone.

We reached the Hotel Rosafa in Shkodër at 2am, to find that, despite the hour and the delay in our arrival, the waiters are all set to serve the evening meal...

Day 1: I awoke to find the bed full of mosquito bodies. I thought it was too late in the year for mosquitoes but these must be the last sluggish survivors.

Today, 28 November, is Independence Day, at least according to the

Democrats who are now in office. The Socialists say the date is 29 November, the day in 1944 when the German forces were finally driven out of Shkodra. Since today is Sunday, offices will be closed tomorrow and both sides will get their way this year.

We walk to the centre of town, where street markets are doing good business with their neat array of leeks, eggs, shoes, cigarettes and bananas. Tables of beige-and-brown *torte*—the one kind of cake I saw in Albania—are for sale in front of a pastry shop. Food is plentiful now, though the prices make anything more than bread and sugar unaffordable for many Albanian families.

I browse among the newspapers, at least two dozen different ones ranging from *Republica* to *Play Boy,* the latter a newsprint tabloid that bears no resemblance to the original. Some 300 newspapers and magazines are now being published in Albania—local, national, party, sports, humour, sex, literary. Aleksandra, Ani's stepmother, strolls with me around Skënderbeg Square. It is teeming with black market money dealers who intone 'dollars, *Deutschmarks*' as I walk past. It seems that anyone who owns a pocket calculator is in the business and, though illegal, it is tolerated and the police keep a careful eye on it.

The square is spacious—the streets overly spacious when one is trying to dodge across them among the cars, bicycles and horse-drawn wagons. That is perhaps the most noticeable change in Albania: the traffic. The eerie silence of the carless society BEFORE has been replaced by a cacophony of horns—hooting, tooting, playing tunes from *Happy Birthday* to *Never on Sunday*. Chaos is inadequate to describe what takes place now. Pedestrians, long accustomed to having the streets to themselves, are reluctant to use the sidewalks. They forget to look before crossing the street. Drivers, most of them just learning, clutch the wheels of aged Mercedes and Volvos and do their best not to hit people (even when they drive down the sidewalk) or other vehicles. Bicycles and horse-drawn carts blithely ignore one-way signs. Policemen wearing white sleeves wave their arms ineffectually in the middle of traffic jams.

But I am not to get acquainted with Tirana today. We are making a short excursion to Kruja, dear to the heart of Albanians because of its association with their national hero, Gjergj Kastrioti Skënderbeg. On the way, we stop to visit Grandmother, dressed all in black for the son who was killed 25 years ago, but her face smile-crinkled in spite of her aches and pains. I translate instructions for medicine she's just received from Germany; a neighbour tells my fortune in my coffee grounds.

Outside Tirana, the houses seem more substantial than the new apartment blocks in town. Mountains rise up blue in the mist; the ubiquitous bunkers look like giant mushrooms, some white, some a poisonous flaking red. A grove of persimmon trees, very bright orange, provides a spot of colour. We pass bedraggled corn shocks, clothes drying on hedgerows, donkeys wearing wooden saddles, and turn right at Fushë-Kruja, which seems to be a village of stove merchants, their wares displayed beside the road.

Then the car begins the ascent into the pine-covered mountains and Kruja Citadel appears like a cockscomb on its ridge.

The tourist trade has been discovered here. Below the fortress is a renovated bazaar whose shop roofs almost touch in the centre of the street. Rugs and alabaster, traditional dress and silver filigree are for sale. Isa buys a round of cornbread, piping hot, a Kruja speciality.

On our climb from the bazaar to the fortress we meet an old woman who allows us to photograph her if we will send her a picture, 'so I can have it for my gravestone'. Two boys sit under a tree playing a game with stones, similar to checkers, that they call *dam*.

The fortress was besieged in 1450 by an army of Turks that outnumbered the Albanians by five to one; the Turks lost more men than the Albanians had soldiers. Inside, we wander around the grounds, looking at the clocktower and the spot where signal fires were lit to warn of the approaching Turks.

At the far end of the fortress grounds are the Turkish baths and the little Dollma Teqe with a small cemetery under an olive tree that Skënderbeg planted, so say two Albanians from Macedonia who have come here on a pilgrimage. 'This is like a monastery, it's a place of contemplation, to be alone with yourself,' says one of them. He adds that Bektashism is a protestant form of Islam and that the Turks allowed Albania to follow this religious philosophy because the Albanians were Janissaries—the elite guard of the Turkish army. Inside the *teqe* are three *turbes*, with comfortable-looking divans and carpets on the floor. The walls are incongruously decorated with new embroidered tea towels.

Kruja's Ethnographic Museum in a renovated traditional-style house on the fortress grounds is a delight; the ground floor is laid out for work with a stall for sheep in one corner. 'Each house had only three or four sheep,' says the guide. 'Their smell is not bad, it is really healthy.'

Richly embroidered costumes have been protected from looters and are displayed throughout the upper rooms. There is even a silk 'cloth of the virgin' that the groom would hang out of the window on the wedding night.

We admire the intricate woodcarving in the museum so our guide invites us to his son's workshop. Florian Guni first learned from his father, then studied with a master carver. Now he makes chairs and tables using the traditional design of the double eagle and floral motifs, as well as models of Illyrian ships.

His workshop is in the basement of the Skënderbeg Museum which dominates the fortress grounds. We tour the museum with its Illyrian Hall full of knives, helmets, pottery and ornaments, and a medieval section where three thrones (replicas) of carved wood represent the three principalities of Shkodra, Durrësi and Arta. The Turkish invasion is depicted in stained glass, and huge chains symbolize the 500 years of Turkish occupation.

Our guide is full of statistics: Skënderbeg could speak five foreign languages and established diplomatic relations with 28 countries. Around 1,000 books have been published about him in 25 languages in 73 countries. He married at the age of 46, his wife was 23, 'but he was a strong man,' says our guide with a wink.

There is a 'tourist restaurant' (it has no other name) in the grounds, a room with six tables downstairs and a café upstairs.

A small hotel is under construction next door. Our plates are loaded with *qofte* (q is pronounced ch), beefsteak and kebabs accompanied by fried potatoes, onion and sliced red pepper. When the raki comes I learn my first Albanian word: *gëzuar*—'to your health'. The lights go out as we eat, heralding many blackouts to come.

North of Tiranë we leave the main road and travel to the northeast, climbing through the limestone hills and olive groves, to the 'Hero City' of Krujë.

We stop by the bazaar, which has been reconstructed since its destruction during National Liberation. Narrow stone streets lead down the hillside, lined by shops with red-tiled overhanging eaves, shading the passersby: old ladies clutching bundles of vegetables, a boy leading a donkey, and a group of schoolgirls in long black uniform dresses with white buttons and bright red neckerchiefs.

The walls and towers of the fortress on the hill are reached up a path to the north gate, past a fountain under a stone porch, with Arabic inscriptions and the carved date '1434'.

The courtyard is dominated by the Skënderbeg Museum, a tall white stone building designed by Enver Hoxha's architect daughter in pseudo-medieval style, and opened in 1982. The view from the parapet looks down on the remains of a minaret, the red roofs of the town, and across the hills to the mist-hazed plain...

Our guide arrives, a short girl in a beige suit, with a rather bossyboots manner, and we go in the entrance dominated by a large stone statue of Skënderbeg and his cronies, posed heroically. The interior of the museum is beautiful, with polished floors and light airy rooms; the quality of display and presentation is excellent.

The only problem is the content of the displays. Apart from a library, with early volumes in Italian and German detailing Skënderbeg's exploits, so little of what is on show seems to be original, and the Albanian passion for including everything related to their heroes is here. So we see a replica of his sword and helmet, reproductions of paintings of him and his battles (the originals being in Tiranë), unattributed photographs of Lear drawings and lithographs, Skënderbeg stamps and Skënderbeg children's toys.

Outside, a Russian-built jeep, with a shiny black leathercloth hood, stands in the courtyard—at least it's original.

Day 2: Aleksandra brings me Turkish coffee as an early morning treat and tells me that if I set my clock for 05.00, I can have a shower tomorrow. Although Albanian houses have plumbing, running water is a rarity. It comes on for about an hour in the early morning so someone has to get out of bed and supervise the filling of various buckets and tubs with the day's supply.

Albania's public utility system is overloaded. Electrical blackouts are a daily occurrence because so many new appliances—TVs, ovens, heaters—have suddenly been brought into a country wired only for lighting. Heating is generally limited to the living room; in Tirana, it is provided by small electric space heaters, in the country, by wood-burning stoves. Natural gas seems to be non-existent. When the power fails, there is no light, no heat, no cooking.

Eternal flame (now out) at Cemetery of Martyrs

Today, we drive past Tirana University and the former Enver Hoxha Museum (now an International Culture Centre) to the outskirts of town. King Zogu's palace is on one side of the road, the Cemetery of Martyrs on the other. The road is lined with magnolias and yellow chrysanthemums. Ani says all Tirana was this well kept BEFORE.

The statue of Mother Albania stands at the top of an imposing marble stairway in the cemetery among pines, palms and cedars. Ani translates the inscription at the base: 'Glory, Infinity of the Martyrs of the Nation'. A red star in its brazier still stands on the hillside nearby, but the eternal flame has gone out.

In April 1985 Enver Hoxha, former teacher of French, tobacconist and partisan leader, secretary of the Party of Labour, was buried here, and his polished red granite tombstone is on the stepped platform next to Mother Albania. A small red and black double-eagle flag flies at the head of the tombstone, and it is guarded by two soldiers at attention, with high black polished boots and automatic rifles: the smartest soldiers in Albania, according to Andrea.

Nearby are the graves of the Party officials, and down the gentle slopes are the graves, many with star and laurel denoting a People's Hero, of 900 men and women killed during the War of National Liberation.

From here you can look down on Tiranë, with the minaret, clocktower and Hotel Tirana clearly visible. On the left, almost hidden by poplars, is the former palace of King Zog, which was an important seizure for the partisan brigades liberating the capital.

There is no trace of Enver Hoxha's grave in the row of honour; his remains were dug up one dark night and handed over to his family. So were the remains of most of the others in the row, on the grounds that they were not martyrs but died in bed (more or less). The only grave left is that of Qemal Stafa, president of the Communist Youth Movement who was killed in 1942, though two yellow chrysanthemums mark the spot where someone else once lay. Farther away, the rows and rows of lesser mortals remain intact.

A couple of guards stroll over from the palace to talk with us. They guess I am Bulgarian 'because of your cap', but when I say I am American one asks in English about my home. He grins— 'Mississippi, Elvis.'

'*Po, po,*' I reply, 'Yes, yes, Elvis.'

We continue our drive to Lundra, a locked and guarded storage depot for various humanitarian and religious organizations, past terraced fields, mostly fallow or planted in grapevines. Our destination is Petrela Castle, situated in the hills about 12km from Tirana.

The Erzeni River flows below the castle, which sheltered Skënderbeg's sister Mamica during battles. It is said that the besieging Turks cut the water supply to the castle and that the Albanians inside lived for two months eating horse meat and drinking blood. Now Petrela's walls are mostly gone and a village has sprung up at its feet.

Another name for the castle is Petralba, 'white stone', though it is now blackened by lichen and time. On the path up is a rock impressed with Skënderbeg's horse's footprint (it is said) and inside a rusty cannon lies on its belly watching over the cliffs. The view is magnificent, silver olives and red-tiled roofs just below, the mountains in the distance tinted a deep autumnal rust against purple. Already I am beginning to associate that colour, fading into blues, then into mists, with Albania.

We return home for a late-afternoon lunch—mealtimes are definitely Mediterranean here—starting with one of Aleksandra's wonderful soups. Lemon is an important ingredient in all of them, adding a delightfully tart twist. Then come chicken and fried potatoes, a green salad, crisp and fresh and seasoned with oil that tastes of fat black olives grown in rich soil, a plate of olives and onions and a plate of pudgy sliced carrots.

In Albania, all courses of a meal appear on the table at once and salads are a communal affair with everybody digging in from the plate in the centre of the table. Sweets are rare; usually oranges, apples and nuts follow the main course. The Albanian diet, if somewhat monotonous, is healthy—for those who can afford what is available.

This evening the electricity blacks out again and stays off. Aleksandra says at least the electricity was reliable BEFORE. Wilma reads her a lecture on positive thinking. 'If you have half a glass of water, is it half full or half empty'—that old hat. Aleksandra says, well, she will just take the glass completely full; would Wilma like to swap places and

live in Albania on US$30 (£19.35) a month?

We sip raki by candlelight while Isa tells about his travels. He was one of the lucky ones, participating in sports events in China and the Eastern Bloc (he still holds the Albanian record for discus throwing). 'We were told not to describe what we saw in other countries but to say they were worse off than Albania,' he says. He told the truth to a few friends ... and to his sons. Yes, he had the chance to defect, but he knew if he did his entire family would be 'exiled' into slave labour. It seems to me that it took more courage to stay than to run away.

Day 3: I rise early. The roosters of Tirana have been crowing since midnight and the baby on the other side of the thin wall is making little burbling cries for his breakfast. But I am not early enough to keep Aleksandra from washing my boots again—an exercise in futility.

After the rain in the night it is a fine day for strolling. I find an art gallery and the market, though all Tirana is a market: vendors set up on the   streets with whatever they can get their hands on—plastic flowers, sunflower seeds, electrical sockets, bananas—always bananas. Under the old regime, bananas could not be imported, so they have become a popular symbol of the exotic. The kiosks display tape measures and disposable razors alongside pictures of pin-up girls.

I stop for a coffee break in the Hotel Dajti, *the* luxury hotel, just to see what kind of foreigners are now coming to Albania. The missionaries look different from the foreign aid people who look different from the businessmen. I suspect a fair sprinkling of con men floating about.

We decide that the other large hotel in Tiranë, the Dajti, is worth investigation. We walk down the Avenue of the Martyrs of the Nation, past the bronze Lenin statue and the Art Gallery, and, behind the trees opposite the statue of Stalin, are the Party cars: Mercedes and black Volvos. The red 'Dajti' lettering fronts a heavy stone and glass canopy, shielding the steps to the entrance.

Inside, a vast reception area and hall contains a bookshop, a souvenir shop and, in a lounge, a television is showing Albanian programmes, watched by some of the foreign businessmen, who, along with trade and political delegations, form the bulk of the Dajti's clientele.

A corridor to the right leads to the bar, and we have cappuccinos and bottled Albanian beer, sitting in comfortable armchairs at a low walnut table. Filip talks about the current troubles in Kosova province between ethnic Albanians and Yugoslavs, and about relations generally with Yugoslavia. A man living in Filip's quarter, a former Democratic

Front member, has been released under an amnesty, after 16 years in prison as a Yugoslav spy. 'When I pass him in the street, I cut him dead.'

The conversation shifts to Britain, and he talks about the National Front. Filip was the guide for a group of fans attending the England/ Albania football match. They were a pleasant bunch, he says, but other groups contained the Front members, who gave the Nazi salute in the stadium as the band played the National Anthem. The Albanians dismissed the gesture, he says, as 'just the behaviour of stupid people'. He imitates the accent of the English fans: 'You bladdy Commies'. Albanians have heard of the sometimes snide British press reports, but Filip's quotation of a Sunday Express *headline, 'Will they kick our fans out of Albania?' is wrong: in fact it was a travel-based item, and the line was 'Will our fans get a kick out of Albania?'*

Later, we drive to the outskirts of Tirana, to the Babru Tunnels. A large part of Albania's military industry is underground and these factories—built in 1971—were designed to continue operation during wartime. One factory is operating at about 20% capacity, stamping precision parts with antiquated Chinese and Czech machinery.

'Why did you build these tunnels?' I ask. The men working there reply, 'We thought you would invade.'

The place is so dimly lit that I wonder how they can see to work. Air vents run across the ceiling and posters in Russian and Albanian, showing cutaways of generators, are plastered to the walls. Someone's lunch of bread and cheese is spread out on the horoscope page of a newspaper.

More men appear. One says democracy is not working. Another asks for concrete suggestions about what they can produce in the factory. 'The things we make are now being imported from Italy more cheaply,' says the director. The workers earn the equivalent of US$24 per month.

The only thing we can do is give some of the men a lift into Tirana.

The metal shutters on the windows [of the Hotel Tirana] raise to give a view over the square. At the lower end stands the recently unveiled statue of Enver Hoxha, whilst opposite us is the bronze equestrian statue of Skënderbeg. The centre of the square has fountains, flower beds and broad open spaces, and enclosing it all is a collection of varied and imposing buildings: the huge, columned Palace of Culture; the Museum of National History, with its mosaic façade; the National Bank; and the minaret and clocktower flanking the Mosque of Haxhi Ethem Bey...

Rasim decides on a tour of the city, and we drive past the seat of the Central Committee of the Party of Labour of Albania; the Art Gallery, with Lenin's statue beside it; the white pyramid of the recently-opened Enver Hoxha Museum; the Qemal Stafa National Stadium; the Higher Institute of Arts (two smart art students on the steps outside—no flared trousers for them); and the buildings and hostels of the 9,000-student Enver Hoxha University.

Day 4: I want to see more of the superb Albanian traditional costumes trimmed in silver and gold so I go in search of the Ethnographic Museum. Ani says it has 'moved around' and he does not know where it is now. Someone at the Ministry of Tourism gives me directions.

I find the *Ekspozita Kultura Popullore Shqiptare* in a concrete building facing a big park where cattle and sheep graze. A market has sprung up on its steps and men play chess and cards in the shelter of its walls. I try the door; it is open but the interior seems dim and deserted. A woman appears from an office on the left. 'Museum?' I enquire, and she replies, *'Prishur, prishur'*. Destroyed. I peer into the dark interior and see broken display cases, naked mannequins, a place stripped bare. Much of Albania's treasured heritage has been looted, sold to collectors and put on the auction blocks of the west.

Disappointed, I walk home through an area of early 20th century villas, much run down, bordering the new jerry-built apartment houses that look as if they would tumble down in a strong wind. Ani says the people are hoping for an earthquake so they can rebuild from scratch. The houses sit in seas of mud in lieu of courtyards, where rubbish piles burn anaemically and mosquitoes breed in open sewage trenches. Though water pipes seldom function indoors, constantly running water outdoors means that even in dry weather the ground is a mess. Cars churn up the mud and the dry spots for walking are shrinking rapidly. In contrast, the streets are immaculate—Gypsy women sweep them daily. The sidewalks are clean, too, except for the occasional banana peel, but be careful: many manhole covers are missing and most of the streets are unlit at night.

Day 5: Last night was stormy but today is wonderfully clear and cold. I start out at the United States Information Service Library in the former Enver Hoxha Museum. Children are gleefully scrambling up its slanting sides and sliding down. He would turn in his grave... On Sulejman Pasha Square I find a Kaffee Balero, a Caffe Aroma and a Kafe Europa (no wonder trying to spell correctly is so frustrating) where I meet Eddie and his girlfriend. Eddie works in his father's book distribution business and I go along on his round of Tirana's bookstores. He introduces me to Isuf Baca, former literary magazine editor and press spokesman for the Ministry of Public Order, now owner of a bookshop.

'Albanians prefer serious literature. They buy books despite the price,' Baca says. 'Yes, Albanians love poetry, but not so much poetry is being written as BEFORE. The young people have left the country and young people are the poets.' He is optimistic about the future; he owns an apartment and his three children want to stay in Albania.

Two librarians from Përmeti come into the shop on their monthly book-buying trip to Tirana. When they leave for the bus station each is carrying two huge, heavy bags.

On the street, we meet a young man dealing in black market visas; he sells about a hundred of them a month. A visa brings as much as US$5,000 (£3,225), he says, but the profit is not so high because the visa has to be bought from someone at a consulate and then the police have to be paid off. The price of a visa depends on the country it is for; the United States is the most expensive. 'Isn't it a risky business?' I ask. He shrugs; he is jobless and must live somehow.

Eddie tells me that the young people in Albania are not on drugs because they can't afford them; however, he says the country is a transit point from Turkey to the West. (Later reports indicate that both marijuana and heroin are used here and that drug-producing plants are being cultivated in the south.)

In the evening we go to the theatre, a play that starts out as a fairly racy comedy and dribbles off into a love story. The acting is good, the small *Teatri Kombëtar* packed. I want to go to the puppet theatre, too, but the troop is away at a festival in Bulgaria.

Day 6: Eddie, his girlfriend and I decide to go to Durrësi, so we find a driver who worked a few months in Austria and brought home an ageing Mercedes-Benz (invariably referred to as Benz-Mercedes). Having a car here is not such a problem, he says, but you have to watch out or your radio and mirrors are gone.

The road from Tirana is lined with hand-painted signs proclaiming *lavazh*—car wash—and the improvised hose-and-bucket brigades are doing good business. We drive through rolling hills and past disused greenhouses, past new flat-roofed houses with grape arbours on their roofs. Many Albanians who work outside the country are building houses here. At Sukëth, one of King Zogu's many villas sits on a hilltop. A train chugs by, a bicycle strapped to the side of its engine. Is this the engineer's transportation home?

In Durrësi, we ask passersby the name of the main square. 'It used to be Sheshi Stalin; now no one knows,' a woman tells us. We explore the ancient ruins—the amphitheatre with its incongruous medieval chapel, the Roman baths—and stop at the Archaeology Museum by the sea. Entry is 100 lekë per person and the doorman patiently tears off 50 paper tickets for each of us: they still bear the old price, 2 lekë.

Day 7: After several attempts, at last I have found the National Museum in Tirana open. The cleaning ladies bustle off to fetch the guide, who explains the exhibits in a mixture of French, Italian and Albanian. He

'Defence of the Motherland is the duty above all duties'

is an Orthodox from Korça. Albanians identify themselves by religion and home town, and never fail to ask yours.

We meet up as a group and walk down the edge of Skënderbeg Square to the Museum of National History, where Filip guides us round.

The rooms are large and airy, and the items are sensitively displayed. The exhibition is laid out chronologically: the ground floor includes prehistoric items, Iron Age implements, Greek and Roman ceramics, mosaic fragments and the exquisite head of the Goddess of Butrint, now returned from Italy.

Upstairs are the weapons of Skënderbeg's battles—huge wide-bladed two-handed swords—and filigreed long muskets of 19th century fighters. Icons, multicoloured tribal costumes, jewellery and domestic items lead up to the rise of Albanian nationalism, the struggle against Italian domination, and the fight against Fascist and Nazi occupation in the War of National Liberation, followed by Albania's achievements over the past 45 years of socialism.

Under a huge painting showing a battle between partisans and Nazi soldiers—Albanians dying heroically, heads back and arms flung wide; Germans dying unheroically, like slumped grey sacks—we begin to realize the nature of this exhibition: we are seeing the official Albanian history of Albania. The sheer quantity of material relating to the period from 1920 onwards is colossal, and this can't be just because of its greater accessibility.

This is not just the heart of Albanian history, but the whole being: the rest is incidental, and important only when it foreshadows 20th

*century triumph—Skënderbeg as the spiritual precursor of Enver
Hoxha. Nothing relating to the struggle is unimportant: the flags,
weapons, books, newspapers and photographs of partisans, shock
brigades, martyrs and People's Heroes, and their shirts, woollen
jumpers, their personal revolvers, Enver Hoxha's leather coat, his
cardigan, his typewriter, his duplicating machine.*

*Some things are enhanced or emphasized: the airbrush haloing the
heroes and heroines, smoothing their cheeks, highlighting their smiles
and glossing their hair, or making certain that the appropriate slogans
on the placards held by demonstrators massing streets and squares
are clearly legible. In the wall-sized enlargement, with workers
parading past us from left to right, the placards and slogans are facing
us.*

*Some things are not there. Filip takes us through the 1930s and the
anti-Zogism struggle, but there is no photograph, no painting, no
drawing of Zog: his image does not exist. And in some of the
photographs there are missing figures, black ink blending with the
shadows in a rallying crowd, or misty airbrushing behind the figures
in a political meeting.*

*As we walk with Filip back up the square to the bus, we are apart
from the group. He chooses from the words we've heard a lot these
past days: Zogite, fascist, spy, traitor, Nazi, chauvinist, quisling. 'Those
people who were missing would be spies or traitors. To include them
would spoil the photographs.' He cites the former Prime Minister
Mehmet Shehu, who, accused of a plot to assassinate Hoxha, committed
suicide in 1981, as an example of the need for vigilance against external
and internal threats, saying 'Shehu worked for the Yugoslavs, the CIA
and the KGB'. Shehu, Hoxha's former partisan comrade, with a
reputation for bravery, ruthlessness and cruelty, and who boasted,
according to David Smiley, of personally cutting the throats of 70
captured Italian carabinieri, was accused by Hoxha of working for
the Yugoslavs, the Americans, and British Intelligence.*

Back at my Tirana home, activity is increasing. There seems to be
some problem with the privatization of the building, and Isa is making
the rounds of bureaucracy to get the necessary signatures to say that
the water and electricity are in order. The raw brick of the stairwell
must be coated, so workmen are mixing concrete on the bare ground
and hauling it up with a bucket and rope. Their sawhorses and pans are
blocking the landing and I must sidle along a six-inch ledge to the
stairs.

Never one with a head for heights, I take a deep breath, hang the straps of my bag and umbrella on my shoulder and take hold of a proffered hand. Halfway across, Isa appears—and sees my just-washed coat brushing against the cement pan! He promptly grabs my other hand and starts picking off the cement particles, dislodging my bag and threatening my precarious balance. The men stop their work to laugh and yell, 'Let her jump!'

Day 8: The sun is shining; I am out of my boots at last. It's almost Christmas and a small market has sprung up on Skënderbeg Square— three tents of dart games, one tent selling plush toy animals and toy guns. A Santa Claus banner streams across the Culture Palace. Some people are carrying Christmas trees home but most still wait for the New Year celebrations to decorate them.

We go walking in Tirana's biggest park out behind the university to see the two lions that have just arrived as a gift from Macedonia. The zoo consists of the lions, one wolf, one fox, one brown bear, an eagle, three vultures, a score of parakeets, a monkey, four pea fowl and a moth-eaten crane. The cages are too small but otherwise the animals seem well fed and cared for.

The park is lovely with its big lake and it is crowded with families out for a stroll. But there is no place to rest, no benches, no fallen trees, and the ground is damp under its blanket of fallen leaves, so we make our way back to town to the big market.

The market is crowded and bustling as people prepare for the holidays. The vegetable stands at the front are full of beautiful leeks, miniature lettuces and spotty cauliflowers, oranges, walnuts, apples, chestnuts and almonds. The meat hall is less delightful, full of whole carcasses and all their parts, and smelling spoiled. Cardboard boxes of chicken imported from France and marked 'keep frozen' are making puddles on the ground.

Tobacco sellers squat in a row in front of the butter-and-cheese hall, and sausages splutter as they cook on little 'rolling stoves'. Anything bought is likely to be wrapped in pages torn from *The Works of Enver Hoxha*. At the back of the market some men have set up a pyramid of tin cans and are trying to knock it over with a rubber ball. Almost everyone is willing to be photographed; when I say, '*faleminderit*' (thank you), their faces light up and some reply, 'Thank you very much,' in English.

We take a break at the Kafe Europa. A little Gypsy boy has taken refuge with a pair of well-dressed young men at the next table; they won't allow the waiter to send him packing. In appreciation he does a fair demonstration of martial arts, then takes up a collection around the nearby tables. He waits until the waiters are out of the way, then scoots out the door and shares his loot with a friend.

Christmas Eve: We have bustled off to the annual Albanian Music Festival in the Congress Palace, the glitzy showplace of the Hoxha regime. The amplifiers are at full volume, the acoustics bad. I am trapped front row centre, sweating in furry boots, coat peeled off in the seat because there is no place to leave it. Every seat is taken, and the TV lights burn like a desert sun.

To a westerner bombarded daily with pop, rock and heavy metal, the show strongly resembles live Musak. Then Sherif Merdani takes centre stage, a hush falls, he sings *When I Am Dead, My Dears*. It holds all the pathos of a gospel song; he composed it in prison. At the last note, the crowd goes wild.

A glimmering of understanding filters into my tired brain. More is going on here than a musical competition. Three years ago in Albania, the girl in the slinky miniskirt ... the keyboard man with the Jesus hairdo ... the kids in tennis shoes and T-shirts could never have appeared on stage.

The second night of the four-show marathon, TV Shqiptar interviews Edi Luarasi, a leading Albanian actress whose career was brought to an end because of this very song *fest*. In 1971, she was among a group of intellectuals who were thrown into jail because they came to the *fest* dressed in western clothes deemed unsuitable by the regime.

'I couldn't sleep after the festival last night,' she says. 'I kept comparing what we can do now with what we couldn't do then.'

It is rumoured that there will be folk dancing tonight, so we hurry to the basement, to what is known as the 'taverna', where Richard and Linda have bagged us ringside seats and ordered rakis and cognacs.

The six-piece band—violin, tambour, accordion, two saxophones and an eight-string bazouki-like instrument—plays a couple of instrumental numbers, the saxophones doing long, swooping solo rallies. The dancers, three men and three girls, appear in costumes which would have delighted Edward Lear: the men in white felt fezzes; white shirts, scarlet, black and gold embroidered waistcoats with deep-scalloped lapels, orange, black and gold sashes and black-braided white trousers. The girls wear white or red embroidered blouses, short maroon bolero waistcoats with gold and silver embroidery, gold-fringed scarves worn as sashes, and scarlet skirts over white trousers. They do their dances folklorique, and most enjoyable too: all very much for the tourists, but then that's what we are.

We would love to be able to describe the dances, but we really can't bring ourselves to write 'they waved their silken scarves above their heads, their graceful movements contrasting with the proud agility of the young brigands', that sort of thing. We don't know the first thing about folk dancing: if they were doing the Albanian equivalent of the triple Arkwright—the double Skënderbeg backflip—we wouldn't have a clue. As long as there is a lot of jolly music, and as long as they don't

fall over, then it's good folk dancing to us.

For their final numbers the band is joined by a girl singer in national costume and a male singer with a deep chest, in a white shirt and a grey suit. The initial incongruity of their love song—the young girl wooed by the ageing baritone—is dispelled by their obvious sincerity.

A house band takes over: bass guitar, drums, guitar and accordion, and they play an odd mixture of jazz standards and Songs from the Shows.

Christmas Day: It's pouring with rain and I am exhausted, so I discard plans to have a look at the religious celebrations in Tirana. The Tare family is Muslim, but we watch the local Orthodox service on television and afterwards have a festive lunch.

Historically the Christian and Muslim religions in Albania have lived together in happy tolerance. There have been pockets of fanaticism, but for the most part the people show a healthy wariness of embracing any one belief too fiercely. If one scratches the surface, one finds elements of the various religions mixed together in surprising ways.

A Muslim describes his best friend as someone he can confide in 'like a priest at confession'. In Lezha, the Catholics attend services at the mosque and pray to Muhammad as they do to their own saints. Throughout the country, Orthodox and Muslim attend each others' services for Easter and Bairam.

Prisons

Visitors may hear stories of the horrors of Albania's political prisons and forced labour camps where dissidents were 'exiled', and may wish to see these places for themselves. It is possible to find them by asking directions from local residents.

Present government policy gives preferential treatment to former exiles and prisoners; nevertheless, some people remained in the camps for lack of any other place to go. Labour camps were at Gradishta, Berati, Lezha and Savra near Lushnja, among other places. The prison at Burrel was notorious as a place of extermination, with torture and starvation taking their toll along with executions. Political prisons were also set up at Spag in the northeast, at Porto Palermo on the coast and at Tepelena.

THE SOUTHERN JOURNALS

Day 1: We finally pull out of Tirana at 13.30, a beautiful sunny day wasted. We pass men driving cows and goats home from the market or resting for lunch by the roadside. A meat market has been set up on the marble base of a monument.

The road climbs through hills of gold and rusty purple with snow peaks and white outcrops of rock in the distance. The sun is already starting to sink when we round a curve and see the huge steel mill, still working fitfully, that heralds Elbasani. Persimmons and oranges are for sale at roadside stands and in the fields, flocks of geese have joined the usual sheep and goats.

Ani does not want to spend the night in Elbasani; he says the people here are aggressive but I find no evidence of this. He stays in the car while Wilma and I explore the old town.

Trees, many still in leaf at the beginning of winter, line the narrow streets. We peek into well-tended courtyards filled with rose trellises; the smell of wood fires and cooking—something we missed in Tirana— wafts from the houses. Almost at once we come upon a classroom where about 30 young girls are studying the Koran. We photograph them; they tell us they cover their hair with scarves only during lessons, not in the street.

Then we find an Orthodox monastery all falling down among its cedars, with the smashed grave of the lexicographer Konstandin Kristoforidhi in the yard. Behind it is a newer-looking church where men on scaffolding are at work on the belltower.

Finally we come out from the walls beside a white villa with rusting army-green cannon in front and red chickens scratching in the yard. This was once the Elbasani Anti-Fascist War Museum but it is now closed, its windows broken, its collection gone. An elderly man and a younger woman stop to talk with us; the woman motions toward the derelict museum. 'Communism, now other system, *inshallah,*' she says.

Night is falling, so we hurry to see the Turkish baths beside the hotel. The town was quiet when we arrived but is now coming to life—we leave town just as a soccer game ends.

Driving along the Shkumbini River we see fallow fields and the skeletons of collective farms. The people have taken for themselves all the building material they could move.

There is no guardrail beside the road, nor a path, so people walk in it. Most of the women are carrying large loads of brushwood on their backs; some are driving cows or goats. A policeman flags us down for the 10km ride into the next town where he works. He says there are blood feuds up in the mountains but no one knows how many have been killed. He likes being a policeman; he earns 4,000 lekë per month. No, he doesn't take bribes as that would endanger his job. Most people who try to bribe him are those coming into Albania without car insurance—it costs 12,000 lekë so they offer the police 5,000 lekë.

We had planned to have dinner in Librazhd, but the police will not allow us to park in front of the restaurant and Wilma refuses to leave the car anywhere else. In spite of the fact that most cars are simply parked on the street, she is quite convinced that if she leaves the car out of sight it will disappear in whole or in part. We drive on, hungry.

Ploughing with oxen on the Kotodesh-Vërri road

At last we reach Pogradeci, a charming town on Lake Ohrid where Ani spent his childhood. His stepfather's mother welcomes us into a small but comfortable home, with striped kelims covering the wide plank floor. She stokes up the wood-burning stove. A slab of red marble sits on the stove—Ani says it keeps the kettle warm without boiling, but Grandmother says Ani used to dry his socks on it.

I am given the honoured guest's place on the divan beside the stove. The divans around three walls are covered with handwoven blankets, along the fourth wall are an iron bed and a chest. A table in the middle of the room is covered with a cloth and on it is a vase of greenery and berries. Family portraits cover the walls. High up in the corner above me is an icon of the Holy Trinity with an electric light bulb in its centre. Icons and a jar of holy water and oil on the mantelpiece leave no doubt that the family is Orthodox.

The television is broken so the young man of the house, a theology student, takes a boom-box from the top of the wardrobe; it blinks red, green, yellow in a mini-disco display, contrasting wildly with the Gregorian chants he plays for us.

The house is spotless though there are only two rooms for six people. We cannot spend the night here, it is too crowded, so we go next door to friends whose house is decorated in the same style. A picture of St Sofia in Istanbul indicates the that family is Muslim. Beside it is a photograph of the oldest daughter at her Orthodox baptism; she converted so she would be able to work in Greece.

Meat hangs to dry from a wire in the ceiling of the living room/kitchen. A small rack for drying clothes is rigged to the stovepipe. The woman of the house brings out a blanket, spreads it on the floor and heats up an ancient electric iron on the stove to iron our pillow cases.

Day 2: I am awakened about 04.00 by singing and clapping, a strange harmonic droning, outside the house. Just as I realize I am not dreaming and gather the courage to brave the cold for a look out the window, the singing stops. There is to be a Gypsy wedding in town. The women of the groom's family sit up all night with him and towards dawn they come to the well for water so he can wash before meeting his bride.

'Are brides still sold here?' we ask at breakfast. There is some argument about this but finally we are told that no money changes hands, though a matchmaker is involved. The wedding celebration lasts three days but the bride dresses in white, western style.

We take an early-morning stroll around the old town of Pogradeci. The smell of wood smoke is pervasive; shoes sit on every doorstep. At the fountains, people are brushing teeth, shaving, washing dishes.

We enter a small enclave where a woman is sweeping up leaves. The whole town is very clean. A man comes to the door of one house and invites us inside—'for five minutes', when we protest that time is short. We stay three hours.

The grandmother—her name is Arta—comes in to greet us. She is dressed in black and complains of a bad back from lifting her invalid husband for years, but she is smiling nonetheless. She has five children; the youngest son (age 43) lives with her. He is a mining engineer but has no work because the mines are closed.

Her daughter-in-law serves small dishes of quince preserves, followed by coffee and cookies, then by local apples. Arta sits on the floor facing us so she can see us better. She is 72, the oldest person in the enclave, mediator of disputes, adviser of young people about to marry or give

birth. She has lived in this house for 47 years.

To our questions about how Albanians have changed, Arta tells us she was born into a wealthy, traditional family. Her friends didn't meet their husbands before they were married, it was all arranged by a matchmaker. But she was a bit more adventurous; when a young man asked for her hand she wanted to see him first and arranged to look out of a window as he was passing by.

Arta was 19, her husband 29 when they married. Traditionally the husband must be older than the wife. Women couldn't work outside the home, so the man had to take care of his wife; she in turn had to be young enough to care for him when he was old.

Arta brings out photos of her courtship and wedding. She and her husband were the first couple in Pogradeci to walk in the streets together before they were married, one of the first couples to hold hands in public. She kissed him before they were married.

'It doesn't matter what people say, someone has to start changes,' she says.

But Arta is a great believer in the family tradition. She has five sisters and visits each one each day. 'If children leave home to work, it is only long enough to earn money and come back. Short-term emigration is common here,' she says.

At noon we leave Pogradeci and backtrack towards Lini, near the Macedonian border. Ani has stopped at a restaurant and bought three takeaway meals of fish. I ask why. He pleads time. I point out that it takes as long to stop and eat as it does to sit in a restaurant, but the damage is done, and we picnic on top of a pass at 0°C. The fish is very good and the view is fine, but the ground is freezing and we have no forks. On the hillside facing us a giant PARTI is still visible written in stone but the ENVER is gone.

We drive along the ancient Via Egnatia, now full of trucks as it is the main road to Macedonia and points east. Then we turn on to a pitted side road that is washed away in places. The villages here look relatively prosperous, with substantial stone or brick houses under construction and a new tractor or two in the fields.

It's time to find a room for the night. We choose a farmstead reminiscent of the fortified farms in southern France. The oldest part of the main building is of dressed stone cut in diamond patterns and half timbered. The windows of the living room are deeply recessed and barred against break-ins, which were unheard of BEFORE. The house faces a steep slope scattered with haystacks. A three-cornered shed of scrap metal houses a small dog chained with a large metal collar, and there are various outbuildings for sheep and goats.

The Leka family invites us to stay the night. In the living room, Grandmother Leka uses a dab of kerosene to light a stove made from an oil drum. As we settle down on the divans, the other family members come around one by one and shake hands with us again, very formally, to welcome us into their home. Grandmother takes a chair beside me and pounds me on the back when something I say pleases her.

The man of the house, Abas Leka, arrives, along with more of the family. Soon six children, a man and a woman are crowded up on the divan on one side of the room while Wilma and I have another divan all to ourselves. Ani is served raki, but Wilma and I must settle for coffee that is being ground by hand in a beautiful old brass Turkish coffee mill.

We ask about the privatization of land. Abas says his family has very little land now; returning it to the original owners is difficult because the population is much larger than when the land was taken over by the state 50 years ago. 'A village of 12 houses then has 100 now.' The new tractors we saw were bought with credit. 'The Greeks gave us credit so every village can have a tractor,' he says. 'They feel this land is part of Greece.'

He has been to school, but there are no jobs for him now. 'The new government promised we could emigrate, but no one wants us,' he says.

'Only the women work,' adds Grandmother.

Abas has three sons and four daughters. 'The tradition is for the youngest son to stay with the parents, but here we prefer the son with the best wife.' His second son remained at home and there is no doubt that Lefteri—the charming, efficient daughter-in-law—is the reason.

Tonight we sleep on the divans near the stove, under handwoven covers filled with wool, so heavy that it is impossible to move beneath them. The pillowcases are embroidered. A nightlight burns over the door.

Day 3: After breakfast, I help Lefteri put away the bedding; when I admire her needlework she takes me upstairs to see more of her rugs and coverlets and a beautiful Butterfly treadle sewing machine made in Shanghai.

The family gives us homemade bread for lunch. Abas accompanies us to keep an eye on the car while we climb up to the Illyrian tombs at Selca. Along the way, we stop at the village school where about 120 students up to age 16 are taught by 20 teachers. The classrooms are basic, the wooden desks and benches of the sort seen only in museums in the West. Each room has a wood-burning stove. We are invited into a classroom and the students stop their French lesson and stand up to greet us, shuffling and giggling. As we leave, they burst into excited chatter. The headmaster, Nesti Qyshko, comes along to the tombs with us.

From the village we climb a steep hill, first through slick mud mixed with slick cow dung, then through sticky clay that tries to keep hold of one's boots. The sun is bright and warm—we are back on the west side of the Thana Pass, which really seems to mark a change in climatic zones. Sheep are grazing among the tombs, a couple of which have been covered with green plastic awnings. A few stones and pot shards are scattered about, but everything movable has been taken away.

We give Nesti a lift into Lini where he lives. On the road to the Via Egnatia we stop to admire a Byzantine footbridge with two lovely open arches and a smaller niche. Like many other bridges and castles in the Balkans, this one has attached to it a legend of immurement—to keep it from collapsing someone must be walled up alive inside it.

Back on the main road, five children have rigged a hose by the roadside and are flagging down cars to wash them. We stop and they hose our car down for 50 lekë. The Bulgarian truckers slow down and toss candy to the children.

In Lini, Nesti takes us to see the mosaics after we promise not to photograph them. It would be impossible anyway, as they are covered with thick plastic and a layer of sand. We can only scrape away a bit to admire the spectacular floor of the ruined basilica.

It is late when we return to Pogradeci. I check in at the hotel on the waterfront and have problems finding room 203 which turns out to be four floors up. There is no hot water, but there *is* a sit-down toilet—the first since Tirana and the first with a functioning flush since the ferry.

We have dinner in the Restorant Poradeci (named for a poet, not for the town), owned by Thanas Gusho. He opened it on Easter Day 1993 in the same place where his family had a restaurant until 1947. He shows us into a cosy back room where a fire crackles and sheepskins cover the seats. Soon our table is heaped with plates of the Ohrid trout called *koran,* salad, potatoes, hot bread and Gusho's tasty homemade red wine, served chilled.

Gusho says he worked for 20 years in the mines; when they closed he started business with US$15 (£9.75) capital, selling tomatoes. He has no problem with food supplies for the restaurant; the farmers come to him to sell their produce. For dessert he brings us apples and chestnuts to roast in the fireplace. 'BEFORE there were so many trees you couldn't gather all the nuts,' he says.

To check out the nightlife in Pogradeci, we stroll to the Disco Diamond, newly opened by Tom Fejzollari who escaped across Lake Ohrid in a homemade boat in 1975, made good in Australia and returned to invest in his native country.

Tom settled in Melbourne, but when Albania opened up in 1991 he decided to build a house in Pogradeci and expand his business to his own country. The disco is a small sideline but is first-class all the way. 'The kids come in after school in the afternoons and couples come to dance at weekends,' he says. 'I pay 24 employees US$50 (£32) a month (better than the standard US$30—£19). If 1,000 Albanian *emigrés* would do the same, it would help boost the economy.'

Day 4: The hotel lobby doors stand open and there is no heating so I go for a stroll among the bunkers by the lake at Pogradeci. When Wilma and Ani arrive, the police will not allow them to stop in front of the hotel long enough to fetch my bag, much less to drink a cup of coffee, so we drive into town to a coffee shop. Ani announces that only men are inside, so we sit obediently in the car and Ani brings out steaming cups for us. I suspect this is a ploy for keeping the car 'guarded'.

The road to Korça is the widest and smoothest we have yet seen. As it begins to climb we stop to buy apples, quinces and walnuts. The road is lined with tree stumps, some of them burned out where people have stopped to make fires for warmth on their way home, some cut for fuel, their stumps ravaged for kindling. It must have been a beautiful avenue once but now the stumps stick up like rotten teeth.

We detour through Maliqi in an unsuccessful search for Bronze Age pilings that were discovered when the swamp here was being drained. 'We haven't seen them in a long time,' the people we ask say vaguely.

Grim factories line the outskirts of Korça, but the town within is lively with kiosks and shops, and the parks are full of fountains, busts and birches. Albania's birch trees were a gift from Kruschev, Ani says.

Korça is known for its carpets so we search for the carpet factory at the edge of the industrial area. We are met in the courtyard by Garo Avakian who has owned the newly privatized factory for just one month. He is Armenian but was born in Albania; his parents came here from Turkey. This was the family business 50 years ago; he and his son and daughter are all weavers.

At the factory, 115 women are at work on 60 looms. The steady thunk of the looms does not stop when we enter. Big windows let in plenty of light, and a large new electric radiator sits between every two looms. The women work seven hours a day, six days a week. They are paid by the number of knots per day; the average salary is 6,500 lekë a month, more than double the usual Albanian wage. The women who work here are specialized and experienced, Avakian says, and they respect design. His very first carpets are still on the looms and won't be finished until January, when they will be exported to Switzerland.

We drive around in circles looking for the road to Voskopoja, famous for its frescos. It takes an hour to cover the 24km on the rough mountain road. We find the local priest, Thoma Samaraj, waiting for a bus at the main square. He is on his way to Durrësi where he studies theology, but takes us to the Church of St. Nicholas instead. The frescos are rich and flamboyant but badly in need of restoration. Why hasn't UNESCO come to their rescue? The village of stone houses and haystacks is very quiet as we drive back into the round mountains with their wide fields of snow.

From Korça, the road south worsens as it climbs into bare, rocky mountains. We pass through Erseka, a town of ugly highrise blocks in a military zone; the road becomes bumpier, the landscape more barren. The sun disappears early behind the mountains as we wind our way through a large pine forest. A lumber camp is the only sign of life for hours and a heavy blackness swallows up the car's headlamps. Once we are startled by a small roadside shrine, a cross contrived of red plastic reflectors nailed to a tree.

At last we see lights up ahead: Leskoviku. It looks like a sizeable town spreading up the mountainside. We stop at the first group of men we see and ask for the hotel. 'It's just in front of us'—one of the men points—'but it is not good, it is better if you come to my home'. So we drive down and round and come to a gate that opens to a large house. The man's wife and daughters come out to make us welcome.

Instead of Turkish divans, the living room has Western-style couches covered with blue and pink flowered throws, and the curtains are an amazing pattern of pagodas, Chinese bridges and mountains interspersed with Christmas balls sprouting ferns—all in purple and red. The walls are pink, edged all around by a white 'frame'. The TV is mercifully out of order.

Leskoviku had a population of 22,000 before the Germans burned it to the ground in World War II; now it has 3,000, the father tells us. He has three daughters, one taking a correspondence course to become a teacher, one just out of school and working in the family shop, the third unhappily engaged to be married. Her fiancé's family doesn't want her to study but she wants to continue school.

Unlike the houses we have visited before, there are no outward signs of religion here—no icons or pictures on the walls. I guess that the family is Orthodox because the youngest daughter wears a gold cross around her neck, but they are Muslim—she wears the cross 'for luck'.

The father is a veterinarian, out of work, so he has set up a food shop and kiosk. Business is not good because he can't buy supplies in Greece—the roads are not open and visas are expensive.

'How do people live here, then?' we ask.

'Wine and raki production, cherries, nuts, wheat, sheep, goats,' he says. 'Cows are good only on an individual basis. It's very mountainous here, lots of snow, and cows have to be kept inside two months of the year. But a cow gives milk 300 days a year and a goat only 120.'

Both the mother and father eat dinner with us; I elect to try goat meat, much to my regret. (It is only when I recover from diarrhoea two days later that Ani tells me Albanian goat meat usually upsets foreigners' stomachs.) After dinner, we have glasses of Albanian tea spiced with dried quince.

We ask about blood feuds. There are none here, they say, the people are peaceful, the town is small. There are only four or five *fis* (tribes) here and they have a strong family tradition. The father has 49 nieces and nephews; the mother says she keeps in touch with family members as distantly related as fifth cousins. They are scattered throughout the country but she visits as often as possible and goes to all the weddings.

'If we don't keep track of our relatives we might marry them and make crazy children,' laughs one of the daughters.

Sometimes young people elope, they say. In that case, the family breaks off from them but usually they make up in the future. If a girl becomes pregnant before marriage, a clever family will see to it that the couple marries, although people who are 'not cultured' may beat the girl.

'Do they ever kill her?' I ask, remembering Ismail Kadare's story in which a girl was thrown into a well. 'It may happen still,' says the father, 'but that's Albanian, not religion. The girl's father would kill them both, the girl and the boy.'

Then the lights black out, and Mother says, 'The trouble is Albania went directly from feudalism to communism with nothing in between to bring progress.'

Day 5: Two of the daughters sit on the bed opposite mine this morning watching intently as I put on my make-up. I discover that I have left my tampons in Tirana. When I explain my plight to the eldest daughter, Entela, she offers me some of the cheesecloth that Albanian women use. However, a shop in town has one package of disposable pads from Greece; the clerk brings it from under the counter as if it were a pornographic magazine.

Entela takes us to see the Holy Spring at the top of a hill. A barren mountain rises up behind it; mint grows there and in summer the scent wafts down.

By mid-morning we are on our way once more into the wild mountains. Fog drifts up from the valley and there is a sprinkling of rain. When we stop at a village to ask directions, two women rush to us with persimmons for sale. When we say we don't want to buy, they give us some.

We are following the Vjosa River to Përmeti. Ani says it is the quietest and cleanest city in Albania but there is nothing to do there. The History Museum is locked, its windows broken.

The road to Tepelena leads through the lovely Gorge of Këlcyra. We stop for lunch at an idyllic spot where little waterfalls tumble down the mountainside. The leaves of the old plane trees are a glorious yellow; I hope the trees won't be cut for firewood, but so much of the countryside has been stripped bare that I fear their days are numbered.

In Tepelena, we drive straight to Ali Pasha's fortress. A plaque commemorating Lord Byron's visit is on the wall and a little boy dances round me pointing a pink water pistol and chanting, 'By-*ron*, By-*ron*.'

As usual, a crowd gathers. In Albania, no matter where you stop—even in the remotest mountains—people suddenly appear to ask where you are from and where you are going. This time, a young man who says he is secretary of the local Democratic Party is the spokesman. He shows us around the fortress, pointing out his vineyards across the river. 'We want to make this a tourist attraction,' he says. 'If a highway

from Durrësi to Greece is built, it will have to run through here.'
Pleading lack of time, we turn down his invitation for coffee and drive
on to Gjirokastra.

*Edward Lear was taken by the Gjirokastër women: 'The quaintest
monsters ever portrayed or imagined fall short of the reality of this
most strange creature in gait and apparel ... suppose first a tight white
linen mask fixed on the face, with two small slits cut in it for the eyes to
look through. Next a voluminous wrapper of white, with broad buff
stripes, which conceals the whole upper part of the person, and is
huddled in immense folds about the arms, which are carried with the
elbows raised, the hands being carefully kept from sight by the heavy
drapery; add to these short, full, purple calico trousers, and canary-
coloured top-boots, with rose-coloured tassels—and what more
amazing incident in the history of female dress can be fancied?' He
drew the fortress, which encircles the top of the hill, and the aqueduct
(which brought drinking water from Mount Sopot), but this has now
gone, demolished during the Zog regime in 1932.*

*In the square outside the Hotel Çaiupi we don't see any of Lear's
women but we do witness a reunion: a group of Albanians, the men in
brown or grey suits, the women in black skirts or floral dresses, greet
a returning expatriate who arrives as part of a German tourist group.
The well-dressed middle aged woman, with a fresh hairdo and imitation
Burberry holdall, looks very much the local girl made good, and is
given a jolly welcome...*

*Afterwards, we wander the narrow and hilly streets: black
cobblestones with bands and diamond patterns of pink or white stones.
The houses have deeply projecting eaves, sheltering large upper-floor
windows: ground floors are often windowless as a protection against
erstwhile blood feud attacks, and are used for storage. We find a place
from where Lear might have made his castle drawing: on a corner in
the shadow of the former mosque, where trees now obscure the large
house with two wings which he included. He thoroughly explored the
town, and 'drew hard while daylight lasted'.*

Of all the towns in Albania, Gjirokastra is the one I most want to see,
enthralled as I am by Ismail Kadare's novel based on his childhood
there in the 1940s. When Ani suggests going to a village for the night,
I refuse. I want to wake in the morning to a view of the city sprawled
over its mountain, so we go to the local hotel which asks US$45 (£29)
for a single room with bath. This is almost triple the rate at other hotels,
and when I ask why, a man leaning against the counter says he has a

friend who rents rooms to tourists.

It can't hurt to go and see, I reason. And sure enough, the house is a delightful old Gjirokastra stone building, high up on the hill, spacious and far and away the most tastefully decorated I have yet seen, with beautiful carpets on the stone floors and oil paintings by an artist friend on the walls. The man of the house, Maksi Bakiri, and his eldest daughter, Katie, both speak excellent English. His wife, Adelina, is head of the Gjirokastra Women's Forum.

At last I have a hot shower and wash my hair because I can dry it beside the wood stove even if the electricity fails.

Adelina is the only one in the family with a job now. It's not a good one, she says; she is an economist with a state-run company and earns 3,000 lekë a month—enough to buy bread. Like most women in town, she brings home a bit extra by producing crochet and needlework for a Greek who pays 200 lekë for 7.5m of crocheted border—three weeks' work.

This area is 65% Muslim, 35% Orthodox; the Bakiri family is Muslim but bemoans the theft of icons from the Orthodox churches.

From the walls, the setting of Gjirokastër is one to marvel at: a circle of mountains around the bowl in which we are at the centre, with grey-white houses trickling down below us. Even the concrete apartment

blocks at the lowest part of the town can be ignored. 'From almost any point you may select, the views ... backed by a sublime horizon of plain and snowy mountain, are as exquisite as indescribable'. Lear was right.

Inside the castle [is part of] the National Museum of Arms [with exhibits] from stone axes to ornate bone-handled scimitars and the filigreed and banded long flintlocks for which Albania was noted, and which were highly sought-after exports to the rest of the Ottoman empire. Real brigand weapons, wonderful, but their doom was sealed by Mr Martini's invention, as evidenced by rows of breech action Martini Henrys in the following room. Edith Durham spelled out the attractions of both guns in 1909: the men '... buy caps and powder, cast their own bullets, and perpetually refill their empty cartridge cases. The ease with which a Martini cartridge is filled is the main reason of that weapon's popularity. As a quick firer it cannot of course compare with the Mauser. But it wounds far more severely, and drops its man when the Mauser fails to stop him .... Many people told me that for a really good old-fashioned wound the good old flintlock with a dram of powder well rammed down, carrying a huge bullet, nails and other fancy articles, was a sure thing at close range'.

The partisan brigades during National Liberation used anything they could get their hands on: captured German and Italian revolvers and rifles, lethal looking home-made pistols (lethal for the user, I would think) and Sten guns dropped by the British, dismissed by Filip: 'these usually came with little or no ammunition'. Thus we are put in our place, although Filip's words are at odds with David Smiley's first-hand account of events with the partisans.

Day 6: We go to the hilltop to Gjirokastra's fortress. It is the second largest in the Balkans, the guide says, though she doesn't know what the largest one is (I guess Kalamegdan in Belgrade). The arched walls of Ali Pashë Tepelena's era in the early 19th century are impressive; the US spy plane shot down in the 1950s is still there, but the fine antique guns have been stolen from the Weapons Museum.

A steep road curves up to one of the two entrances to the castle. Walking up, we pass some of the Chinese and Russian built military trucks which are still in use. Despite the fact that links with the Soviets were severed in 1961, and with the Chinese in 1978, there is no problem over spare parts: there is a factory in Tiranë.

The castle entrance is imposing: a high vaulted tunnel with arched alcoves leads to a T-junction with a cavernous three aisled hall. The castle houses the National Museum of Arms, and, spotlit in the aisles, are German and Italian field guns, mortars, machine guns and an Italian armoured car, 'captured from our enemies' says Filip, 'during the War of Liberation'. The Second World War is rarely referred to as such: it is 'The War of Liberation', 'National Liberation' or just 'Liberation', and 'the Nazis' or 'the Fascists' were the foe, rather than 'Germans' or 'Italians'.

On the walls of the castle is a reminder of more recent concerns: a captured USAF spy plane stands on the grass. Whilst we wait to be photographed

in front of such a trophy, Filip explains: 'Two of our planes forced it down. To use the military term, we put it in inverted commas'. He demonstrates a flanking force-down with his index fingers. The plane, a Lockheed T33 Shooting Star—a T-Bird—is a 1950s built, two seater single jet trainer (still flown by the Greek air force), its black USAF markings on nose and tail, and its silver paint crisply maintained. We had known that we might see this curious exhibit, but had failed to find references to its capture and the identity or fate of its pilot. He was released, Filip tells us, after being tried for spying.

We finally locate the house where Enver Hoxha was born, once a museum but now locked tight. Just a few doors away is the Ethnographic Museum where we have better luck. A caretaker motions for us to wait and soon returns with the English-speaking curator. She shivers in a light sweater as she shows us through the house. When I ask where I can buy carpets, she says she has a few handloomed ones. 'The Italian tourists like them but they didn't come this year,' she says.

The house where Enver Hoxha is said to have been born, in 1908, is a large building much restored and extended from what was presumably a more modest structure. It houses the Museum of the National Liberation War: Hoxha was anxious that it did not become a shrine, explains Filip, as he did not wish to encourage the cult of personality. One or two eyebrows are raised.

Inside are documents and photographs of Albanian nationalists from the last century through to National Liberation, photographs of Nazi atrocities and mass arrests, and a painting of two local heroines: the teenage Gjirokastër girls who were hanged, by the Nazis, from a tree in the square outside the Hotel Çaiupi.

The rooms have been exquisitely restored, with carved and painted ceilings, doors and wall panels, richly coloured kilims, and low divans around the walls.

On our way to the coastal town of Saranda we drive in circles for an hour trying to reach Shën Kollit Church at Mesopotam. Children beside the road say the people who now own the land tore down the bridge. The only possibility is to ford the river but it looks deep and the weather is cold, so at last we give up.

In Saranda the mild sea air and a lemon sun provide delightful relief from the cold mountains we have travelled through for the past two days. The Butrinti Hotel on the sea front sends us farther down the road to the House of Relaxation, which has hot water. I sit on my balcony—it is warmer outside than in—sipping tea and gazing at Corfu. The hotel is beautifully situated right on the sea, surrounded by pines, palms and oleanders still in bloom. There's a rock beach so white it looks painted. (It *is!*)

A warm, clear morning gives our first daylight view around the bay, with the neat houses of Sarandë terraced behind a broad promenade shaded with palm trees. It's the type of setting which mass tourism has obliterated with high-rise hotels in most other Mediterranean resorts.

The northeastern bulk of Corfu looms across the channel, the scene of the Incident in 1946 when the British destroyers Volage *and* Saumarez *were damaged by mines, with 44 men killed. The boats returned to Corfu, where the* Saumarez *was found to be beyond repair. Lengthy proceedings in international courts eventually awarded £900,000 damages to Britain against Albania, although there are arguments that the mines could have been laid by the Nazis, Greece or Yugoslavia. Britain insists on retaining, in the Bank of England, the Albanian gold seized from the Nazis—or at least that part which covers the Channel award: there are American and Italian claims on the remainder.*

Soon Ani appears with an army pal and a policeman friend, and we all go into town to a fish restaurant. The restaurant is furnished with plastic tables and chairs and the tablecloth is not particularly fresh, but the fish is. Army and Police make short shrift of two bottles of Albanian Riesling, drinking from tumblers and topping off the wine with 7-Up.

We return to our hotel to find a busload of would-be refugees resting in the lobby. They have come from Elbasani and hope to walk across the Greek border in the dark of the night.

Day 7: This morning there are patches of blue among the clouds and no whitecaps, just a slight rippling of the water. The day promises real warmth. Ani's army friend is going with us to the archaeological site of Butrinti, south of Saranda.

We stop at a guard station just at the neck of the Ksamili Peninsula; Army speaks with the soldiers on duty and they allow us to climb up a steep hill to the ruins of a grey stone monastery that blends with the silver leaves of the old olive trees. Behind a rusting gate is a church with ruined frescos dribbling from its dome; it is possible to make out a crucifixion and a row of 12 prophets flanking God, or maybe Moses. Recent smoke and wax streak the niches. Candles have been stuck into broken bottles and six mouldy lemons and two oranges have been placed on the hacked-off remains of the altar. A fresh new icon hangs on one wall.

I stir up gnats and mosquitoes in the undergrowth. Along the outer wall, which is intact to about 3m high, loopholes look out over Butrinti Lake on one side and the sea on the other. This was a defensive place as well as a religious one. I ask Army its name and he says *Manastir*—Monastery. Did the names die with Hoxha?

I am determined to find out and ask everyone I meet if they know about it. Finally at the Institute for Cultural Monuments, a document seems to indicate that it is Çuka Monastery—but there are several other monasteries in the Saranda area as well.

From this point on the peninsula, it is one minute by *scaff* (some sort of small, fast boat) to Corfu. The Greeks patrol carefully. 'We used to shoot, now they shoot,' Army says.

On the road again, we drive between lake and sea. Fluffy clouds reflect in the lake, ducks make Vs in the water. The land is terraced for olive groves and pigs root under the trees. A shiny white ferry moves

in the distance—there is a daily ferry service between Kerkira (Corfu Town) and Saranda, and in summer the ferry is full of day-trippers coming to visit the Butrinti ruins.

We stop at the state restaurant on the hilltop. The view is marvellous but the restaurant has no fish though it is surrounded by sea and lake, no olives though surrounded by olive groves. We take a look in the kitchen at the thin, cold slabs of beef already cooked and congealed in their fat, and decide to move on.

Down by the ferry landing at the small channel that connects lake and sea, just at the gate to the Butrinti ruins, a small private restaurant has set out a few tables in the sunshine. We eat there, watching the ferry, which consists of cross planks and wooden treads attached to four metal pontoons, being pulled back and forth, back and forth on a cable. The ferry connects the road to six villages farther south and to the Vrina Plain, known for its vineyards.

A guard allows us to park inside the fence surrounding the ruins and for once Wilma and Ani leave the car unattended. We tramp along shady lanes to the baths and temples, amphitheatre and Roman houses. Almost everybody who was anybody in Albania has been here, from the ancient Greeks and Romans to the Venetians and Turks, and one can easily spend a half day poking about in the undergrowth for their traces. It is impossible to get near Asklepios' Temple because of a stagnant moat and all the mosaics are covered with sand, as usual, but there is enough to explore. Army plucks leaves of delphinium and gives them to us to chew; they taste like the Dentine gum that I loved as a child.

The path circles round the ruins and comes out near the lake. The tinkling of sheep's bells floats up as we climb to the fortress—it looks so new and I can't find a Venetian lion.

Equipped with leks, we drive south for 16km on the peninsular road to Butrint, through the orange groves with the Ionian Sea on our right and the saltwater Lake Butrint on our left: the isthmus is about 1km wide.

The entrance to the ruined site of Butrint (the ancient city of Buthroton) is at the foot of the hill next to a cable-hauled ferry barge, near two 18th century Ottoman fortresses. A path leads through the trees to the ruins, where we are met by a local guide who speaks in Albanian, whilst Rasim translates.

A small theatre, with 19 tiers of seats, is flooded at its lowest level, and we teeter carefully along the wall foundations. Our guide tells us that the inscriptions, in tiny Greek letters on the left-hand wall, are the names of the slaves who built the theatre. Maybe so, but they are neatly cut and someone went to much trouble to record mere slaves: I think an Albanian reminder of Graeco-Roman society's more unacceptable characteristics could be more likely.

We wander through this most beautiful setting (aware of the mosquitoes which have fed on some of us), past the baths, a fountain, the remains of houses and shops, to the circular baptistry. A layer of gravel protects the mosaic floor, but two small areas are cleared, and layers of polythene can be raised to lift the gravel in other places, revealing some of the 69 images of birds, animals and plants. The large 14th century basilica, with a wide nave and aisles, is close to the path which leads to the Lake Gate: a small sally-port in the colossal dressed polygonal stones which form the base of the perimeter walls.

The path follows the walls, past a large well dedicated to nymphs (or used by brides-to-be on the morning of their wedding, if the guide is to be believed) and on to the Lion Gate: the heavy lintel, lower now than its original height as a result of earthquakes, has a relief depicting a fight between a lion and a bull.

At the top of the hill is the museum: a cool, well-displayed exhibition of archaeological finds, including fragments of statues, inscriptions, jewellery and utensils. Outside, from the walls, is a marvellous view down on to the ruins and the trees and across to the lake, the fortresses and the marshes.

The path down to the bus passes a replica of the Goddess of Butrint: a marble head discovered by Italian excavations, taken to Italy, but now returned to Tiranë—a stunning Aphrodite (or, say some, a head of Apollo)...

Arriving in Sarandë, we continue past the Hotel Butrinti, and walk along the broad pedestrians-only promenade. I sit on a wall, to have my photograph taken in front of a sculpture of three girl workers heroically picking grapes, when we are joined by a dark-skinned woman with a white plastic bag, who tries to beg money. Easily put off, she sits on the wall for a rest and a cigarette (a tipped Partisani). As I offer her a light, Andrea misses the photographic opportunity of the holiday: 'This is Me with an Albanian Gypsy who made Friends with Me'. I am not amused.

The town is smart and clean, and has three main streets running parallel to the sea. Like all Albanian towns, there is hardly any litter, and Western advertisements are replaced by political slogans and pictures of Enver Hoxha. Even the remote hilltops have PARTI ENVER spelled out in white stones, and, at the roadsides, on schools and factories and official buildings are signs and exhortations: RROFTE PARTIA YNE POPYLLON—Long live the Party and the People; RROFTE PPRSH—Long live the Party of Labour of the Republic of Albania; and LAVDI SHOKU ENVER HOXHA—Glory to comrade Enver Hoxha.

You can sense the closeness of Greece: the women in black skirts and coloured blouses and cardigans— not skirts and trousers as in the north—and the black-scarved black-clothed widows.

In the late afternoon we drive back to Saranda and take a look at the excavations in town. Then we head for Himara. This will be the most dangerous road, Ani says, and it is indeed horrendous. Narrow and much patched, it hairpins its way up into the mountains that are turning pink in the sunset. Cotton candy clouds waft above our heads and we catch a glimpse of silver sea.

We drive through a huge herd of sheep and goats, and on through

Shën Vasi, a stone village whose monument with three red stars is still intact. In Qeparo the locals advise us to take the high road because there is construction on the coast road, so we go up, up, up into the night.

In the mountains the darkness is palpable. The sky is full of stars but they cannot penetrate the forest around us. At last we see the lights of a village—Piluri—spread out on the mountainside like the Big Dipper fallen to earth. Ani says that because Piluri was 98% anti-communist it got no roads, no schools, no medical care. That's why it is so isolated.

In Himara the soft yellow lights of the Restorant Goro on the seashore are doubly welcome after the thick darkness in the mountains. The plastic chairs are a bit too low for the tables—Wilma says she feels as if she is at Alice in Wonderland's tea party—but the room is freshly painted white with blue trim and the red cloths are clean. We have local wine, a plate of olives and cheese, the tasty local fish called *merlutz*.

Things just happen in Albania. It sometimes takes time, but while we sit and eat, wheels are turning and suddenly doors open or someone with a room to rent appears. This time a room has appeared a couple of doors down from the restaurant. The family has gone to Greece and rents out their apartment to tourists. For US$5 (£3.25), I spend the night in a three-room apartment with kitchen, the bedcover neatly stacked and ready, the water in the barrels fresh. There is no heat but the weather is mild and the blankets plentiful.

Day 8: I wander down to the restaurant to wait for Ani and Wilma. Turkish coffee is prepared on a camp stove and for breakfast there are eggs, fried cheese, bread and a plate of honey.

Today we are going to one of Ali Pashë Tepelena's fortresses at the Bay of Porto Palermo, completely inaccessible BEFORE because it was situated on a top-secret submarine base. It is a 20-minute drive south of Himara down a gravel road, still fenced and guarded. A huge tunnel leads from the bay into the side of a mountain; Ani says the tunnel can accommodate two submarines.

The castle stands out pinkish on its little peninsula; an armed guard watches as we photograph it but makes no effort to stop us. We drive into a seemingly deserted base where PARTI ENVER survives on a couple of barracks walls along with newer graffiti in praise of DEEP PURPLE, and begin the climb up to the fortress.

It seems very small, its walls low. An arched chamber is dimly lit by a couple of skylights, and a bit of marble shows through the dirt on the floor. The walls look about 3m thick. We grope our way among the maze of arched rooms and find marble steps to the top. Ani says that when the fort was finished Ali Pasha himself attacked it from the sea to see how strong it was.

A naval guard wanders in and is soon joined by another; the first man unceremoniously passes over the gun and cartridge belt to him. Their uniforms consist of blue trousers and navy jackets with stars still on the buttons, but they threw away the red stars that were on their caps. There is a shortage of shirts—some men do not have shirts at all and some wear T-shirts of varying hues under their jackets. The officers sew tiny strips of white cloth around their jacket collars in lieu of shirt collars.

Eventually the guard says that the officer wants to see us. We go to the barracks and wait while someone tries to get through to him on a crank telephone. A dead eel lies on the filing cabinet.

When the officer arrives, we are not questioned but simply exchange small talk and then we leave. As we drive away we meet two soldiers toiling up the mountain with a huge bucket of water, then another three with an even bigger pot.

Back at Himara we stop at a house to photograph dolls. From time to time we have noticed modern plastic dolls stuck up on posts or fences. Here, three are strung on wire over a gate. When the owner of the house comes out we ask why the dolls are there. He says he will tell us if we come in for coffee.

The house has two storeys with a large balcony, a terrace, a grape arbour and tomato vines. Huge geraniums are still blooming, and cats wander around the yard. There is running water in an outdoor sink; the water spout is fashioned from a metal pipe labelled 'poison' in red and marked with a skull and crossbones.

The man makes coffee over a camp stove. He has six children, all working in Greece—his 'eyes are dropping tears' because he misses them so much. He was born in France; Wilma asks if he could get a French passport and live there but he says he doesn't want to. He likes it here. He wants to renovate this house as a bed-and-breakfast for tourists. The dolls, he says, are to keep away the evil eye. Some people string up garlic, but he wants to be more modern.

Above Himara beach is the old town full of square stone houses. The cobbled streets are narrow and stepped, the houses cluster together, and chickens scratch in the yards. We stop to talk; a woman gives us oranges, putting the peel on a low wall to dry—she uses them to scent her house. Her husband was an 'exile' in Lezha; they have just come back to reclaim the family home.

The road from Himara is full of traffic—people drive to the town for oranges and olives. At the top of a pass there has been an accident. The drivers are shouting at each other, there may be a fight. A small traffic jam develops. Finally someone calms the drivers and gets them to move on.

From the mountain top we see Dhërmi beach—it is beautiful but littered with bunkers. The hotel is boarded up and the tiny pink, blue and white cottages of corrugated tin are shut tight. A baroque boy-with-fish fountain spouts water; there are orange groves and honeysuckle. Is the place empty because the former owners are demanding the land back, or are we simply here out of season?

Day 9: My friend Manfred has arrived in Tirana on holiday from Germany, and we decide to make a short tour to the 'museum city', Berati, with a car arranged through Albturist. Our driver, Ilir, speaks only a few words of English but has placed a dictionary on the dashboard beside a Koran and we manage to communicate very well.

We drive out of Tirana past the large textile mill, formerly named Stalin, but now both name and bust are gone. At Kavaja—famous for its carpets—kelims flap in the wind by the roadside to tempt tourists. The state carpet factory has been converted to making shoes but is selling off the remainder of its stock. I buy a small rug for US$10 (£6.50) but must wait for the boss to come and sign my receipt—'We must be correct'. The women who accompany us to the car are visibly upset when I photograph a faded propaganda poster on one of the factory walls.

The road leads through a plain reclaimed from swampland; seagulls trail behind the tractors and the shepherds are all carrying umbrellas. Villages of square brick houses are surrounded by fences woven of sticks; the yards are full of hay stacks, geese and turkeys. We meet many ox carts on the road.

We turn off the main road toward Divjaka, circled in green on my map as a 'place of touristic interest', and take a long, straight road that would feel at home in the Mississippi Delta. Divjaka village is congenial, and when we stop to photograph we are surrounded at once by a group of schoolboys. '*Allemagne*?' they ask, and I say, 'America'. One boy grins broadly. 'English,' he says, and struggles out of his backpack to dig out his English textbook. Manfred, who has a Germanic horror of dirt, remarks on how clean the people are.

Past Divjaka, we enter pine woods and soon reach the sea—actually a calm bay almost completely surrounded by crab claws of land. The hotel seems to be open and people are strolling around, possibly a school class on a weekend excursion. Ilir gets out his camp stove and makes Turkish coffee for 'Lady' and 'Sir', as he persists in calling me and Manfred.

Back on the main road, we stop for diesel. The station is the usual two tanks inside an iron cage, like some dangerous animal at a zoo. The most popular tanks say Aral and Agip and they often stand side by side in the same cage but these are never the brands of fuel in them. Neither is the type of fuel necessarily that marked on the tank: diesel may be pumped from one marked 'Super Benzine'.

Ilir is not happy with the fuel here, however, so he tanks up from his reserve canister. He uses state fuel which is sometimes hard to find in Tirana, he says. There is another station on the outskirts of Berati and this time he fills both car and spare can.

Berati's old town rises above us and we spot a surviving ENVER spelled out on the blue mountainside. The Hotel Tomori (named for one of the mountains here) sits on the Osumi River bank behind a charming park. Our room is terrible but the balcony opens to a wonderful view of the white stone buildings climbing up the mountainside.

We have a late lunch at the hotel, the usual choice of *qofte* or *biftek*, Merlot wine and Glina mineral water. The waiter does not bring the bill; a hierarchy still functions here. The bill man says he can speak 'a little' English, then proceeds to talk to me in Italian. In the evening we go bar hopping with Ilir. Coffee costs 20 lekë, Skënderbeg brandy 40 lekë per glass. Ilir says the brandy was very good BEFORE but hard to get; now it is easy to find but not so good.

Promptly at 21.00 as promised, the hotel desk man, accompanied by one of the little Gypsy boys who hang around on the steps, brings a heater to our room. It is the heater from the lobby. Two bricks serve as the missing leg of the apparatus. It is huge and barely fits between the beds but will not produce enough heat to endanger the bedding. However, there *is* hot water for a shower downstairs in room 107.

The journey south to Berat, partly retracing our route of two days ago, but branching left at Lushnjë, takes two hours. We stop at the Hotel Tomori for lunch, at the bottom of the hill topped by the fortress, in a square next to the minaret and domes of a former mosque. Like Gjirokastër, Berat is a 'Museum Town', with planning regulations governing new buildings. Here too, the houses are clustered together, with their white façades and large windows banked up the hillside: 'a view that combines Tyrolese or Swiss grandeur with all the pretty etcetera of Turkish architecture', said Edward Lear.

Lunch is in a large skyblue room, with the tables end to end in a horseshoe shape, banquet style. A fat and jolly waitress serves us a salad of lettuce, spring onions, pickled gherkins and carrots followed by meatballs with leeks and peas, a piece of ginger sponge cake, and tinned cherries.

A steep path leads up to the main entrance to the castle, through a tall grey gateway in the perimeter walls, pierced by twin dark cannon ports beneath the crenellations. An Albanian boy overtakes us, riding

a chestnut pony bareback up the track. The gate leads to narrow streets between well kept houses with deeply overhanging eaves: at one time the citadel contained over 300 houses and 20 churches.

We arrive at the former Orthodox church of St Mary, tucked in an alley, with an Albanian woman sitting on the steps knitting. We had been told we were to see the works of 'an Albanian painter', and, dreading a show of romanticised peasant girls, we were intending instead to go off exploring. Thankfully, some tiny spark of curiosity takes over, and we stay with the group.

Inside the church, Filip greets the guide, an old friend from university, with a hug and kisses on both cheeks, and we are introduced to the works of Onufri, 'an Albanian painter'.

Onufri was a 16th century icon and fresco painter, who may have studied in Italy, and who is known for the greater degree of realism which he introduced to the formalism of icon painting. But the most impressive qualities to our eyes are the colours, the brushwork and the composition. The colours are extraordinary for 16th century paintings: Onufri was known for his red—'Onufri red'—but he used mushroom, greys, turquoise, flattened greyed pink and muted greens.

Restoration of the paintings has cleared away the varnish gunge, still visible on a couple of panels flanking the iconostasis, and you can see the steady matt drag of the brush, crisp and flat, dry and even. No greasy butter smearing, just good, solid, honest painting, and lines and echoes and rhythms and joy in the putting on of paint and making marks on surfaces; and the compositions or the images, are stunning. An icon of John the Baptist, the saint winged and looking out at us, but also carrying his own severed head as the symbol of his martyrdom, is a Rossetti painting of Janey Morris, a Proserpine, in a turquoise so stinging that you have to go up close to try and find the secret, but it's just wonderful paint mixing.

*The iconostasis of carved and gilded wood shines down the aisle
from behind the hanging lamps with ostrich eggs bracketed into their
chains, and a sadly damaged Christ Pantocrater in the dome looks
down on a deeply carved pulpit.*

The Onufri museum is, as they say, a little gem.

*Out again, in the citadel compound, we walk around the grassy spaces
between the foundations of houses and shops, climbing to the edge of
the perimeter wall, by the restored church of St Mëhill—St Michael.
Overlooking the steep drop down to the Osum Valley, it is a picturesque
if fairly standard Byzantine church, with a red-tiled cupola and dormers
over tiny windows in vertical rows inside terracotta arches, but with
the unusual feature of white stone for the lower walls set off against
the same white stone on the upper walls but with flat terracotta slabs
in the courses: one band of slabs in the horizontal, two in the vertical.*

*We clamber up the slopes next to the church, and, on the northern
side of the citadel, is a restaurant overlooking the terraced olive trees,
the green plain, and the grey snowy mountains beyond. The
schoolchildren out in the yard next door are in good voice, singing a
partisan song for our benefit.*

Day 10: Ilir drives us to the Berati's citadel and we wander among the
quiet lanes. We meet only a group of small boys who, when they see
our cameras, scramble to the top of the ruined minaret to pose and
wave. A dog barks down at us from a garden wall; the streets are steep
and stepped.

The door of the Onufri Icon Museum is locked and we are unable to
rustle up someone with a key. Nearby is a school; a boy is ringing the
bell for recess and children are tumbling noisily out the door, so in we
go. The teachers welcome us, then three girls aged 14 appear, one of
whom, Esmeralda, speaks good English. The teachers excuse them
from class to show us the town.

We walk to the lovely little Byzantine church which sits alone, back
to the ruined minaret that looks like a factory chimney, past neat white
houses with their courtyards, stacked over one another above the white
cobbled streets.

Esmeralda invites us to her home. We enter through a minute
courtyard full of green plants, with a sink at one side that seems to
have running water. We are not allowed to remove our shoes so we
tiptoe over the carpet and sit down for raki and candy, followed by an
orange and an apple. Esmeralda's mother peels the orange first, giving
Manfred and me half each, then does the same with the apple. When
we leave, she presses four oranges into our hands. Such hospitality

leaves one in a quandary—it is terribly impolite to refuse gifts but the people have so little to eat that one feels guilty for accepting. We try to solve the problem by giving the oranges to Ilir for his children.

We go back to the lower town. The History Museum is closed for renovation but someone invites us in anyway. We get as far as a lovely Turkish Room when the director arrives, horrified that we are seeing the place in such a dishevelled state, and sends us to the Ethnographic Museum instead.

The curator Alma Naci, whose English is excellent, tells us that Berati is 2,400 years old. The citadel contains remains of all the ages of the city—large stones from the Illyrian walls, red masonry between the Byzantine stones. 'Once there were 42 churches within the walls—every important family had its own church,' she says.

We have coffee in the Turkish Room, then go with Alma's friend, Enriketa, to the city library where we explore the stacks, looking at book titles—most of the English material consists of medical journals though there is no medical school in town. We have coffee with the library director, Balil Gjini, a poet from Gjirokastra, and when we leave Enriketa presents me with a bouquet of autumn flowers.

The drive to the monastery of Ardenica takes much less time than I had estimated. The roads, though slippery because it is raining, are the best in the country. The monastery, surrounded by a wall and a grove of cypresses on its hilltop, was not destroyed in the 1967 crackdown on religion but was turned into a museum. Now its church has been reconsecrated and the monastery itself is a hotel with 11 rooms. It is usually booked up by Italians during the hunting season, but the season been cancelled this year so we are the only guests.

e concierge speaks German and converses exclusively with

Manfred. This seems typically Albanian; even when I pay entry fees, Manfred is given the tickets and the change.

Our room in the hotel is huge, the beds covered with two sheepskins each; there are a table, chair, mirror and TV set, and best of all a big new electric radiator. The toilet flush works and the hot water heater registers 70°C.

After settling in we visit the church. Skënderbeg is said to have married Donika here, and that is what saved it during the crackdown on religion. The head waiter speaks excellent English and translates the history of Ardenica as told by our concierge:

> 'The birthday of St Mary, 8 September, used to be a big celebration here. It was a trade fair as well as church services, and that was the first element of tourism in Albania—people came from as far away as Greece and Macedonia, and of course they had to sleep and eat here. Orthodox and Muslim sat down together at the tables.
>
> 'Ardenica was saved because its priest was a very intelligent man. When the students came to destroy the church in 1967, the priest said, "The key is not in my hands but in the hands of the state." He had been hard at work reminding the local teachers and government officials that Skënderbeg married here.'

We have an early dinner at the hotel so the staff can go home to Lushnja. Manfred and I go into the empty restaurant, but Ilir fetches us into a small lounge with low tables and a fireplace, both floor and chairs covered with sheepskins. The television is on loud, and a party of four is celebrating at another table.

Halfway through the meal the electricity fails. The waiter brings in stubs of candles from the church and we have a romantic dinner with candles stuck on to the mantelpiece and in the ashtrays.

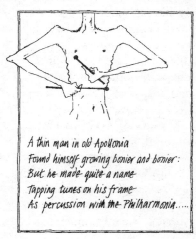

A thin man in old Apollonia
Found himself growing bonier and bonier:
But he made quite a name
Tapping tunes on his frame
As percussion with the Philharmonia.....

Day 11: In the late morning, we drive to Fieri—a bustling, pleasant city—and take the road to Apollonia, a major archaeological site 10km farther toward the sea. Apollonia's museum seems to have been stripped bare. A young man offers me a terracotta head—it's probably genuine. I photograph two boys beside the city wall, and they try to sell me gangrenous Illyrian coins. Behind the 2nd century Temple of Diana two men are playing cards; they are selling a lovely cameo.

At Fier we make a loo stop at the Hotel Apollonia in the main square, facing an apartment block with three huge banners: ORGANIZIM, DISIPLINE and EMULACION.

On the narrow, bumpy road to the west of Fier the pillboxes and bunkers multiply: groups of four or five, lines and clusters. Richard and Linda, our new chums from last night, seem bent on breaking the 'be sensible' recommendations on photography in Albania, and are gleefully snapping groups of sheep which happen to be standing in front of the most impressive bunkers.

We pass a group of schoolchildren exercising with wooden rifles in their schoolyard. Military training for all pupils is an element of the tripartite educational system of 'learning, productive labour, and physical and military training'. Filip, who is sitting near us, explains about the system of national military service (two years for all able-bodied males, with university students usually commissioned, and a large reserve force).

The ruins of Apollonia spread up a hillside, above the green plain through which flows the once-navigable River Vjosa, and the former monastery and church stand on a ridge flanked by olive trees. Edward Lear was here in 1848: 'The exterior of the building offers nothing picturesque—but inside ... everywhere evidences of past ages meet the eye—a strange mixture of ancient Greek stones,

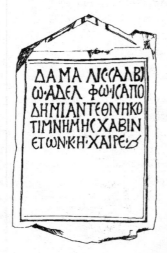

Roman columns, medieval cornices and capitals, later Greek brickwork, and Turkish galleries.' His description still holds, although the church of St Mary, then 'in a ruinous condition', has now been restored and there is a small museum in the upper floor of the convent, and a well displayed collection of sculpture, inscriptions and fragments of architecture in the cloisters. All the items are dated according to the Albanian system: in an atheist state the abbreviations BC and AD are no longer acceptable, so BC becomes PES—Para erës sonë, before our era, and AD dates are normally unaccompanied by initials.

Lear's overnight stay, in a 'barn-apartment ... not obtrusively luxurious', was disturbed by 'very asthmatic goats'. The next day he went to see 'the single Doric column—the only remaining token of Apollónia above ground'. We find a great change since then: the façade of the six columned temple of Artemis has largely been restored, and excavations are still in progress, exposing shops and houses, walls, streets and mosaics.

A more recent visitor, Eric Newby, came across a partly undesecrated Christian cemetery here (and was accused by his driver, who Newby thought was a member of the secret police, of photographing the nearby defences), so Andrea and I climb to a higher spur to investigate. No signs of a cemetery, but we do meet a quintet of giggling Albanian ladies, scarved and gumbooted, in skirts over trousers, shouldering long-handled shovels. We decide against attempts to climb higher when a soldier materializes, Jeeves-like, and we understand his look of warning: the gun emplacements on the far side of the hill, passed on our way here, were formidable. Maybe the cemetery is at the top of the hill, or perhaps it has now been obliterated.

Richard arrives back at the bus late but triumphant: on the pretext of photographing a fig tree, he had managed to include a group of soldiers in the shot. A subversive sub-group seems to be forming...

On to Vlora: we pass a large animal market where two major roads converge and see a mosaic monument of *Partizanis* still in good condition. A lovely mosque stands in the centre of Vlora and many small motorboats are moored along the seashore. At the beach we stop at the private Gloria Bar and Restaurant for espresso. Nick, the proprietor, brings us oranges on the house.

Past Vlora the road starts to climb, giving superb views of cliffs dropping down to the sea, but soon the mountains back off and we drive once more along the shore. At Orikumi, we get as far as a military base in search of Greek and Roman ruins but this time find none. 'All the archaeology has gone to Greece,' say the people we ask.

Going south, the road climbs again and roughens on its way up to the Llogara Pass. A new tourist camp has been built at the top, 11 comfortable prefabricated cabins brought from Germany, each with bunks for four, shower, hot water heater, fridge and TV. The camp restaurant is attractive, the prices reasonable, the food good.

We would like to come back in summer and go hiking here.

THE NORTHERN JOURNALS

I did come back in summer, but not to Llogara. This time I headed north from Tirana to the Albanian Alps. My first acquaintance with this area had been through Edith Durham's book *High Albania*. Although much of the trail she followed in 1908 is now in Montenegro and Kosova, I found a great deal of what she wrote about almost unchanged.

The group trek that I had planned to join did not materialize so I simply flew into Tirana alone with the vaguest of plans. 'This is what I want to see, is it possible?' I had written to Isa, the father of my friend Ani. 'Of course it is possible,' he said. 'Everything is possible in Albania.'

Albania defies planning and organization but somehow things work for the traveller who is willing to improvise. Time and flexibility are essential for getting off the beaten track, and it is advisable to have an Albanian-speaking friend or guide to accompany you.

Day 1: The journey north has begun. Isa has found a university student, Ari, who is eager to practise his English and will go along as translator. We take a bus to Lezha; it stops outside town at a Uji i Ftohtë (Cold Water) and the passengers fill their drinking bottles. 'Lezha water is the water from God,' says Isa.

Lezha is the town where Skënderbeg was buried in 1468. 'This was the most beautiful time for Albania—the 25 years of Skënderbeg,' says Ndue Perleka, our guide at the site of the tomb, a memorial built around the remains of St. Nicholas Cathedral, later a mosque.

Just before he died, Skënderbeg convened a second Council of Lezha in the fight for Albanian independence; it was also attended by Lekë Dukagjini who is credited with the *Code* that is still the law in much of the country today. Perleka says there was always rivalry between the two leaders but that during Skënderbeg's last battle at Kiri three days before his death, he was so ill that he turned the leadership over to Dukagjini.

'After his death, Skënderbeg's wife, Donika, and his son, Joni, went to Italy. Four branches of the family still live there—in Puglia, Naples, Florence and Venice. They are now in the 20th or 21st generation. King Zogu was a descendant of Skënderbeg's sister, Mamica, but in Albania we don't count heredity along female lines,' he says.

'Once Lezha was the most beautiful city in the Balkans,' Perleka continues. 'Archaeologists have found coins here from Rome, Romania, Spain, Austria and Egypt, which proves that it was an important commercial centre even when it was called Lissus in ancient

times. It was a great city, with schools, temples, institutes.'

Lezha has no active history museum now. Its exhibits have been stored to keep them from being stolen, as have the things from the ethnographic museum whose home has been reclaimed by its former owner. 'We want a new museum to combine history and ethnography, but we don't have the money,' Perleka says.

The half-hour climb up to Lezha's fortress—the site of ancient Lissus—is steep and hot, but worth the effort. There is no guide here so we ask a shepherd about the fortress.

'It was built in Illyrian times,' he says, 'and then rebuilt in the Middle Ages to keep out the Turks. You can see the different eras in the shapes of the stones. There are Roman parts, and Byzantine. Many years ago the Mongols came here and after them the Austro-Hungarians and then the Turks.'

It is a very large fortress, a grey tumble of stones where tortoises and lizards bask. Tufts of wool are caught in the briars or scud across the ground like miniature tumbleweeds. We find the entry to a tunnel, then climb up on the ramparts for the pleasant breeze coming in from the sea. The fields below make a neat patchwork of green and yellow. We have a view of the sea in the distance and of the colourful market on the banks of the Drini River in front of Skënderbeg's tomb.

Many Lezha folk, both young and old, still wear traditional dress. The women wear white pantaloons under a white skirt covered with a black apron. Some of them cover their black headdresses with white scarves. Colourful woven belts are wound round and round the waist with tassels dropping down at the back. All the women have a regal bearing—is it because of the dress or because people with such bearing have the pride and self-confidence to wear the dress?

***

We arrive in Lezhë in the late morning, after a journey of 40km, and stop by the banks of the Drin, at the Skënderbeg Memorial.

In January 1468, 25 years after uniting the Albanian nobles to combat Turkish domination, Gjergj Kastrioti Skënderbeg died in Lezhë and was buried in the cathedral of St Nicholas. In 1968, 500 years later, the ruins of the church were reconstructed as a memorial to the national hero. It is a restrained and impressive place, the walls lined with plaques listing his victories, a slab on the floor with replicas of his horned helmet and massive sword (the originals are in Vienna, taken there during Austro-Hungarian rule), and a bronze bust in front of a large red mosaic with the black double eagle in bronze:

*'In January 1468
the national hero,
Gjergj Skënderbeg,
was buried here.'*

Skënderbeg's coat-of-arms, and now the Albanian emblem. Fresh wild
flowers have been placed on the slab, and around the neck of the bust.
   I'm puzzled by the Albanian spelling of his name—Skënderbeu—
but Rasim explains. 'Skënder' is 'Alexander'—shades of James
Skinner, he of Skinner's Horse, hailed by his Indian soldiers as
'Sikander Sahib'—and 'beu' is as the Turkish 'bey'. So, Alexander
Bey.

Southwest of Lezha is a hunting lodge once owned by Mussolini's
son-in-law; it is now a hotel and I am determined to spend the night
there. No bus runs the 5km into the countryside, so we negotiate a
taxi. It is late afternoon and the hotel staff says that yes, rooms are
available but we can't check in until the manager arrives. So we sit on
the ground in the shade beside a little pond and wait.
   Weeping willows—lotus trees, Ari says—droop into the water. They
are here, he tells us, because once there was a monster who demanded
sacrifices. The most beautiful girl of the region had to come to this
spot so that the monster could kill her. As the girl waited, she cried so
much that her tears made this pond, and just as the monster arrived
she turned into a tree. That tree is called *me lotue*, 'to cry', in Albanian.
   It is much cooler here, with the trees and the water, than in town.
Frogs are screeching in the pond and insects jabbering. Finally the
manager arrives; he is a friend of Isa and we get our rooms. There is
hot running water for a shower. The lodge is made of rustic stone and
wood, the rooms panelled in dark wood. The bathroom mirror has

wood, the rooms panelled in dark wood. The bathroom mirror has been hung so high that I can barely see the top of my head when I stand on tiptoe, but there is a well-lit walk-in wardrobe with a full-length mirror and plenty of space for hanging clothes. There is even a minibar, stocked with two airline-size bottles each of ouzo and ginger ale. At dinner, Isa tells me they cost 70 lekë. 'Don't drink them, that's too expensive.'

We look into the tourist dining room, the seats covered with sheepskin, white cloths on tables beautifully set with wine glasses. But Isa says the 'people's restaurant' is 20% cheaper and the food comes from the same kitchen, so we settle for a plainer table and blue-checked napkins. The woodcarved chairs are lovely. We have *biftek* for three with all the trimmings and beer for less than 1,000 lekë. As in restaurants throughout the country, the bill is added up on a tiny scrap of cardboard cut from a cigarette carton because paper is in short supply.

Afterwards we sit at a picnic table by the river in the soft darkness, and Isa tells about his travels during his sports days, when he would sleep in parks or airports and save his hotel allowance to buy shirts and shoes. His family and friends expected him to bring things home. He is trying to make the point that I have splurged on this hotel (it cost 2,000 lekë for me, 300 lekë each for Isa and Ari).

Day 2: We get a lift back to Lezha and from there take a bus (tickets cost 5 lekë per person) to the beach at Shëngjini 8km away. A picture of an icon is pasted to the sun flap of the windshield and a cross hangs from the rearview mirror. In front of me is a Muslim with a flamboyant red moustache, wearing a peaked white fez; yes, he will be happy to pose for a photo.

The reasonably good road winds around the base of the mountain. We pass through a bit of marshland, then through farmland with neat stone houses. At Shëngjini the wide sandy beach sprouts colourful umbrellas; plenty of bikinis are in evidence. Two rusting wrecks protrude from the water—the *Bashkimi* and the *23 Nëntori*—two of the ships sailed to Italy by desperate refugees in 1991. The beach is full of bunkers. 'We were very proud of our bunkers,' Isa says, so seriously that I am sure he is laughing at me.

We have lunch at a beach restaurant. Afterwards I stay under its awning sipping water while Isa goes off to visit friends and Ari walks out to the beach 'to expose my body to the sun' and study the dictionary.

A taxi driver offers us a ride to Shkodra for 500 lekë. We cross the Drini—it was narrow and a murky green at Lezha, but here it is wide and sparkling blue, the way people imagine the Danube to be if they have only heard the song.

Rozafa Fortress south of the city comes into view long before we reach Shkodra. It is striking on top of its sugarloaf mountain and the path leading up to it looks even steeper than the one to the fortress at Lezha.

Shkodra is spacious, with an atmosphere of leisure—perhaps even a breath of the *belle époque*—that I fall in love with at once. Isa checks

hotel prices; we choose the Park Hotel at the Grand Café, a lovely art deco building, with a flat rate of 800 lekë per person, foreign or Albanian. There is still etched glass on the doors, but many layers of paint disfigure the beautiful ironwork of the stair rails and the rooms have been newly painted shocking pink. This is the only surviving building by Kol Idromeno, a local architect; it is all original, built in 1900, and has always been called the Grand Café, the new owner tells us.

In the late afternoon we stroll around town looking for the places that I want to visit. There are many bicycles here—maybe two or three per family—because the city is so spread out. The people of Shkodra were the first to get bicycles; when private cars were allowed, they were also the first to get cars, Isa says.

The *Muzeu Popullor* will be open in the morning; beside it is a park and down the street is the Franciscan Church (its interior still outfitted as a theatre, which it was during the Hoxha regime) and its neighbouring convent. The newly renovated Catholic Cathedral (a sports palace during the regime), that was reconsecrated by Pope John Paul II, is farther from the city centre, near a cedar-shaded graveyard, together with its convent (believed to have been headquarters of the secret police).

The cemetery obviously predates the communist era—several tombs bear 1900 dates—and I wonder how the crosses and religious statues (albeit headless) survived the Hoxha regime. A group of elderly men who are sitting on a tomb gossiping offer a variety of explanations.

'It was protected like a museum,' says one. 'Look over there, German graves from World War II were there, but they have been destroyed.'

'For a long time it was closed and no one was allowed in, not even those who had family buried here,' says another. 'It was reopened in 1990—the people opened it by force.'

Cemetery wall in Shkodra–how did the crosses survive? It is obviously old.

Northwestern Albania was more influenced by Rome than Constantinople and Shkodra and its surroundings have remained a bastion of Albanian Catholicism. Before 1967, Shkodra was about 35% Catholic but now that people from the surrounding mountains have flocked into the city it is about 50-50 Catholic and Muslim. Perhaps a hundred Orthodox families live here.

We find an area of narrow streets and low Turkish houses interspersed by villas. Shkodrans have a penchant for painting their gates and doorways pastel colours, creating a pleasant effect. Many of the houses have shady courtyards.

We retrace our steps and explore the area on the other side of our hotel. Down a street lined with linden trees, pines and magnolias we find the huge City Park with sparkling fountains and crowds of people strolling or sitting on the grass. Isa, I discover, knows the best ice-cream shop in every town; the one in Shkodra is at the edge of this park. The ice-cream is made in an antiquated electric crank machine; it tastes like the hand-cranked ice cream I remember from my childhood and costs 30 lekë for two scoops.

Isa and Ari wonder at my obsession with street names but have made

it a game to see who can find out the name of a street first. We stop people and ask them, we go into shops and ask, we constantly search for signs. 'How do you find your way around without knowing the names of streets?' I want to know. 'If you ask, you can get to Istanbul,' replies Isa. The same principle applies to bus stops. They are seldom marked; people simply know where they are.

For dinner, we wander into a tiny restaurant with six tables. Isa has a word with the cook and we get plates of fresh fried tongue, liver and yogurt. The bill for three people comes to 525 lekë, but Isa thinks we were overcharged.

Day 3: Breakfast doesn't seem to be on any menu, but if you ask, you can usually get fried eggs. Most people eat *pilaf* and *fricassee,* a thin stew of chicken lights and livers.

Ari and I make the rounds of Shkodra's *Muzeu Popullor* with a guide. 'We have no proper museum,' he laments. 'The owner wants this house back and we have no money to build a new one. The objects outside are being destroyed by the weather.'

Most of the exhibits are on the ground floor, but the guide takes us upstairs to a photo exhibition. There is an archive in Shkodra of 500,000 negatives from 1856 onward—the oldest in the Balkans, he tells us. It is a real photo chronicle of the city, of its people, of many buildings that have been destroyed: a small 13th century church that was dynamited in 1967, and a mosque that was also blown up. There are pictures of the traditional-style houses with *çardhaks,* of which only 10 or 15 survived, and of the Shkodra market. It once had 2,500 shops and was the biggest bazaar outside Istanbul.

We follow the road northeast to the village of Mes, where the river Kir, a tributary of the Bunë, is crossed by the lovely 18th century stone bridge, built by the local feudal lord Mustafa Pasha Bushati. Just four metres wide, it has 13 stone arches, with the largest—over the river—23 metres across and 13 metres high. Around this central arch are eight stout metal hooks, but no one can explain what they are for: hanging chains as a barrier? banners? dead donkeys to ward off

the uninvited? We wander across for our first real encounter with Albanian soil.

We are summoned back on the coach. Pilo's bus, which he obviously loves, has a posh horn system with which he not only scares the pants off other road users, both human and animal, but also uses to call us on board when he thinks sightseeing time is up...

We are wary when taking photographs, because of the inevitability of including, unwittingly, soldiers or people who might object to being photographed. Two old men, in dark suits but wearing white felt skull caps, cycle by, and groups of young girls carry white and yellow blossoms.

To Rosafa castle, on a hilltop on the outskirts of the town. Edward Lear in 1848 described the 'odious paved paths' up the hill, but this might have been coloured by the meal of 37 dishes with which he was met at the summit. The path now is not so odious, though the grey-white stones are well polished and slippery. The track looks out over the Leaden Mosque, pillboxes in the fields, and the rooftops of the town.

The entrance to the fortress (with a memorial on the wall to victims of the Nazis) is an impressive barbican: a deep tunnel with guardhouse alcoves, casemates, and meurtrières, with a right-angled bend into the main courtyard. This is a large oval enclosure, with steeply battered walls and both round and square towers, containing the ruins of former dwellings, and a mosque built on the ruins of a church. From one side there is a sheer drop down to the river, which has the chevron catch-fencing of a fish farm linking across from islands to riverbanks.

While we have been touring the museum Isa has been arranging for someone to show us around Rozafa Citadel and for transportation to Thethi. To reach the fortress, we take a bus to the outskirts of Shkodra, then climb for about 20 minutes. At the top, our guide Zamir Tafilica tells the legend of Rozafa.

'Three brothers were building the fortress walls. They worked from sunrise to sunset but during the night the walls fell down. One day an old man passed by and they asked him what was going wrong. 'Are you married?' asked the old man, and they answered, 'Yes, and we have many children.' So the old man told them that the wife who brought their food the next day must be walled up alive to make the fortress strong.

'The victim was to be chosen by chance but the two older brothers warned their wives. The third brother was honest and when his wife Rozafa brought the food it was her fate to be walled up. 'I will do it for the sake of the people, but with one condition,' she said. 'You must leave one eye free so I can see my baby, one hand free to stroke him, one leg free so I can rock his cradle and one breast free so I can nurse him.'

'The fortress was completed and was strong; and to this day mothers who have no milk come here, scratch the stones of the wall, mix the dust with milk and drink it so they can feed their babies.'

The restaurant in the fortress grounds is closed; so is the museum. It's always open, I am told, but not today—the usual story. We climb on to the walls for a view of Taraboshi Mountain (it gave its name to a brand of Albanian cigarettes) and of the three rivers: the Kiri and Drini converge, then flow into the Buna at our feet. A neat village of tiled-roofed villas sits just across the bridge; it is called Baçallëk from the Turkish *bacha*—a yard of flowers. The settlement was built after the earthquake of 15 April 1979, but only people with good *biografi* were given the houses.

Biografi. The word has cropped up again and again. During the Hoxha regime, detailed files were kept on each citizen. Those with good *biografi* got the good jobs, the perks; those with bad could very well end up in prison or 'exiled' into forced labour.

On our descent from the citadel we pass a bunker built into the hillside where a family is living. Down below a Gypsy settlement has sprung up on the site of the old market. On the hill above is a large house built

'On 29 November 1944, partisans of the 23rd brigade raised the victory banner here, completing the liberation of the Motherland from Nazi-Fascist occupiers and traitors to the country.'

ME 29 XI 1944 PARTIZANET E
Br 23 S. NGRITEN NE KETE VENO
FLAMURIN E FITORES OE SHENOI
ÇLIRIMIN E PLOTE TE ATDHEUT
NGA OKUPATORI, NAZIFASHISTE
DHE TRADHETARET E VENDIT.

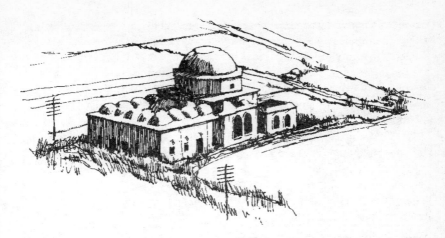

for government functionaries, now used as a residence for foreign dignitaries.

Over a very good lunch of grilled chicken at a roadside restaurant (it has no name) below the fortress, Tafilica tells us that Shkodra was always very beautiful, very traditional. 'Shkodrans are gentlemen,' he says. 'Many poets, artists and intellectuals lived here; our Catholic priests were scholars and philosophers. But much has been destroyed. Shkodra was a centre of anti-communist activity, though now there is a lot of protest against the present government, too. During World War II, the Germans were here and Shkodrans expected the Allied Forces to help us. But at Yalta, we were given to the communists. Most of the intellectuals and artists fled, first to Europe, then to the United States. Little countries' politics depend on big countries,' he sighs. 'But if Europe wants peace, it must ensure peace in the Balkans.

'Shkodra has four heroes who were killed in anti-communist protests,' Tafilica continues. 'There were three demonstrations by students who wanted to pull down the Stalin and Hoxha monuments. At the third, police sharpshooters killed the four leaders. The army didn't shoot, only the police.'

We return to Shkodra in the late afternoon, just as the *muezzin* is sounding his call to prayer. It also seems to be the call to reconvene in the cafés.

The Luigj Gurakuqi Museum is closed; it has been returned to its owner but perhaps a visit can be arranged. Paulin Perja, local historian and co-author of a guidebook to Shkodra, says the owner is a good man—he is unemployed but he protects and cares for the house. One night he fought with five people who tried to break in.

The museum birthplace of the poet Migjeni (1911-1938) is also

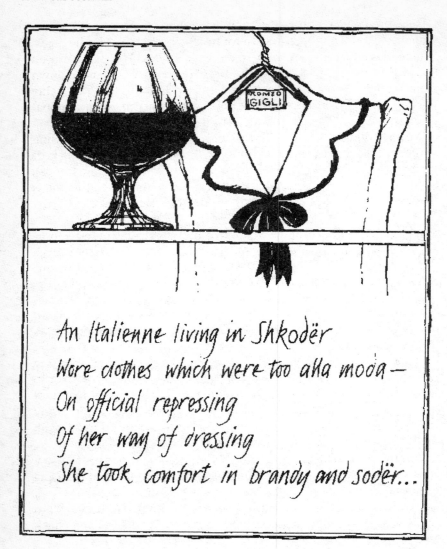

An Italienne living in Shkodër
Wore clothes which were too alla moda—
On official repressing
Of her way of dressing
She took comfort in brandy and sodёr...

closed. Migjeni (an acronym for Millosh Gjergj Nikolla) is considered Albania first contemporary poet. He died young of tuberculosis, and wrote only 200 pages—'but,' says Perja, 'his pen was so strong!'

On the street that runs from the radio station to the stadium is the lovely old house where Ramiz Alia, Albania's last communist leader, was born and lived until the age of seven. It is also where the 'folk hero' Oso Kuka was born and is therefore being renovated as a museum. We go in to admire the woodwork and the ornate chimneys, though exhibits are not yet in place.

Near the hotel I stop at the cubbyhole shop of silversmith Marin Gjonej. Shkodra has been known for its silver since the Middle Ages. 'There was a factory here with 70 employees,' he says, 'but it closed and now everyone works privately. Jewellery used to be handed down from mother to daughter because that was the only thing of value women owned. During Hoxha's time, people asked for traditional designs, but now modern jewellery is more popular.'

We have dinner tonight in the former *hammam*. Inside, it is sparkling white, bright carpets cover the floors and modern tapestries (one is of Elvis) decorate the walls. The small rooms provide charming nooks and crannies for quiet conversation, but even though the ceiling fan is creating a breeze we decide it will be cooler to eat outside.

Day 4: We meet Perja at the Shkodra museum. He has found a four-wheel drive vehicle to take us to Thethi (the bus runs only once a week) but it is raining today so we decide to wait until tomorrow. Shkodra is the rainiest town in Albania, Ari says. We while away the showers under the awning of the Grand Café. A little street girl of about five appears. She is enamoured of my watch and tries to take it off my wrist. Even when Isa tries to shoo her away with a few lekë, she lingers, gazing.

By mid-morning the sun is shining again so we take a bus the 32km from Shkodra to Velipoja, a lovely beach almost on the Montenegrin border. The narrow asphalt road winds past hayfields and flocks of geese, past sheep sheds with straw roofs, then climbs into stony mountains. The earth is red, the stones grey and white. Ari points out the Black Summit and then we descend to the coast.

Velipoja is a real holiday village—still state owned—with low concrete flats painted in pastels, sprouting satellite dishes. Soon Albania will have as many satellite dishes as it has bunkers.

The surf is stronger here than at Shëngjini and behind the beach is a shady area of fig, pine, mimosa and poplar trees where many snack bars have been built.

On the way back to Shkodra we detour to Shiroka on the shore of Lake Shkodra to see another of King Zogu's villas. It is painted a very gaudy pink and sits at the top of a very long flight of steps. The town has not been developed for tourism though the lake is beautiful here. Many people drive their cars right into the lake to wash them.

Day 5: Promptly at 08.00 the four-wheel drive arrives and we begin our journey from Shkodra to Thethi, travelling on a road built in 1937. It is crooked and stony and the only other traffic on it is the occasional blue snub-nosed flat-bed truck packed with people. It takes four hours to get to Thethi by bus but only 2½ by car, says Perja; if you hike, it takes two days.

The Albanian Alps begin just outside town. A PARTI ENVER survives on the mountainside. We pass a cemetery whose tombs are ornamented with mosaics; Perja says the decorations on some tombstones show pagan elements.

'Only sheep and goats can be raised here,' he says. 'The shepherds used to take their flocks to the fields near the sea, as far away as Kruja, like nomads.' There are many caves in the limestone mountains, and underground rivers drain into Lake Shkodra.

The road passes through Boga, a village where rich Shkodrans once had summer villas. The boulders are getting bigger, the forests thicker, reminding Perja of a legend. There was an old shepherdess, he says, who took her sheep into the mountains on the first day of April because that was the beginning of good weather. This made March angry and he said, 'Brother April, give me two days more to show this old woman how strong I am.' April agreed and March sent such snow and cold that the old woman froze to death. Now all over northern Albania the

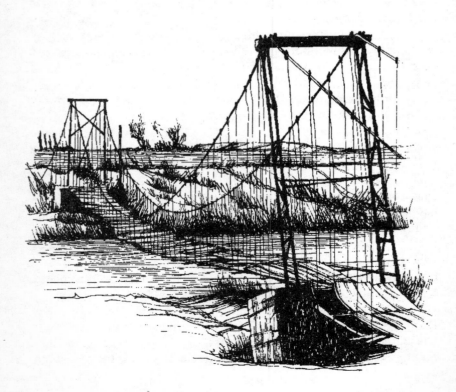

tall pine trees represent the woman and the stones her sheep.

There are many such stories, Perja says, that used to be sung by roving bards.

The holiday village at Thethi has been abandoned, but substantial stone dwelling houses are scattered over the mountainsides. Albania's northern mountain villages are very spread out; it is hard to recognize them as cohesive settlements in the context of compact northern Europe.

We scramble up a mountainside to a large stone house, climb a stile and cross a log bridge over Thethi's waterfalls. The water of the Shala River is very clear; it has been harnessed to a working mill. We go up a path past more falls and rapids, past fields of alfalfa to a stone *kulla*, or tower. This type of building, with one low arched door, is unique to northern Albania—the place of refuge during blood feuds. Someone finds ladders and we climb up to the third level of the dim interior. The only daylight is provided by four loopholes and three tiny windows.

'This tower is 200 or 300 years old; it belongs to the tribes of Shala,' says the young man who opened the door for us. 'Long ago there was a feud over property in which 18 people were killed in one fight and 15 men took refuge in this *kulla*.

'Blood calls for blood,' he says. 'According to the *Code of Lekë Dukagjini,* land problems could also be solved by payment in gold or by changing boundaries, but people seldom had money and they did have guns.'

The *Code,* attributed to Dukagjini who lived in the 15th century, was probably handed down from earlier days. It sets forth very strict, specific rules and punishments concerning everything from land to dowries to hospitality.

'We still live by the *Code,*' the young man says, 'but there are no feuds now. Thethi is a civilized place.'

Jezerca, the highest peak in this region, rises up over the village. It takes three hours to hike around it to Valbona in northeast Albania, and there is no road for cars. Yugoslavia begins behind the mountain.

At one of the big stone houses in the village, we ask if we can buy food. The family serves us salad, eggs, pork, cheese, bread, wine and raki. Over lunch I ask again about the *Code of Lekë Dukagjini*. Yes, it is traditional for the parents of the bride to give the husband a bullet so that if she tries to run away he may kill her. Since the bullet is the parents', no revenge blood is required. But now, of course, she is not killed.

'Are there any Albanian Virgins in Thethi?' I ask. Only one now, I am told. She smokes, sits in the council with the men and has all the

rights of a man. According to the *Code,* which considers women to be property with no rights—'a woman is a sack, made to endure'—a woman can refuse marriage, but if she refuses one man she can never marry. She can then dress as a man and inherit property as a man.

What about traditional dress? The woman of the house owns a *xhublet,* the black woollen suit with a wide bell skirt ornamented with silver buttons and colourful embroidery. If we wait a moment, she will put it on for a photograph. It includes stiff black embroidered leggings that have to be hooked on and silk scarves tied at the waist.

Day 6: It is time to leave Shkodra for the northeast. Buses go to Komani at 05.30 and 09.00, we are told, and from there the ferry leaves at 11.00; surely we need not take the early bus. But the 09.00 bus does not materialize, so Isa organizes a car.

Along the way, the driver tells us about himself and his family. His son who works in Germany escaped during Hoxha's time and the rest of the family was 'exiled' to work in the copper mill near Komani. 'My father was a Communist during the war and was imprisoned by the Fascists. Then the Party put him in prison,' he says.

We pass a military installation where Isa's brother was killed in an accident at the age of 20. 'I buried my brother and that same day went to a sports competition and won two gold medals. We had a slogan, *Triumph from Adversity,*' Isa says bitterly.

We cross the Drini River which has been dammed to create the Vau i Dejës, Komani and Fierza Lakes and provide much of the country's electric power. A big ugly dam towers over Vau i Dejës village. Our driver points out a clump of cedar trees where a little Romanesque church used to be. On an island in the lake are the ruins of seven churches and nearby is the Shurdhahut fortress.

The lake is deep blue and there are outcrops of green rock on the mountains. Some of the mountains have been strip-mined bare. 'There are copper and magnesium here,' says our driver. 'This is the poorest place in Albania; it has no school at all.'

It takes a little more than an hour to reach Komani, where we drive through a dimly lit tunnel to the ferry landing. A crowd has already gathered. The ferry arrives at 11.30, a rusty tub but with plenty of life jackets on board. It casts off at 12.45 for the two-hour trip across Komani Lake to Fierza.

It is hot and windy on the open deck but the view is marvellous. The water is deep green and the rock formations are a constantly changing pattern of colour and shape: red, brown, grey, white, in folds, crinkles and layers. Fingers of the lake disappear into the wild mountains and there are occasional coves with small beaches that seem accessible only by boat.

At Fierza we hurry off the boat so as not to miss the bus to Bajram Curri. I am confused when Isa says we are going to Tropoja when we are actually going to Bajram Curri—there is a Tropoja village about 17km away, 'but there's nothing there but birds,' says Isa. He explains that Bajram Curri is the capital of Tropoja District and people generally speak of the district.

Bajram Curri is a small, sleepy town, more barren than those in northwest Albania. Poverty is more obvious here; it can be seen in the lack of traffic, in the food, in the clothing. Foreigners are more noticeable—Red Cross and European Union representatives with their fancy four-wheel drives. In other areas of the country, local people also have jeeps, but not here.

This is the birthplace of Sali Berisha, the current president of Albania, but he hasn't done anything for it, the people complain. Just look at Gjirokastra, Hoxha's hometown ...

We climb a hill in the blistering heat, past a sports arena and a park where children are rolling metal hoops around the rim of an empty fountain. The Shkëlzen Hotel is named for the mountain facing us. The hotel is a bit seedy, but it will have hot running water in the evening. I ask whether there is time to go to Valbona 36km up into the mountains for the night, but we are told the hotel there is closed.

Late in the afternoon we stroll down the main street past the larger-than-life statue of Bajram Curri in front of the local museum. I photograph two men in fezzes, one dressed all in black, the other all in white. I never find out whether they are dervishes.

Ari asks if he can spend an hour visiting a friend here; the friend's father had a bad *biografi* and was sent to Bajram Curri to work as an engineer. Now he wants to return to Tirana but cannot find housing there.

This is the only major town in Albania where Isa has never been before, but he has friends here nevertheless. We stop at a snack stand to have coffee with one of them; Isa spots a big bottle of Italian mineral water and buys it at once. It turns out to be the only bottle in town. Inadequate water supplies are a major problem in this region. In spite of the many rivers and springs, people in some mountain villages must walk four or five hours to get water.

At about 20.00 a great gurgling in the hotel pipes heralds the arrival of water here and I rush to shower and wash clothes before it goes off again. The towels provided by the hotel are about the size of tea towels.

For dinner we try the Logu Restaurant upstairs in a wooden building on the main street. The *biftek* cooked on a wood-burning stove is the best we've had yet. We ask for knives and are given what I suspect is the one kitchen knife to share. The bill comes to about 500 lekë for three people.

Day 7: The search for transportation to Valbona begins at a café with one of Isa's friends, who brings along two local historians, Elez Qerimi and Ahmet Imeri.

People here wear traditional dress only on special occasions, they tell me. The men wear a costume called *tirqe* and a vest called *xhamadan* flared at the bottom and worked in silver thread. A unique carpet called a *sexhade* is made in this region; it is very thick and the motifs are Persian.

This part of the country borders Kosova and the two areas are spiritually very close. It is the country of Lekë Dukagjini—known as *Rrafshi i Dugagjinit*, literally the 'smooth part of Dukagjini'—and covers an area on both sides of the border with Kosova from Gjakova Peja Prizreni to Priština, including large mountainous areas and the Kosova Plain. There are many *kulla* villages here; the men tell me that *kulla* refers both to the sanctuary towers and to the fortified stone houses where people normally live. The houses are particularly beautiful in Qerret i Epërm, they say, but the road is so bad it can be reached only on horseback, and the journey takes five hours.

At 10.30 our wheels arrive, a van with bench seats and vinyl flooring in the back and lavender plastic roses stuck to the windshield. Today is the anniversary of the Revolution of 24 June 1924, so on the way out of town we stop to visit the house of the patriot Shpend Balia, where the first assembly of Bajram Curri met in an attempt to overthrow King Zogu. Inside the house is a loom to which a paper pattern for a carpet is clipped; skeins of coloured wool hang on the wall. The women here are weaving a *sexhade*.

The road runs along the mountainside above the Valbona River; the water is so clear that the rocks on the bottom are visible. It is about 7m deep here, says Qerimi. Farther along the river runs more swiftly; perhaps white-water rafting would be good. The rocks in the river are very yellow and when wet they glisten like gold. The road is stark white, the grey peaks forbidding. There are foxes, wolves, wild pigs and bears in the mountains, the men say.

We stop for water, clambering down a slope to a place where we can drink. ENVER is painted in white on one of the boulders; trout swim in a quiet pool below.

Near Dragobi, a scattered village of *kullas* with their distinctive wood-shingle four-sided roofs, we drive into a rock slide. The car in front of us has to be pushed but we get a running start and make it across. It takes about 1½ hours to reach Valbona; this road is better than the one to Thethi and can be managed easily without a four-wheel drive.

Valbona is a village of a few stone houses cupped in a wide valley. The river is almost dry here, leaving a rocky bed bleached white by the sun. The mountain with snow on its peak is Kollata; Jezerca is out of sight.

We go on to Fushë e Gjehve (Cattle Plain) about 3km from Valbona. There are horses at the spring but no cattle in sight. This would be an excellent spot for picnicking or pitching a tent.

Qerimi knows an old man who lives on the edge of the village and who may have a *xhamadan*. He doesn't, but he does have a horse harness decorated with blue, yellow and red weaving and a mirror. It is mostly for decoration, but also protects the horse from the evil eye, he says.

For dinner we go to the Jezerca Restorant down some steps just off the main street of Bajram Curri—it is quite good and for the first time lettuce is included in the tomato, cucumber and onion salad. For dessert, Isa finds the local ice-cream shop just a few steps away.

Day 8: On our way out of Bajram Curri, we are parading downhill with our luggage and a delegation of seven in search of a *sexhade*. The carpet we find was woven ten years ago by a woman for her dowry. It is heavy and beautifully made with the typical multicoloured fringe. The patterns for the *sexhade* are handed down from mother to daughter and the wool comes from *rude* sheep which have very thick fleece.

A woman always makes a *sexhade* for her marriage. The work is so difficult and takes so long that before it is done she begins to lament, 'Whoever will finish this carpet for me can have my husband.'

The ferry across Lake Fierza to Kukësi doesn't go from Fierza but from Gropaj, and there is no bus. I leave Isa to haggle about the price of a car while I photograph a particularly attractive wooden saddle. It occurs to me that the people watching are having a big laugh about the American journalist taking pictures of the rear end of a horse.

The car Isa finds has a whole garden of plastic flowers planted on the dashboard and curtains in the back decorated with pictures of

Marilyn Monroe. It bumps along a bad road that winds around mountains to the top of the dam, where we get out and walk past a forest of electrical power masts down to the ferry landing. This ferry carries no vehicles.

It is 40°C and there is no shade. The only thing to indicate that this is a harbour is a small snack bar and a crowd of people, half of whom are police. Realizing that there will be no toilet on board for the four-hour trip, I begin to look around for a sheltered spot. Finally in desperation I find a place under a footbridge, in full view of the road but away from the crowd, and decide to take my chances that no one will come down the road.

The ferry lands at 11.35 and casts off at 11.50. Once we get under way there is a cool breeze and we stand on the bow beside a small goat that tries to take a bite out of my skirt. When I photograph it for the colourful braided rope it is wearing, its owner brings me a bowl of the cherries she is taking to market. Not to be outdone, I get out my instant camera and take a picture for her. She gives me another bowl of cherries and asks me to find a job in Germany for her son.

We sit in the cabin talking with the captain of the *Drini*. It is so rusty that I wonder how it manages to float, but the captain is proud of it. The ferry is private, as all of them are now. It makes 21 stops on this trip, just bumping against the shore where people want to get off or on. Most of them scramble up or down the hills from nowhere; few houses are in sight. Now and again a small rowing boat hitches a ride, its occupants holding on to the side of the ferry.

Eventually the mountains give way to hills and we pass a farmstead on a slope of yellow and green fields, a flock of sheep grazing at the edge of the lake and a small cemetery set in a grove of trees. The forests here are mainly pin oak, and not so many trees have been cut down here as in the southern part of the country.

Kukësi has no proper port, either, though it is a sizeable town. We simply hop on to the ground and take the short cut straight up the hill to the tourist hotel. A paved road winds around the hill but no one uses it. I slip and slide and complain but make it to the top, panting for breath and dying of thirst. The sun is blistering.

I want a shower and a toilet but Isa drags me into the hotel's souvenir shop to look at Kukësi carpets. They are machine-made remainders from the factory now closed and the patterns strike me as unimaginative after the lovely examples we saw in Bajram Curri. Water is what I want now, not carpets.

The hotel is relatively new and in reasonably good repair. A European Union flag hangs over the balcony. Isa takes the desk clerk to task because a single room costs 2,500 lekë while a double is 4,000; he reckons I should pay only 2,000. 'Single supplement,' I explain. 'That's capitalism.'

Then I ask what time the water will come on and unwittingly make an enemy for life of the desk clerk. 'There is no water,' he says. 'Maybe tomorrow'. I reason aloud that perhaps I should rent a cheaper room: why pay for a shower if there is no water? Everyone begins talking at once, explaining why there is no water (though the hotel is almost surrounded by the lake), saying the rooms without showers have baths (which they don't) and ending with 'I am only the desk clerk, you can talk to the manager tomorrow.'

During this upset, I decide that having a private toilet is worth the few hundred extra lekë but am unable to get a word in, so I just stand there laughing at the absurdity of it all and that makes everyone angry.

Finally I am shown to a room and assured that there will be water in the sink tonight, but 'the shower is special—it works only on Sundays and Mondays.' However, a couple of hours later all the water comes on, so I rush to the drill of flush, bathe, wash underwear, fill the water jug. The towels here are wonderfully big bath sheets.

It's too hot to go out before dusk, but then we wander along the lake front toward town, once more eschewing the paved road for a bumpy track full of holes. There is no *passeggiata* here, but little groups of people gather on the plain above the lake. Some of them build fires and roast meat.

One of Isa's friends has a restaurant where we have dinner. Boiled eggs accompany the *biftek* and the tomatoes are the tastiest yet.

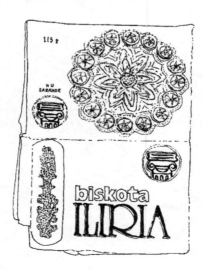

Day 9: The Kukësi museum is closed; its building was sold to a local dissident and former 'exile' under the government programme of restitution. It sits alone (though nearby the foundation of a large mosque has been laid) overlooking the lake, surrounded by a new picket fence and a small garden of tomatoes and beans.

The new owner of the house, Isa Elezi, spent 8½ years in forced labour near Elbasani. He was allowed to return to Kukësi in 1977 though he had no job. His wife, whom he met in Elbasani, is a nurse. She was allowed to work but could not advance in her profession because of him.

When communism started to crumble in Eastern Europe, Elezi felt something must happen in Albania, too. 'I had nothing to lose, so I was one of the people to start the Democratic Party in Kukësi,' he says. He and 15 friends—artists, historians, writers—founded the local party branch and remain staunch supporters. 'But the government has to create more jobs or the communists will win again,' he says. 'There is always that danger. The government must bring in foreign investors.'

The house was built for Enver Hoxha, but after Hoxha became ill and could no longer visit Kukësi it was used as the local ethnographic, archaeological and history museum. However, it had been built as a house and was not suitable for a museum. The city fathers decided to move the exhibits to an old hospital but thus far have not been able to secure it properly, so the museum exhibits remain in storage.

When Elezi was given the chance to buy the house his family and friends helped him raise the money. There was opposition from local Hoxha supporters but he succeeded. 'I feel I have a right to this house,' he says. 'When Hoxha came to power he took a valuable carpet from a rich man in Elbasani who opposed him and put it in front of his own door. When anyone came to the door he would tell them 'wipe your feet on that carpet because it is the carpet of the rich man.' That's why I wanted this house.'

Elezi's family owned property here before the Hoxha regime, 'but it's at the bottom of the lake' which flooded large areas when the dam was built.

I thank him for his time, and he says time is the only thing they have here.

Day 10: When I open the door of my hotel room this morning I discover that the lock does not work properly. I have slept (and left my cameras unattended) in an unlocked room in a town about which Wilma once spun me a tale of visitors sleeping with knives and guns because the populace is so fierce. What nonsense!

On the plain above the lake, women from the town have spread wool—some dyed a deep purplish red—in the sun and are beating it as it dries. Other women are spinning with wooden distaffs. We go back to visit Elezi, and to meet some of his friends.

Sulejman Dida is a poet and journalist who spent a year in Italy. Once he wrote political poems but now he writes love poems. 'We had to read foreign poets such as Pushkin, Byron and Shakespeare in secret,' he says. When I ask whether one can become a revolutionary by reading Byron he replies, 'I saw that the great poets oppose regimes that are against free thought.'

Kukësi seems so far removed from the world that I wonder if it is a good place to work. 'The moon is more visible away from city lights; poems are more beautiful in the villages,' Dida says.

When Nazif Dokle, a specialist in local ethnography, arrives everyone begins to advise me on where to trek. Kroi i Bardhë, the White Brook,

on the other side of Mount Gjalica is the best, they agree. It is a nature area, with wide fields 'like England' and forests. Shishtaveci is another good place and Bicaj on the way to the White Brook is beautiful. Gjalica is rich in flora and fauna, and from its summit on a clear day you can see all the way to the Adriatic Sea on one side and to Skopje on the other.

There are two fortresses, one in Bushati and one in the hills at Pecë, both about 8km away. The village houses are *kullas* but all their churches and mosques have been destroyed.

Dokle describes the music, the traditional dress, the customs and the handicrafts of the area. 'The traditional men's suits are white but since Skënderbeg's death a black thread runs down the side of each leg in mourning,' he says. 'Fan Noli (a leading Albanian politician and historian exiled in the 1920s) theorized that the Kastrioti family was originally from this region and moved on to Kruja.'

Weddings in Albania last three days, wakes about a week. It is an Albanian tradition for women to wail a formal lament for the dead man, telling the story of his life.

'The area known as Luma is especially rich in folklore,' Dokle says. 'It is known for its ballads, for epics that show the complexity of the human spirit. *Rude* sheep are still raised and Luma has a strong tradition of weaving. The traditional dress is called *Veshje e Bardhë*; its motifs can be traced back to Illyria. The White Drini is the border of Luma and Kukësi is in the middle of it.'

Yes, the *Code of Lekë Dukagjini* is very strong here. The *besa* is especially respected. (*Besa*—truce, promise, word that once given is honoured to the death—has no exact translation into English.) There are also many taboos and superstitions: people do not kill snakes because they believe that humans descended from the snake, so if it dies the family will die. On 21 March each year, the owner of an orchard holds a sword against an apple tree and says 'Give me apples or I will cut you down.' The tree is so frightened that it produces apples. When women cut their hair, they collect the snippings and burn them or hide them in a hole in the wall so no one can use them to work bad magic.

'Enver Hoxha wanted to destroy all that was Albania, but he couldn't destroy the customs and beliefs,' Dokle says.

Dr Muhamet Beluli, an archaeologist, says the remains of Kukësi's cultural heritage date from prehistoric times to the Middle Ages. However, the most important Illyrian tombs in the area at Qinamokx were flooded when the dam was built.

Ruins of fortresses can be seen along the White Drini at Pecë, Bushati,

Domaj and Va-Spas, he says. A grand ancient town was discovered at Demastion; the coins found there were taken to the museum in Tirana from which some have been stolen.

'The culture here is the same as that in Kosova, and evidence shows that this was ancient Illyria's Dardania,' he says. (This is a major bone of contention with Serb archaeologists.) Beluli named his son Dardan because he was born during a dig in the area. 'We are now trying to teach our history to the young people,' he says. 'This is important in a democracy because now we can know what we were.'

DRIVING THROUGH THE HEART OF THE COUNTRY

Sheer pigheadedness got me where I am today—on the ferry from Trieste to Durrësi again, this time behind the wheel of a fire-engine-red four-wheel drive. It's much too flashy for my taste but was the only thing I could lay hands on at short notice. Manfred says it will be stolen as soon as I turn my back; I say no one will touch it because only the Mafia drive cars like this in Albania.

Big Red was baptized in a thunderstorm in the Austrian Alps. Now it is baking in the July sun on the top deck of the *Espresso Grecia*. The ferry is due at Durrësi at 14.00, actually arrives in sight of the harbour at 17.00 and pirouettes in the bay for an hour waiting for a Dalmatian ferry to leave the one berth.

I elbow my way to the front of passport control but Big Red is blocked in. At last I make it to the down ramp, where I must hang on a steep incline hoping the brakes hold while the car in front of me gets a thorough check at customs. When it's my turn, I get papers quickly and am directed into one of several queues. Nothing seems to be happening here until a boy of about 10 approaches and offers to take me to through the police check.

He does an admirable job and I offer him a dollar. 'No,' he says, 'customs costs US$20. Give me the money and I will take care of it.' I say I'll pay it when I actually get there, so finally he settles for a dollar and gets his ears boxed by an official who suddenly appears. Of course, there is no US$20 fee.

Day 1: I am driving Big Red because I want to get deep into the heart of Albania, to places where buses don't go. The Lura Lakes are my main destination. Everyone I meet sings their praises but ends by saying, 'The roads are too bad, you can't get there.' It's all the reason I need to go.

Isa, Ari and I drive out of Tirana at 06.30 to take advantage of the cool of the morning. Temperatures will hit 40°C during the day. We stop at a restaurant at Milot for breakfast—it's safest to stick with *pilaf* and salad, I have discovered. When I ask for the toilet, I am directed to 'nature' across the railway tracks by the river. This is the Mati, in midsummer dried up to a trickle that children use as a wading pool. The bleached rock bed is wide with a promise of springtime torrents but now I swear there is dust on the water.

At Rubiku a delightful little church perches on a hill above the town but we can find neither the road to it nor the person who has the key. At Kurbneshi I slow to a crawl searching for a café and Big Red is immediately surrounded by a crowd. Everyone, it seems, wants a ride to Lura. We make room for an elderly man who directs us along a road that follows the Uraka River, through a spacious landscape of rolling hills and gentle mountains. The valleys are wide and planted in grain and the cows and goats seem glossier than elsewhere. We pass through villages of stone houses roofed with tin or wooden shingles. I like it here, I can breathe better than when I'm surrounded by high mountain walls.

At Gryka e Selishtës we make a photo stop at a tumbled down church surrounded by a newer cemetery. One of the tombs is decorated with reliefs of wine pitchers, donkeys and a man with a gun, but no one can tell me the story of who is buried there.

Gur-Lura seems to be the end of the road. We pass a hospital where white-clad nurses are spreading white sheets on the bushes to dry. Our passenger alights and when I refuse payment goes to find someone who can tell us how to get to the Lura Lakes.

The young man he finds looks underneath Big Red and decides the car is high enough to tackle the road, which is gravel for a short distance, then rock. 'There are 11 Lura Lakes in all,' he says, 'but only seven can be reached by driving. The others are on the tops of mountains.' Gur-Lura used to be a tourist spot but the hotel is abandoned now. The villagers are hoping for restructuring; an enterprise from Durrësi is to rebuild the nearby resort that was used by party functionaries.

There are a charming little church with its windows all bricked up and a mosque under construction in the middle of town. We try to get lunch at a couple of places but very little is available: we settle for boiled eggs, cheese, a packet of French butter cookies and beer.

At 13.30 we set off on the rock road surrounded by yellow wild flowers and purple thistles. Little streams babble across the road. Finally we spot a tiny lake and begin to count. At the third lake we get out to take a look and come upon a crew of lumbermen. This lake is called Rasave, they say. Farther along, we meet three small boys who know the names of four other lakes.

The lakes are still and quiet, some full of waterlilies, all surrounded by lightning-blasted trees. I don't want to be up here in a thunderstorm.

When we reach lake number six I see a soccer ball soaring above the treetops. I stop to look—I *do* see a soccer ball. We round the curve and come upon the last lake—Luleve, Flower Lake—where a group is having a picnic.

By this time in my Albanian travels it comes as no surprise that Ylli, one of the young men at the picnic, is a friend of Isa. 'Out here in the middle of nowhere,' I say, 'what else should I expect?' Ylli is an army officer stationed at Peshkopia. He and his friends often come here. 'It is the most beautiful place in Albania,' they say. 'Songs have been written about its beauty.'

They apologize that most of their picnic food is gone, but cut a watermelon for us. We must come back with them to Peshkopia, there is no hotel in Burreli now, they say. The road is bad but I will drive between their two jeeps.

It is getting late and a thunderstorm is rumbling in the distance. Just as we reach our vehicles the storm breaks—driving rain, hail, lightning dancing. The road is awash and we are between the other two jeeps, bouncing over the rocks. I try to avoid sending up enough spray to get the brakes wet. Luckily the downpour is soon over, settling into a steady rain that smells like springtime. The jeep ahead of me stops—it's not a breakdown, everyone piles out to pick wild strawberries.

Because I am night blind and want to get out of the mountains before dark, we go on ahead. However, there are many forks in the road and we have to stop and ask, and ask again. Isa holds an extended conversation with one man. Yes, this is the road to Peshkopia, but a truck has broken down blocking the road 2km away. The pantomime our informant performs is quite alarming. 'You can't get past the truck and there's no place to turn around,' he says.

After a bit of nail-chewing we decide to try anyway. We don't know where the other road leads, dusk is falling, there are no villages or even single houses here. In exactly 1.7km we come upon the truck but Big Red can just squeeze by. The truckers say it is an hour to Peshkopia. For the next four hours it is an hour to Peshkopia.

We have wasted quite a bit of time asking the way but so far our friends have not caught up with us. 'A crossroads is coming up and we are much nearer to Burreli than to Peshkopia,' Isa says. 'Would you rather go to Burreli?'

I look at the fading light and at the state of the road. I have been sitting behind the wheel for ten hours.

'Burreli,' I say.

Just at that minute the two jeeps with our friends pull up behind us. 'Don't worry, we can take you in,' says Ylli. We don't know either road, so maybe it is better to go with people who know the way, I decide.

The road into Lura is not particularly bad. Rocky, rough, but hardly frightening. The road out is a nightmare. The next day Ylli says, 'It's a good thing you *couldn't* see.'

But I can feel. I can feel the emptiness at the edge of the rocky road, the yawning gorges, the nothingness below the hairpin curves. Narrow, twisting, always in the mountains, never once descending to a valley.

As we're travelling southwards to Durrës
I'm once more beset by my wurrës:
I don't want to utter
My last words in a gutter,
Slaughtered, by big trucks and
                    lurrës...

I know from studying the map we are at 2,000m.

Without Ylli's lights in front I would go over the edge—there are points at which I cannot see the road. To make matters worse, albino frogs are swarming, brought out by the rain, impossible not to run over, making the tyres slick.

At one point I am driving so slowly that Ylli stops and comes back to Big Red.

'You're tired,' he says.

'Very tired,' I admit.

'This is where the army trains its drivers,' he says.

I try to laugh: 'If I get us out of here alive, will I be a certified Albanian army driver?'

On we go. Isa sits calmly, now and again directing me to the right, closer to the mountain face, but with a 'you can do it' air of confidence that is contagious. 'Talk,' he says. 'Stay awake.'

'I couldn't go to sleep if I tried,' I say. 'But I don't believe there is such a place as Peshkopia. If there ever was, they've moved it, moved it to China.'

Eventually, of course, there is such a place as Peshkopia. About 75km from the last lake we come down out of the mountains and cross two wooden bridges with runners so askew that I fear for Big Red's tyres. 'They were damaged in World War II,' Ari says. 'I'd have said in Skënderbeg's time,' I reply.

By 23.00 we have checked into the hotel and crashed a wedding party. It is at the only restaurant still open; a little table is set up for us behind the band and we are brought bowls of yogurt and *pilaf,* and a big glass of raki for me.

Day 2: We meet Ylli again so I can thank him properly. He invites us to his home in one of the ramshackle highrises up the hill. Inside it is neat and clean and there is a fine stove in one corner of the living room with a kettle boiling. Ylli is 33 years old; he doesn't have much hope for a better life for himself, but he does for his two children.

'Next time, I'm going to trek into Lura,' I say.

'It's a wonderful place for trekking,' he tells me, 'and for cross-country skiing in winter. Another good place to trek is the Korabi Plain surrounding Albania's highest mountain. The best time to climb Korabi is mid-June to mid-August.'

This is borderland, a stone's throw from both Macedonia and Kosova. An army friend of Ylli's was killed by Serbs last year near the border. The Korabi Plain has always been a battleground between Serbia and Albania, he says.

Peshkopia has a market, a mosque and a health spa. The water here contains sulphur and reaches 42°C, good for rheumatism and female complaints. The spa clinic has 50 baths and can accommodate 600 people.

'The villages around Peshkopia are very traditional,' Ylli says. 'The houses are *kullas* and the rooms are furnished as in Roman times, with only skins on the floors and a fireplace as furnishings. Radomira is a village of lovely *kullas*, as are Murri and Selishta that we passed in the dark last night. Dodës Fortress is nearby, but only a tower remains. There is a good road, 96km, from Peshkopia north to Kukësi, called 'the road of the young people' because it was built by the youth in Enver Hoxha's time,' Ylli says.

But we head back west and the main road from Peshkopia to Burreli comes as a relief. It is high and winding part of the way, but paved and wide enough for two cars to meet; there are even a few concrete guardrails here and there at the steepest drops. We pass a man lying asleep on one of them—I hope he is not a restless sleeper.

Then we are once again in hill country, red clay hills and houses made of red brick from the clay. Bulqiza, a mining town, is high and cool with a strong wind blowing. This is Mati, the district where King Zogu was born. We all yell 'photo stop' at once and I pull up beside a cemetery—just a few graves beside the road. The Muslim ones are Turkish, Ari says, because they have both head- and footstones; Albanian Muslims use only headstones.

Across the road, however, is what attracted us: a beautiful, big traditional-style house, three storeys tall with a balcony and a big gate with arched doors. It was built in the first half of the 19th century; the top floor was added at the beginning of the 20th century. The owner invites us inside. He used to live in nearby Klosi but has now reclaimed

Byzantine bridge near Vërri

the family home. It has nine rooms almost bare of furnishings, with tobacco hanging to dry beside one of the fireplaces and strings of onions beside another.

The road is fine now and Isa asks why I don't drive faster. 'Because,' I say, 'there are still lots of curves. I can't see what is in the road around them, but something always is—a herd of sheep, a cow or two, bent-over roadsigns, children playing ball.' As if to prove my point, just at this moment a man at the top of the hill spots Big Red and begins running helter-skelter for the road. I slow down, expecting him to step into my path to flag a ride. But no—he has left his wheelbarrow in the middle of the road and is racing to move it.

Burreli comes as a pleasant surprise. It is a relaxed and spacious town and the kiosk owners seem to have had a contest to see who could paint the most interesting scene on the roofs. The regional museum is closed, but the Tarzan panorama restaurant in the city park is open and serves a fine *biftek*. The owner, Vjollca Cubaj, takes me to the terrace for a view over the round mountains and wide valley, across to the remains of King Zogu's home. 'Everyone here loved Zogu,' she says. 'During Hoxha's time, Burreli was all Zogist and it suffered.

'When my grandmother was a little girl, she used to play with the prince's son,' she says. 'One day they were playing a game rolling bottles full of stones when the prince appeared. He was so struck with the beauty of my grandmother that he took off his crown and rolled it in the game.'

'The place where we're standing used to be full of trees, just like a jungle. That's why the restaurant is called Tarzan,' she says.

Vjollca's husband Myftar Cubaj is an artist who paints under the signature Mikalis. He is an expert on the traditional dress of this region. 'It is a much smaller region than Vlora, but we have many more costumes,' he says. 'One of the most interesting is in the area of Baza. The people are Catholic and embroider motifs of the cross on their dress. During the Hoxha regime they had to disguise the cross so they made a very elaborate design with flowers and many colours. But it was still a cross.

'You can see by the old houses here how advanced civilization was,' he says. 'The houses are more beautiful and more comfortable than in some other regions, they have baths and guest rooms. There is a big difference between the people of north and south Albania,' he adds. 'In the north, people were stronger, and the only things they wanted from life were a traditional suit, a gun and a house in which to bring up their children. But in the south, people would go abroad to work— they were clever, but not as tough.'

We go into the taverna of the Tarzan to see one of Myftar's murals. It is a wedding scene, a mixture of modern and traditional dress much as one sees now. It is in three parts: the couple meeting, their wedding, their family. 'It would have been prohibited to paint this scene BEFORE,' Myftar says. 'We were not allowed to show courtship.'

Day 3: Having survived the Peshkopia road, I decide I can tackle driving through the Alps to Vermoshi, Albania's northernmost village. We go back to Shkodra to look for Çel Leka, an electrical engineer who can tell us about Vermoshi.

Çel lives in a village called Sterbeq right on the shore of Lake Shkodra, past a derelict collective farm. 'They cut down a lot of trees to build this farm, but the land is not good,' he says. 'A lot of chemical fertilizer was used, but it didn't help. The people were very poor; the peasants had only cornbread to eat and only families with babies got a half-litre of milk a day.'

Çel's brother, Islam Leka, is home for a visit. He escaped from Albania in 1964, swimming for four hours across Lake Shkodra despite a bad leg. Montenegrin fishermen pulled him from the water and hid him from the search party. He was sent to a camp in Slovenia, then was able to settle in Sweden. 'The way I felt then, I wanted to get out dead or alive,' he says.

Night is falling as we drive back to Shkodra. A long, long line of cars is going in the opposite direction toward the Montenegrin border: fuel is being smuggled quite openly into Yugoslavia. Drivers fill their tanks for the equivalent of around US50 cents per litre, drive across the border, syphon it out and sell it for around US$1.50 to US$2.50 per litre, leaving just enough in the tank to get home.

The roadside is lined with canisters, barrels, plastic bottles full of fuel for sale. Along this road, four spanking new service stations are pumping fuel. On a larger scale, on the drive from Durrësi to Shkodra we count two dozen fuel lorries; just one is an unusual sight in the rest of the country.

Day 4: We parked on the street last night and early this morning Isa comes round to tell me Big Red still has its ears—its outside mirrors. At breakfast Ari says that Isa doesn't want to travel on Tuesday, it has been an unlucky day ever since Skënderbeg lost a battle on Tuesday. Though I have heard this story before, I suspect a ploy to give me a day off after several days of strenuous driving before we head into the mountains over what all and sundry assure us is a very bad road.

'All right,' I say, 'let's just stroll around Shkodra and maybe have lunch at the lake.' So we go out to Shiroka and sit for a while on an anchored boat that has been turned into a bar, watching goats graze at the edge of the lake and children splashing from rubber boats.

Then we visit Zogaj, a lakeside village almost on the Montenegrin border, where carpet-making is a traditional cottage industry. About 16 families weave kelims on looms at home but now the market has dried up. The European Community sent help a couple of years ago, they say, but not much came of it.

Day 5: The road to Vermoshi is not nearly so bad as its reputation. It is asphalt for the first 50km, then gravel for the remaining 45km, and I drive it in three hours including photo stops. We pick up a hitchhiker who lives in Vermoshi; he invites us to his home.

His new stone house sits beside an old one on a big stretch of land with green fields and a plum orchard. There is a substantial sheep shed; a hobbled horse is grazing in the pasture. A wooden cross hangs over the door (and on every house in the village) and on the living room wall are pictures of the Pope and of Gjergj Fishta, a cleric and author early in this century. This is staunchly Catholic country.

Vermoshi is one of those spread-out villages with 330 houses and more than 1,200 people. The people raise sheep, pigs and cows, and grow corn and potatoes. Winters are hard. There is ample snow for skiing from November until April and it is good countryside for trekking in summer, especially the pass at Budaca to the south. Going north, it is just 15 minutes to the Montenegrin border.

In communist times the villagers had special *Zonë Kufitare* (border zone) stamps in their passports and no one else could come to Vermoshi. No one was allowed to walk around alone then; anyone who did was sent to prison.

The mountain to the left is Kerrshi i Djegun and the Liqenve Pass is in front of us. It takes two hours to walk to the top. Behind the mountains is a place called the Garden of Bears, and then there's Yugoslavia. But a stretch of the border also runs along the other end of the village at Vermosh-Velipoja, a field full of bunkers.

We meet two young men dressed all in black. They have come from Detroit for the funeral of a brother—'He was 24 and died of a heart attack,' I am told. There is another funeral in the village, too. I wonder... 'Do you still live by the *Code of Lekë Dukagjini*?' I ask.

'Oh, yes. Yes, of course. We are free birds now, we can do what we want,' says one of the men from Detroit, 'but we will never lose our traditions. We kept them through communism and we will always keep them.'

BACKTRACKING: ELBASANI AND VLORA

Day 1: I am sure there is more in Elbasani than I saw last December, so Isa finds a shared taxi in Tirana that is going there and I get a second look.

Elbasani now has traffic lights, but our guide, Miranda Gurmani, who keeps the souvenir shop at the Hotel Skampa, says that many people don't understand them so they simply ignore them. Just below the bus station near the PTT is a lovely new mosque with a lead roof. The Turkish baths have become Disko Hamami.

We wander into the old town behind the fortress wall and stop at the café facing the main gate. Its bar is made of original columns from the fortress. On our left is the King Mosque, painted white, its windows bricked up, its minaret gone. This is the place where last December schoolgirls were learning the Koran. This time we walk through the schoolroom into the carpeted main room with its *mihrab* and *minbar*. The building is in need of repair, but the man who shows us around says most of the money sent to Elbasani has gone for other building projects or to buy books.

A few streets farther along, workmen are busy renovating the old Orthodox monastery. The tomb of Konstandin Kristoforidhi in its yard has been repaired. We stand at one side of the yard admiring the ensemble of the monastery, its cedars and the spire of the Catholic church in the background.

Miranda laughs because I photograph the many roofed gates that lead into the courtyards of the houses. She says the smooth white-painted stones beside the doors are where the old people sit of an evening to gossip with their neighbours and passers-by.

Within the walls, the museum that traced the history of Elbasani from Turkish times to World War II is shut, but the Ethnographic Museum across the park is open. Its collection is impressive, comparable in richness to the museum at Kruja.

Pasha Kaplan Memorial

I particularly like the array of sheep's bells made of iron and bronze. Each bell had its own distinctive sound so the shepherd knew exactly where each sheep was, says museum director Kreshnik Belegu. There is also a beautiful little inlaid chest that held a silversmith's tools. At the end of the 19th century, about 100 families in Elbasani worked gold and silver, mostly as jewellery and ornamentation for rifles and knives.

The clothing on display includes beautiful gold braided vests that were handed down from generation to generation. Early on only men wore such sumptuous vests but after the 19th century they were made for women, too.

Day 2: Isa's youngest son, who is studying medicine in Italy, will arrive by ferry at Vlora, so we pile into Big Red and head for the coast to meet him. Just outside Kavaja we stop for lunch at Skënder Ismaili's restaurant—a real delight with good food, good service and an A1 toilet.

The approach to Vlora runs through hills covered with olive groves where cicadas are humming in the heat of the day. Vlora's streets are wide and spacious; I recognize the mosque that looks like a Byzantine church and the market hall. The beach is full of people trying to escape the heat.

Because the family home will be crowded, I check in at the House of Vacations of Workers up on the hill. My room is reasonably comfortable, but a giant has gone through Albania hanging bathroom mirrors too high to be of use. The shower is positioned over the toilet square and there is no little wooden platform to place over it: I decide not to risk breaking a leg in the Black Hole of Calcutta and make do with a splash in the sink.

From my balcony, the view over the beach and bay is marvellous. I can see Sazani Island in the distance, but I'm told we can't go there; it is the site of a military installation.

We do drive up to Kanina Fortress, however, about 5km up a four-wheel-drive road. The fortress is still a military base, with stone barracks and a couple of watchtowers scattered among the ruins of the old fortifications, but we are allowed in and are shown around.

'This was one of the most important fortresses in all Albania,' says our guide. 'It was the biggest fortress in Albania, bigger than Rozafa in Shkodra. Kanina was the strongest fortress in Illyria and it repulsed the Turks even before Skënderbeg fought them. It was the last fortress to fall to the Turks. It once belonged to a noble family—to Gjergj Arianiti, father of Donika, Skënderbeg's wife.'

'Ah, so Skënderbeg's marriage to Donika was political,' I say.

A couple of towers, a couple of gates, five cisterns and a few stretches of walls with their layers of Illyrian, Roman and medieval stones remain. The main grounds give a view over the sea and Kanina village just below, noted for its honey, figs and donkeys.

On the drive back down the mountain we pass the entry to a derelict factory tunnel where faded slogans remind us 'We must protect socialism, be good soldiers and sailors ...' A man bringing water uphill stops us and offers us a drink.

In Vlora we take a look inside the mosque, built for soldiers, according to the guide, since there is no balcony for women. However, women come here now. The mosque was used for storage during the Hoxha regime, then as an atelier for artists. On 11 January 1991 it was reopened as a mosque but was in such poor condition that the people raised money for its restoration. Our guide points out an old plane tree in the yard that has grown in the shape of a cross. 'Vlora is about 70% Muslim, but the religions respect each other,' he says.

A Hoxha villa in Vlora, now empty, perches on a cliff over the bay. We pass it on the way to 'The Castle', a point of land where a new restaurant has been built; it serves good grilled fish. We sit on the terrace overhanging the sea long after darkness falls. Below us a motor yacht sets out, running without lights—probably someone is smuggling refugees to Italy. A 'ticket' costs US$1,000 (£645) and the Chinese Mafia here can fix up a passport for another US$1,500 (£967).

We park Big Red on the beach where a couple of young men who own a snack bar will keep an eye on it. One of them has family property up on the hill and asks me to look at it and advise him how to develop it for tourism. We go up into beautiful olive groves and orchards just a 10-minute walk from the beach. He wants to attract Italian tourists because Vlora is located so conveniently for Italy and many excursions can be made from here. Do I know any investors who might be interested?

Next day Big Red is intact but covered with bird droppings. I want to get it washed before the paint is damaged, so we stop at a *lavazh* in Kavaja. For 250 lekë Big Red gets a thorough scrub down, inside, outside, underneath. Albanian car washes, I decide, are the best in the world.

GOODBYE TIRANA

These are my last days in Tirana, and I stroll through the warm twilight already savouring a feeling of nostalgia. The scent of linden blossom mingles with the acrid smoke of strong Albanian cigarettes.

In the six months since my first visit to Tirana the city has acquired a bit of spit and polish. Shiny new snack bars with colourful awnings and rows of bottles glittering against mirrors have sprung up in the parks, replacing some of the jerry-built ones of the previous winter. Brightly lit grocery shops contrast with the lively street markets. A few stores and cafés are putting up marble façades. Though the 'caged' fuel pumps are still around I have seen several real service stations, too.

But in some ways times are harder. Prices are rising constantly; telephone rates have skyrocketed since December. Aleksandra's job is gone and her pension barely pays the electric bill. She spends her days watching soap operas on television—it's not the story line but the clothes and lifestyle that interest her, she says. TVSH is running the same advertisements as in winter, mostly for sweets, soft drinks and cat food... in a country where many people can hardly afford to eat.

The electricity does not fail once during my summer visit—after all, no one is using heaters—but the water no longer comes on in the house so heavy buckets and barrels have to be carried up the steps each day. The sewage pipes in front of the family's block of flats are in place and fair progress is being made in levelling the courtyard. How nice it would be to plant grass and trees there.

I make the rounds of meeting old friends and new people, looking into the nooks and crannies that I missed in winter. The hot sun is debilitating, but all in all I prefer the dust of summer to the mud of winter.

'Do you know about Dervish Hatixhe?' I ask the Tare family. Yes, Aleksandra goes there often to pray for her son who is in Germany and whom she hasn't seen for three years. 'Yes, we pray to her like a saint.'

Dervish Hatixhe's house is set back from the street and a row of beggars lines the path to the door. Inside is cool and dim. Carpets cover the floor as in a mosque and there is a row of *turbes* of Hatixhe and her family. The stream of visitors is steady ... remove shoes, kiss the scarves draped over the *turbes,* touch the portraits, leave gifts of milk or sunglasses or food wrapped in newspaper. Many visitors light candles and place them in a niche filled with sand.

Mother Rukije of Dervish Hatixhe welcomes me with a kindly sparkle in her eyes. She shows me photos of the house when it caught fire just

a couple of months ago—an electrical fire, only the *turbes* were saved...
a miracle. Twenty workers rebuilt the house in 20 days.

The markets are overflowing now with summer produce: tomatoes,
cucumbers, eggplant, okra, cherries. I buy herbs to brew for tea: one
for the stomach, one as a pick-me-up and one that is supposed to heal
cracked feet—should I really drink it?

At the art gallery I see a watercolour by Spiro Vllahu of an Orthodox
church in Tirana, and I want to find it. We walk to the lake, to Shën
Prokopi. 'You won't find the church in your picture, though a church
has existed here for a long time,' says the caretaker, who belongs to
the Shundi family, one of the oldest Vlach families in Tirana. 'In 1967,
all the church's ornaments and mosaics were destroyed and it was
turned into a restaurant. But the people never forgot the church. They
came and prayed around the building, and when they went for a walk,
they never said "Let's go to the lake," but "Let's go to Shën Prokopi."'

Back at the art gallery I meet Vllahu. A strong religious theme runs
through all his work. He has painted many Albanian churches both
Catholic and Orthodox, existing and destroyed. He spent seven years
in prison under the old regime. He had studied art in Russia and when
Albania broke off relations with the Soviet Union he was accused of
being a spy.

I also meet five women artists at the gallery. Eleni Laperi Koci (who
speaks good English) is director of the gallery as well as a painter,
Mariana Eski is a painter and fashion designer, Zana Varvarica is a
sculptor, Ikbal Beli and Zanfira Heta are painters.

They deplore the difficulties of balancing life in Albania with a career
in art. There are the demands of husband, children and home, there is
not enough space to work, paints and paper are in short supply. That is
why they decided to form an association of women artists to help each
other by sharing books and working to get exhibitions in foreign
countries and to meet foreign artists. The association has 18 members;
though about a hundred women in Albania have studied art, few of
them are able to follow that career.

'We are trying to find ourselves now,' they tell me. 'Under the old
regime, we were told what to do and we did it. Now we are
experimenting with the spiritual side of our lives.'

Zanfira invites me to her home, a low brick attachment to a block of
flats with a covered porch and grapevines on trellises. Paintings cover
every inch of the walls; she pulls stacks of drawings from under the
beds and couches. She asks if I am married and says she envies my
freedom.

'Linda go?' asks Isa. Of course, Linda always goes, though she is not always quite sure where. Aleksandra is dressed up in pearls and high heels, and I hope I won't embarrass the family with my clunky sandals. But this time we aren't going to visit friends or relatives. We are going out for *parfait*.

We stroll to one of the new snack bars in the park. It is almost dark, about 21.00 on a late summer day, and the streets are full of people of all ages. Cars have not curtailed the *passeggiata*. In the cool of the evening couples and families come out to enjoy the air, to meet friends, to have *parfait*—a slab of ice-cream with crushed nuts all wrapped up in aluminium foil. Tasty, but I prefer the ice-cream from those antiquated crank machines.

Another evening we take the bus to visit Isa's parents. They live at the edge of town in a cottage that somehow was not swallowed up by the big blocks of flats. They have a sheep, two dogs, a few chickens. Grapevines lend coolness to the yard and everyone sits on the front porch in the evenings, or under the arbour playing chess. I sit and watch, sipping a deliciously cold glass of *kos*.

On the crowded bus home we meet a friend of the family. She talks to me in careful German; she worked in Germany cleaning a church but had to return home to care for her sick mother. She is a trained calligrapher, 'but we take whatever jobs we can get,' she says.

We wander into the Institute of Cultural Monuments to enquire about the monastery at Ksamili and find a gold mine of information— Sulejman Dashi, specialist in Islamic architecture. Descriptions bubble over as his talk jumps from city to village, church to mosque, and he makes sketches in my notebook as he goes.

'There was a book printed in China about Albanian cultural monuments, very good quality, but you can't find it any more,' he says. 'There's a church in the Kavaja region with a Norman floor plan... Have you seen the mosaics at Arapaj?... Tirana once had 30 mosques but only five with minarets ... There were two forms of mosque, the cupola-style and the roof-style and people preferred the roof-style because it was bigger and more elaborately decorated. In 1955, there were 1,050 mosques in Albania. Around 800 survived, but only 30 were protected as cultural monuments.

'The *teqe* is another example of Islamic architecture,' he goes on. 'It is a sort of convent for dervishes. *Teqes* are different from mosques: in the first place, nationality comes before religion and in the second place, each has its own building style.

'Several different types of Islam came to Albania during Turkish times,' he says. 'Halveti the oldest order, Kadri the order of Dervish

Hatixhe, and Rufai. The Bektashi order was quite different from other forms of Islam. It baptized with wine as the Orthodox, confessed as Catholic and recognized both Christ and Muhammad as prophets. There are interesting Bektashi *teqes* at the village Melani near Gjirokastra and near Skrapar.'

As we near the border, the number of pillboxes increases, and a gate in the barbed wire is slid back, letting the bus through, past a sentry box and into the compound.

We unload our cases and say farewell to Pilo, Rasim and Filip, who have done their jobs well and patiently, despite our constant questions. If they were irritated, it never showed.

Outside the customs house, we rummage for passports and suitcase keys, and talk to a tall, friendly official in a dark brown suit. Two guards, rifles slung casually, eye us as we chat, whilst a third stands, legs apart, watching us from his platform at the barrier, opposite a flagpole with the red and black double eagle flag.

Finally allowed into the customs house, we are searched fairly perfunctorily, and we pick up our cases and pass the barrier, making the return stagger across no-man's land.

At the Yugoslav side, where Stefan, with his Hertz bus, greets us, we are searched thoroughly, presumably for Albanian literature.

On the bus, one of the group offers us an unnamed bottle of Albania aperitif, bought earlier and apparently undrinkable. It is fairly foul, dark brown like alcoholic gravy, clinging to the side of the glass like engine oil, but it is drinkable, and sees us through Montenegro—'little Montenegro down on the Adriatic Sea', which gave Jay Gatsby a medal—into Herzegovina, and downhill to Dubrovnik.

***

It is 2 July, the anniversary of the day in 1990 when Albanians desperately seeking asylum stormed the fence of the German embassy in Tirana. Today Ramiz Alia, the last of Albania's Communist leaders, is sentenced to nine years in prison.

Appendix

LANGUAGE

Albanian is a musical but difficult language that most philologists agree is descended from ancient Illyrian. It is spoken with a lisp reminiscent of Castilian Spanish; occasionally a French-sounding word surfaces (*qen,* a bit like *chien* - dog), but for the most part Albanian bears no resemblance to major Western tongues.

A very quick, very basic language course with cassette suitable for tourists is *Albanian Language Course Using the Proven Listen and Read Method* narrated by Gazmend Goci. It can be ordered from Wim Heiwegen, PO Box 183, 8170 BT Vaassen, Netherlands.

A more extensive course, *Colloquial Albanian* by Isa Zymberi, is published by Routledge. Language courses combined with visits to Albania can be arranged through travel agencies.

There are 36 letters in the Albanian alphabet, including eight double letters treated as one. Letters that differ from the English include:

c	as ts
ç	as ch in *much*
dh	as th in *the*
ë	as u in *nurse* (but often silent at the end of a word)
gj	as du in *endure*
j	as y
ll	as l
nj	as n in *news*
q	similar to ch, with a hiss
rr	trilled (as in Italian)
sh	as sh in *she*
th	as th in *the*
x	as z in *zinc*
xh	as j in *John*
y	as u in *Hugo*
zh	as su in *leisure*

Tunugasheta
tunooasheta

Useful words and phrases

Two delightful phrases of greeting often pass between guest and visitor: *Mirë se ju erdhet* (It's good that you came) answered by *Mir se ju gjetëm* (It's good that we found you).

Hello	Tungjatjeta (literally 'long life')
Goodbye	Mirupafshim
Good day	Mirë dita
Good evening	Mirë mbrema
Good night	Natën e mirë
Please	Lutemi
Thank you	Faleminderit
Do you understand?	A më kuptoni?
I don't understand	Po unë nuk kuptoj
What is your name?	Si ju quajne?
My name is ...	Me quajne ...
Do you speak English?	A flisni Anglisht?
Do you speak Albanian?	A flisni Shqip?
Yes	Po (shake head)
No	Jo (nod)
Excuse me	Më falni
Please repeat it	Lutemi, përsëriteni
This	Ky (m) Kjo (f)
That	Ai (m) Ajo (f)
Where is ...	Ku eshtë ...
What	Çka, çfarë, cili
Who?	Kush, cili, cila, cilet, cilat
When?	Kur
Why?	Pse
Do you have ...?	A keni ...
How much does it cost?	Sa kushton kjo?
I like ...	Me pëlqen ...
Good	i Mirë (m), e Mirë (f)
Bad	i keq (m), e keqe (f)
Big	i madh (m), e madhe (f)
Small	i vogël (m), e vogël (f)
Much	Shumë
Little (few)	Pak
Expensive	i shtrenjt (m), e shtrenjtë (f)
Cheap	i lirë (m), e lirë (f)
Left	i majtë (m), e majtë (f)

(handwritten margin notes: mirupafshim, Mir dita, mir mbrema, lutemi)

Right	i djathtë (m), e djathtë (f)
Straight ahead	Drejt
North	Veri
South	Jug
East	Lindje
West	Perëndim

Emergencies

Doctor	Mjek	Pharmacy	Farmacia
Sick	Sëmurë	Police	Policia
Hospital	Spital		

Numbers

1	Një	18	Tetëmbëdhjetë
2	Dy	19	Nëntëmbëdhjetë
3	Tre	20	Njëzet
4	Katër	21	Njëzete e një
5	Pesë	30	Tridhjetë
6	Gjashtë	40	Dyzet
7	Shtatë	50	Pesëdhjetë
8	Tetë	60	Gjashtëdhjetë
9	Nëntë	70	Shtatëdhjetë
10	Dhjetë	80	Tetëdhjetë
11	Njëmbëdhjetë	90	Nëntëdhjetë
12	Dymbëdhjetë	100	Njëqind
13	Trembëdhjetë	200	Dyqind
14	Katërmbëdhjetë	Thousand	Një Mijë
15	Pesëmbëdhjetë	Million	Milion
16	Gjashtëmbëdhjetë	Billion	Miliard
17	Shtatëmbëdhjetë		

Time

Hour	Orë
Minute	Minuti
Second	Sekondi
What time is it?	Sa është ora?
Three o'clock	Ora tre
It's half past one	Ora është një e gjysëm
It's 10 minutes to one	Ora është një pa dhjetë
Afternoon	Pasdite
Evening	Mbërëmje
Night	Natë
Noon	Mesditë
Midnight	Mesnatë

Days of the week

Monday	e henë
Tuesday	e martë
Wednesday	e merkurë
Thursday	e enjte
Friday	e premte
Saturday	e shtunë
Sunday	e dielë

Today	Sot
Tomorrow	Nesër
Yesterday	Dje
Every day	Cdo ditë
This week	Këvë javë
Next week	Javën tjetër
Last week	Javën qe shkoi

Months

January	Janar	July	Korrik
February	Shkurt	August	Gusht
March	Mars	September	Shtator
April	Prill	October	Tetor
May	Maj	November	Nëntor
June	Qershor	December	Dhjetor

This month	Ky muaj
Last month	Muaji i fundit
Next month	Muaji(n) tjetër

Seasons

Spring	Pranverë
Summer	Verë
Autumn	Vjeshtë
Winter	Dimër

Weather

It's hot	Është vapë
Cool	Fresk
Sunny	Me diell
Raining	Bie shi
Snowing	Bie bore

Places to eat

Breakfast bar	Mëngjezore
Snack bar for *byrek*	Byrektore
Bar for men only	Bufe
Café	Kafe
Cafeteria	Rosticeri
Restaurant	Restorant
Pastry shop	Pasticeri

Food and drink

Breakfast	Ha mëngjes	Grapes	Rrush
Lunch	Drekë	Ice-cream	Akullore
Dinner	Darkë	Lamb	Qengj
Beer	Birrë	Meat	Mish
Coffee	Kafe	Oranges	Portokalle
Cognac	Konjak	Pastry	Pasta, embëlsira
Juice	Lëng	Pepper	Piper
Milk	Qumësht	Pork	Derri
Tea	Caj	Potato	Patate
Water	Ujë	Rice	Orizi
Whiskey	Uiski	Salad	Sallatë
Wine	Verë	Salt	Kripë
		Soup	Supë
Apples	Molle	Sugar	Sheqer
Beefsteak	Biftek	Veal	Viçi
Bread	Bukë		
Butter	Gjalpë	Cup	Filxhan
Cheese	Djathë	Fork	Pirun
Chicken	Pulë	Glass	Gote
Egg	Vezë	Knife	Thike
Fish	Peshk	Napkin	Pecete
Fruit	Fruta	Plate	Pjate
Goat	Dhi	Spoon	Lugë

Sightseeing and travelling

Airport	Aeroport	Postcard	Kartoline
Automobile *	Makina	Railway station	Stacion i trenit
Boat	Barkë	Receipt	Faturë
Book	Libër	Room	Dhomë
Bus	Autobus	Souvenir	Kujtim
Church	Kisha	Square	Sheshi
Customs	Doganë	Street	Rruga
Ferry	Traget	Ticket	Bileta
Mosque	Xhamia	Timetable	Orar
Museum	Muze	Train	Tren

Signs

Attention!	Vini re!	Stop	Ndal
Entrance	Hyrje	Toilet	Nevojtore
Exit	Dalje	Watch out!	Kujdes!

* You will save yourself embarrassment by not using the English word *car;* the Albanian *kar* means 'penis'!

FURTHER READING

Some of the books listed are now out of print and may be difficult to obtain.

Books

A Guide-book to Albanian (phrase book) 8 Nentori Publishing, Tirana

Allcock, John B & Young, Antonia (eds) *Black Lambs & Grey Falcons: Women Travellers in the Balkans,* Bradford University, 1991

Amery, Julian *Sons of the Eagle,* Macmillan, 1949

Amnesty International *Albania: Political Imprisonment and the Law,* 1984

Bland, William *A Short Guide to Albania,* The Albanian Society, 1989

Bland, William and Price, Ian *A Tangled Web,* The Albanian Society, 1986

Blue Guide Albania (2nd edition), A & C Black, 1996

Durham, Edith *High Albania,* Virago, 1985

Elsie, Robert (ed and translator) *An Elusive Eagle Soars: An Anthology of Modern Albanian Poetry,* Forest Books, 1993

Fitzherbert, Margaret *The Man Who Was Greenmantle,* John Murray, 1983

Gjeçov, Shtjefën (collected and arranged), Leonard Fox (translator) *The Code of Lekë Dukagjini,* Gjonlekaj Publishing Co, 1989

Hall, Derek *Albania and the Albanians,* Pinter, London, 1994

Halliday, Jon *Enver Hoxha, the Artful Albanian,* Chatto

Hamilton, Bill, photography by Bhasker Solanki *Albania: Who Cares?* Autumn House, 1993

Hibbert, Reginald *Albania's National Liberation Struggle: The Bitter Victory,* Pinter Publishers, 1991

Hudhri, Ferid *Albania and Albanians in World Art,* Christos Giovanis AEBE, 1990

Hyman, Susan *Edward Lear in the Levant,* John Murray, 1988

Jones, Lloyd *Biografi: An Albanian Quest,* André Deutsch, 1993

Kadare, Ismail: Books available in English by this leading Albanian writer include:
Chronicle in Stone (an excellent portrait of Gjirokastra), New Amsterdam, 1987
Doruntine (the legend of a young man who returns from the dead to keep his promise), New Amsterdam, 1988
Broken April (blood feuds), New Amsterdam, 1990
The General of the Dead Army (the Italian occupation), New Amsterdam, 1991
The Palace of Dreams, (totalitarian nightmare), Morrow, 1994
The Concert, Harvill, 1994

Lear, Edward *Journals of a Landscape Painter in Greece and Albania,* Hutchinson, 1988

Monuments of culture in Albania 8 Nentori Publishing, Tirana

Newby, Eric *On the Shores of the Mediterranean,* Harvill Press, 1984

Pettifer, James *Blue Guide Albania, 1994,* A&C Black, London; WW Norton, New York

Pollo, Stefanaq and Puto, Arben *The History of Albania from its Origins to the Present Day,* Routledge & Kegan Paul Ltd, 1981

Smiley, David *Albanian Assignment,* Chatto and Windus, 1984

Vickers, Miranda *The Albanians*, I B Taurus, 1995

Ward, Phillip *Albania: A Travel Guide,* Oleander Press, 1983

Winnifrith, Tom (ed) *Perspectives on Albania,* Macmillan, 1992

Newspapers and Magazines
Albanian Economic Tribune, published monthly. Rr Qemal Stafa 262/1, Tirana, Albania. Tel: 042 24301/33214; fax: 32027

Albanian Telegraphic Agency News Bulletin, weekly mimeographed bulletin. Bd Marcel Cachin 23, Tirana, Albania. Tel: 042 24412; fax: 34230.

Balkan News, tabloid published weekly with two to four pages devoted to Albania. 480 Mesoqhion Ave, 15342 Athens, Greece. Tel: 301 601 6705; fax: 4600.

Illyria, tabloid published twice weekly in English and Albanian, focusing on Eastern Europe and the Balkans. 2321 Hughes Ave, New York, NY 10458, USA. Tel: 718 220 2000; fax: 220 9618.

INDEX

accommodation VII, 17-20, 78, 81, 88, 96, 97, 99, 105, 109, 113, 129, 131, 132-133, 135-136, 139-140, 144, 149, 151, 152, 156, 160, 164-165, 167, 175, 179, 183-184, 185, 190, 191, 199
Acrolissus 88
addresses 11, 168-169
Adriatic Sea 3, 4, 5, 72, 78, 88, 92, 94, 187
Africa 60
agriculture (see *farms and farming*)
airlines 31, 45
airports 31, 39
Albanian League 8, 87
Albanian Life 12
Albania Report 12
Albanian Society 12
Albanian Virgin 177-178
Albanische Hefte 12
Albanoi 6, 7
Ali Pashë Tepelena 8, 56, 67, 68, 69, 72, 73, 74, 76, 78, 83, 137, 141, 150
Alia, Gjergj Elez 96
Alia, Ramiz 4, 10, 93, 174, 204
alphabet 6, 92, 205
Alps 3, 5, 94, 99, 161, 176
Amantia 78
Ancona 31
Angevins 7, 51
Anglo-Albanian Association 12
Antes 7
Antigonea 67
Antipatrea 82
Aoos River 79
Aphrodite 75, 148
Apollo 75, 79, 148
Apollonia 7, 36, 44, 79-80, 82, 158-159
Arapaj 44, 55, 204
Arbania 7, 47
Arbëresh 49
Arbëria 7, 44, 78
Arbers 7, 92
archaeology museums:
    Apollonia 80, 158-159
    Butrinti 76, 148
    Durrësi 54, 119
    Tirana 44
architecture 50, 57, 61, 62, 69-70, 78, 83, 84, 91, 92, 93, 94, 96, 97, 99, 108, 119, 131, 135, 139, 140, 144, 150, 152-153, 154-155, 167, 168, 174, 190, 195-196, 198, 204
Ardenica 80, 156-157
Arianiti, Gjergj 199
Arianitas (feudal family) 7
Armenians 5
arms 69, 92, 93, 96, 108, 120, 141-142, 150, 195, 198
art and artists 32, 36, 45, 62, 79, 113, 115, 154, 173, 185, 195, 199, 202
Arta 108
Asklepios 75, 146
athiesm 6, 9, 43, 83, 92, 156-157
Aulon 78, 79
Austria, Austro-Hungarian Empire 6, 8, 18, 51, 80, 88
Avars 7

Babru Tunnels 115
Baçallek 172
Baikal, Lake 60
Bajram Curri 19, 21, 29, 36, 95-97, 179-182, 183
Balia, Shpend 96, 181
Balli Kombtar (see *National Union*)
Ballshi 30, 44, 80
Ballshaj (feudal family) 78, 88, 89
banks, banking 15
bards and ballads 96, 177, 187
Bari 31
Barleti, Marlin 88
Barmash Gorge 66
Barmash Pass 66
Barthelemy 79
Basil II 7
Bashtova Citadel 82
bathing (see *swimming*)
Baza 195
bazaar (see also *markets*) 39, 50, 107, 109, 169
BBC 26
beaches 4, 25, 36, 54, 55, 72, 77, 78, 81, 88, 94, 144, 151, 160, 166, 175, 199, 200
beer 24, 62, 113
Bektashi 49, 87, 108
Belgrade 141
Berati 4, 7, 9, 29, 30, 36, 39, 42, 82-85, 87, 126, 151-156
Berisha, Sali 10, 179
besa 187
Bicaj 187
Bilisht 29
biografi 172, 180
black market 13, 15, 27, 106, 118
Blinisht 98
blood feud (see *feuds*)
Boboshtica 64
Boga 94, 176
books 32, 117-118, 156
border crossings 29, 60, 88, 103
border formalities (see also *visas*) 13, 103-104, 189, 203
border incidents 71, 193
Borova 66
Borshi 4, 76
boundaries 8, 42
brandy 24, 33, 152
bridges 45, 73, 83, 89, 94, 99, 132, 144, 169-170, 172, 177, 193
Brindisi VII, 31
Britain, British 69, 78, 144
Buallit Pass 100
Buçimas Plain 62
Budaca 197
Budi, Pjëter 100
Bujan 95, 96
Buletini, Isa 93
Bulgaria, Bulgarians 5, 7, 27, 30, 51, 56, 59, 60, 82, 111, 118, 132
Bulqiza 100, 194
Buna River 4, 88, 172
bunkers VI, 105, 107, 151, 158, 166, 171, 172, 175, 197, 203
Burreli 29, 99, 100, 126, 191, 194, 195
buses 27, 29-30, 54, 95, 97, 104, 161, 164, 165, 170, 171, 175, 176, 178, 182, 189, 198, 203

Bushati 187
Bushati, Mehmet 91
Bushati, Mustafa Pashë 94, 169
Bushatllijtë 88
Buthrot, Buthroton (see *Butrinti*)
Butrint Head (Goddess of) 41, 75, 120, 148
Butrinti 7, 36, 41, 73-76, 145-148
Butrinti Lake 4, 73
Byron, Lord 67, 137
Byzantium and Byzantines 7, 47, 51, 53, 55, 56, 59, 60-61, 72, 73, 78, 82, 83, 87, 88, 89, 92, 98, 132, 154, 155, 163, 199

Caesar 55, 77, 79, 87
cafés 22, 46, 85, 108, 113, 117, 123, 133, 167, 173, 175, 198
Çajupi, Andon Zako 8, 70
Cakrani 7
Calabria 49
caravanserai 56
çardhak 50, 93, 169
carpets (see also *sexhade*) 31, 33, 58, 62, 70, 82, 85, 96, 107, 128, 135, 142, 144, 151, 183, 197
cars (see *driving*)
car rental 29, 151
Catholic (see *Roman Catholic*)
Cemetery of Martyrs 45, 56, 110-111
cemeteries 45, 63, 107, 127, 159, 167, 176, 190, 194
Ceni River 94
Çermenika Mountains 56
Çeta 82
Charles of Anjou 7, 49, 78
Childe Harold's Pilgrimage 67
Chimarra 77
China, People's Republic of 9, 141, 204
cholera 13, 43
Cika Mountains 77
cisterns 70, 89, 199
climate (see also *weather*) 5, 127, 194, 197
clothing 16, 124, 148, 150, 166
Code of Lekë Dukagjinë 161, 177, 187, 197
coffee (see also *cafés*) 22, 109, 131, 151, 152
Communist, Communism V, VII, 4, 9, 10, 57, 64, 83, 102, 111, 115, 127, 137, 149, 173, 178, 184, 197, 204
Comnena, Anna 53
Comnenus, Michael 55, 83
Congress of Lushnja (see *Lushnja, Congress of*)
Constantine XI 72
Constantinople 27, 51, 83
Conte di Cortellazo, Geleazzo Ciano 88
Corfu 7, 72, 79, 144, 145, 146
Corinth 7, 79
crafts (see *handicrafts*)
credit cards 13, 15
crime 13, 131, 189
Crusades and Crusaders 7, 51, 59, 100
Cuba, Embassy of 45
Çuka 73, 145
currencies 14-15, 31, 34
Curri, Bajram 96, 180

Currila 53
customs and immigration (see *border formalities*)
customs and manners 17, 129-130, 151, 155, 182, 187-188, 195, 197
Cyril 60, 61

Dangëllia 70
Dajti Mountain 55
Dajti National Park 5, 55
Dalmacia Fortress 97
dance 25, 124-125
Dardania 96, 188
Dardha 65
Dars 100
dates 17, 159
David of Selenica 64
Delvina 72
Demastion 188
Democratic Front (see *National Liberation Front*)
Democrats (Democratic Party) 10, 26, 106, 137, 185
Deutsche-Albanische Freundschaftsgesellschaft e.V. 12
Dhërmi 36, 77
Diber 29
Dimitrios of Thessaloniki 73
Dionysos 75
Dionysus of Syracuse 7
discos 24, 25, 58, 60, 133, 198
distances 30
Divjaka 4, 36, 152
Divjaka National Park 5, 81, 152
Dodës Fortress 193
Domaj 188
Domosdova Plain 59
Donika 156, 161, 199
Dragobi 96, 181
Dragot 67
Dratsch 52
dress (see *clothing, traditional dress*)
Drini River 4, 87, 88, 91, 94, 99, 163, 166, 172, 179, 187
Drinos River 67
driving 27-28, 98, 99, 106, 119, 128, 133, 152, 175, 178-179, 181, 182-183, 189-194, 196-197, 198, 200, 201
Dropulli Plain 71
drugs 118
Dubrovnik 48
Dukagjini (feudal family) 7, 87, 95
Dukagjini, Lekë 161, 181
Dukati 78
Durazzo 52, 54
Durham, Edith 22, 141, 161
Durrësi 4, 7, 19, 25, 26, 27, 29, 30, 31, 36, 51-55, 56, 82, 88, 98, 108, 119, 135, 139, 189, 190, 196
Durrës, Belle of 41, 53
Dušan, Stefan 7, 82
Dyrrachion 51

earthquakes 49, 53, 67, 79, 83, 87, 116, 172
economy 10, 111, 115, 128, 133, 135, 140, 165, 201
education 57, 58, 62, 93, 127, 132, 136, 155, 179, 198
Egypt 5, 161

Elbasani 7, 19, 26, 29, 30, 44, 51, 56-59, 127, 144, 184, 198
electricity (see also *hydroelectric power*) 4, 13, 15, 96, 105, 110, 112, 116, 121, 137, 157, 201
embassies and consulates 12, 39, 45
emigration and emigrants 5, 8, 42, 49, 62, 92, 130, 131, 133, 139, 144, 166, 173, 196, 200, 204
Encheleana Fortress 60
entertainment (see also *discos, music, theatre*) 24-25
Epidamnos (see also *Durrësi*) 7, 51
Erseka 29, 66, 135
Erzeni River 51, 56, 111
European Union (Community) 45, 81, 179, 197
exiles (see also *forced labour*) 113, 126, 151, 178, 185

Facists, Facism 9, 100, 120, 121, 142, 178
family tradition 5-6, 131-132, 136, 161
Fani River 98
farms and farming 4, 73, 82, 105, 111, 127, 131, 133, 136, 152, 163, 183, 190, 196, 197
ferries 31, 74, 94, 95, 97, 145-146, 178, 179, 182, 183, 189, 198
festivals 62, 69, 72, 79, 123, 157
feudalism 9, 39, 47, 48, 57, 63, 70, 83, 100, 137
feuds 127, 136, 177
Fieri 27, 29, 30, 79, 80, 158
Fierza 94, 95, 179
Fierza Lake 4, 95, 97, 179, 182
Finiqi 72, 73
Fishta, Gjergj 197
flag 48
Flag Pine 78
folk dress (see *traditional dress*)
folklore 124-125, 187
food and drink (see also *restaurants*) 22-24, 58, 106, 107, 108, 112, 123, 129, 130-131, 133, 136, 150, 152, 153, 165, 169, 171, 173, 177, 184, 189, 190, 201
football 45, 115, 127, 190, 191
forests 5, 73, 76, 77, 80, 81 92, 98, 107, 133, 135, 137, 152, 175, 176, 183, 187, 195
France, French (look in chronological) 79, 80, 88, 123, 131, 132, 151, 205
Frashëri, Naim 8
Frashëri, Sami 8
frescoes 53, 59, 60, 61, 63, 64, 77, 80, 81, 84, 85, 87, 135, 145, 154
Friends of Albania 12
fruit 56, 62, 64, 73, 95, 107, 127, 133, 136, 137, 151, 183, 191, 199
funerals 187, 197
Fushë-Arrëza 97
Fushë e Gjehve 96, 182
Fushë-Kruja 107
Fushë-Lura 98

Galicija Mountain 59
garages 28
Genthius, King 89, 92

Gepides 7
Germany, Germans 6, 9, 42, 52, 68, 69, 136, 142, 167, 173, 178, 183, 204
Gërmenj 66
Ghegs 5, 58
Gjakova Peja Prizreni 181
Gjalica Mountain 97, 187
Gjërë Mountain 68
Gjirokastra 19, 26, 29, 30, 31, 33, 36, 39, 67, 68-71, 139-144, 153, 156, 179, 204
Glaukias 7, 51
Glina 71
Gllavenica, Epitaph from 42
Golem 25, 36, 55
Gorica 29
Goths 59
Gradishta 126
Greece, Greeks 3, 4, 5, 7, 8, 10, 24, 25, 30, 31, 42, 44, 51, 62, 64, 65, 67, 68, 71, 72, 73, 74, 75, 77, 78, 79, 83, 92, 120, 131, 136, 137, 139, 140, 142, 144, 145, 146-147, 151, 158, 160
Gropaj 97, 182
Grykat e Hapëta 96
Gryka e Selishtës 190
Gubuleum 97
Guiscard 55
Gur-Lura 98, 190
Gurakuqi, Luigj 92-93, 173
Gypsies 5, 58, 116, 123, 129, 148, 153, 172

Haxhi Bektashi Veli 49
Halveti 46, 204
hammam (Turkish baths) 39, 49, 58, 71, 93, 107, 127, 175, 198
handicrafts (see also *carpets, silk, silver, woodcarving*) 33, 47, 56, 82, 83, 84, 88, 96, 107, 187
Hani i Hotit 29, 88
Hatixhe, Dervish 43, 201-202, 204
health care (see also *medicine*) 14, 190
heating 18, 110, 128, 131, 133, 135, 140, 149, 153, 156
Hekali 80
hiking (see *trekking*)
Himara 21, 76-77, 148-151
Himara, Cave of 77
Hofburg (Vienna) 49
holidays (see *public holidays*)
hotels (see *accommodation*)
housing 97, 105, 107, 116, 119, 121, 128-129, 131, 136, 150-151, 155, 180, 193, 201, 203
Hoxha, Enver V, VI, VII, 9, 10, 26, 41, 43, 45, 55, 60, 63, 66, 68, 69, 91, 102, 104, 109, 110, 111, 115, 116, 117, 121, 131, 142-143, 145, 148, 150, 152, 173, 176, 179, 181, 185, 187, 194, 195, 199, 200
Hungary 48
Huns 7
hunting 88, 156
Hunyadi, Jaños 47
hydroelectric power 4, 95, 97, 179, 183
hydrofoils 31

Ibe 56
ice-cream 168, 203

icons and iconostases 60, 61, 63, 66, 80, 81, 84, 128, 145, 154, 155
Idromeno, Kol 167
Illyria, Illyrians VIII, 7, 44, 51, 56, 58, 59, 67, 72, 73, 77, 78, 79, 80, 82, 87, 89, 92, 96, 108, 155, 163, 187, 188, 199
Illyrian language 6, 205
Illyrian tombs 41, 54, 59, 132, 187
immunizations 13
immurement 132, 171-172
Incident of 1946 144
income (see *economy*)
independence 8, 105, 161
industry 56, 62, 79, 82, 98, 115, 127, 135, 141, 151, 178, 199
insurance, automobile 27
insurance, health and accident 14
International Association of Medical Assistance for Travellers 14
Ioanina 29
Ionian Sea 3, 4, 72, 77, 78, 147
Iskenderia 88
Islam (see *Muslim*)
isolation 9
Italy, Italians 5, 7, 8, 25, 31, 41, 42, 49, 74, 88, 120, 121, 142, 144, 148, 156, 166, 200
Italian, occupation 9, 42, 44, 52, 57, 68, 78

Janina 8
Jezerca Mountain 3, 94, 96, 177, 182
Jews 85
Justinian, Emperor 39, 56, 83

Kadare, Ismail VIII, 68, 139
Kadri 204
Kalasa River 72
Kamenica 72
Kaneo 61
Kanina 199
Kanina Fortress 79, 199
Kapllan, Pasha 46
Kapshtica 29
Karaburuni Peninsula 78
Karavastas Lake (Lagoon) 4, 81
Kastrioti (feudal family) 7
Kastrioti, Gjergi (see *Skënderbeg*)
Kavaja VIII, 33, 54, 81, 82, 151, 199, 200
Kavalje 82
Këlcyra Gorge 4, 67, 137
Kerrshi i Djegun 197
Kiri 161
Kiri River 88, 94, 169, 172
Kliment of Ohrid 60, 61
Klosi 99, 100, 194
Kolgecaj (see *Bajram Curri*)
Kollata Mountain 96, 182
Kolonja 70
Komani 94-95, 178, 179
Komani Lakes 4, 94, 95, 179
Konispoli 29
Kontakuzeni 68
Kopor 31
Korabi, Mount 3, 99, 193, 193
Korabi Plain 193
koran (fish) 23, 60, 133
Korça 7, 8, 24, 26, 29, 30, 31, 33, 58, 60, 62-63, 81, 119, 133-135
Korça Plain 62

Koritza, Republic of 62
Kosina 66
Kosova 3, 4, 5, 10, 29, 95, 113, 161, 181, 188, 193
Kosova Plain 181
Kotodeshi 59
Krraba 56
Krraba Mountains 56
Kroj-Lura 98
Kristoforidhi, Konstandin 58, 127, 198
Kroi i Bardhë 186
Kruja 7, 19, 21, 30, 33, 36, 39, 47-50, 56, 100, 106-109, 176, 187
Kruja Citadel 41, 47-50, 51, 107-109
Ksamili Peninsula 4, 73, 145, 204
Kuçova 82
Kuka, Oso 93, 174
Kukësi 19, 29, 30, 33, 97, 182, 183-188, 193
kulla 94, 96, 97, 100, 177, 181, 187, 193
Kuna 4
Kurbneshi 98, 189
Kurt Pasha 83
Kuwait 18

Labova e Vogël 71
Laçi 98, 100
lahuta 96
Lana River 43, 45
language VII, 6, 13, 58, 62, 92, 119, 205-209
laundry 35
League of Nations 8
League of Peja 8
Lear, Edward 109, 139, 141, 153, 158-159, 171
Lekëli 67
Lenin 41, 113, 116
Leskoviku 66, 135
Leusha 19, 66
Lezha 4, 7, 29, 30, 36, 87-88, 126, 151, 161-165, 166
Lezha, Council of 87
Libohova 71
Librazhd 128
lighting (see *electricity*)
Lini 59, 130, 132
Liqenve Pass 197
Lissus 87, 88, 161
Llixhat 58
Llogara National Park 5, 161
Llogara Pass 77, 160
Lombards 7
London Conference of Ambassadors 8, 95
looting VII, VIII, 17, 116, 141, 158
Luarasi, Edi 124
luggage 16, 103
Lukova 76
Luma 187
Lundra 111
Lura Lakes 4, 36, 98, 189-191, 193
Lura National Park 5, 189-191
Lusnie 82
Lushnja 29, 30, 81, 82, 126, 153, 157
Lushnja, Congress of 8, 39, 82

Macedonia 3, 4, 5, 27, 30, 36, 59, 60-62, 64, 99, 107, 123, 130, 131, 193

Maliqi 7, 62, 135
Malit Pass 97
Mallakastra Highlands 80
Mamica 51, 111, 161
maps 33, 41, 42, 92, 97
markets 46, 61, 62, 70-71, 78, 106, 113, 116, 123, 127, 163, 172, 193, 201
marriage (see *weddings, women's issues*)
Martaneshi Mountains 4
Mati district 100, 194
Mati River 4, 98, 189
Marusium 82
Mborje 64
Medical Advisory Service for Travellers Abroad 14
medicine (see also *health care*) 14, 106
Melani 204
Merdani, Sherif 124
Mehmet II, Sultan 56, 88
Melissopetra 29
Mesi 94, 169
Mesit Bridge 94, 169
Mesopotam, Church of 72, 144
metals 31, 57, 59, 95, 97, 100, 179
Methodius 60
Migjeni (Millosh Gjergj Nikolla) 97, 173-174
military 73, 76, 78, 79, 103, 111, 135, 145, 150, 158, 159, 160, 178, 199
Milot 98, 100
mineral/thermal springs 4, 47, 56, 58-59, 66, 67, 71, 82, 109, 137, 152
mines and mining (see also *metals*) 97, 100, 129, 179, 194
minorities 5, 58
Mirdita 98
Moissi, Alexander 53
monasteries
Ardenica-80-81, 156-157;
Apollonia-80;
Elbasani-127, 198;
Ksamili-145;
Shën Liezhri i Oroshi-98;
Shën Pjëtri dhe Pavli-64;
Shën Prodan-64;
Sveti Naum (Macedonia) 60;
Sveti Pantelejmon (Macedonia)-61
Montenegro 3, 4, 5, 8, 88, 91, 93, 96, 161, 175, 196, 197
Morina 29
mosaics 41, 61, 53, 55, 59-60, 72, 74, 75, 80, 132, 147, 204
mosques 17, 39, 41, 46, 50, 53, 54, 57, 61, 63, 71, 78, 83, 84, 85, 87, 89, 91, 92, 155, 160, 185, 187, 193, 198, 199, 204
Mother Albania 45, 110, 111
Mulleti, Sulejman Pashe 39
Murad I, Sultan 7
Murra Pass 99
Murri 99, 193
music and musical instruments 25, 31, 33, 54, 62, 93, 96, 104, 105, 123-125, 129, 155, 187
Muslim (see also *religion*) 6, 49, 58, 66, 95, 168, 194, 200, 204
Mussolini 88
Muzaka feudal family 82, 83
Myzeqe Plain 82
Myzyri, Isuf 58

Naples 48
Narta 78, 79
Narta Lake 4
National Liberation Army 9
National Liberation Congress 66
National Liberation Front 9
National Liberation Movement VI, 9
National Liberation, War of (see *World War II*)
National Resistance 8
National Union VI
nature parks 4, 5, 55, 60, 81, 88
Naum of Ohrid 60
Nazis 9, 120, 121, 142, 143, 144, 171
Newby, Eric 159
newspapers 106
night clubs 24, 25
Niš 48
Noli, Bishop Fan 9, 82, 93, 187
Normans 7, 51, 55, 59, 73, 78, 204
nuts 62, 70, 95, 133, 136

Ohrid Lake 4, 29, 36, 59, 60, 65, 128, 133
Ohrid pearls 61
Ohrid (town) 61-62
olives 56, 73, 78, 85, 145, 146, 151, 200
Onchesmos 72
Onufri 59, 63, 84, 154, 155
Orikumi 78, 160
Orthodox (see also *religion*) 6, 46, 57, 58, 60-61, 63, 64, 66, 71, 72, 77, 80, 84, 154, 168, 202, 204
Ostrogoths 7
Osumi River 82, 152
Otonete, Battle of 99
Otranto 31
Otranto, Gulf of 78
Ottomans (see *Turkey and Turks*)

paganism 92, 176
Palasa 77
parking 26, 196, 200
parks (see also *nature parks*) 43, 44, 62, 85, 123, 168, 201
Partizani VI, 41, 66, 160
pashalics 8, 67, 88, 89
Paskali, Odhise 87
passeggiata 72
passports (see *visas*)
Pazhok 56
Pece 187
Peja, League of 8
Pelasgians 7
Peliom 62
Peqini 56
Pera 29
Perlati 98
Përmeti 24, 29, 30, 66-67, 137
Perondi 82
Peshkëpi 71
Peshkopia 3, 29, 30, 31, 99, 191, 193-194
Petrela 36, 51, 56, 111
Philby, Kim VI
Phoinike 72
photography 33, 107, 121, 123, 127, 151, 152, 155, 158, 159, 165, 169, 170, 178, 182, 183, 198
Piluri 149
Piluri Pass 76

Pindus Mountains 4
plaš (fish) 60, 61
Plloça 78
Podgorica 29
poetry and poets 118, 173, 186
Pogradeci 19, 21, 29, 30, 59-60, 61, 62, 128-130, 132-133
Pojan 79
Poliçan 85
pollution 36, 54, 56
Pompey 55, 77, 79
Pope John Paul II 167, 197
Pope Leo XIII 98
population 5
pornography 24, 104, 137
Porto Palermo 76
post 26-27
pottery 82
Prespa Lake 4, 64-65
press, the (see also *newspapers*) 10
Preza 36, 51
prisons 53, 69, 89, 126, 178, 197
Priština 181
privatisation 11, 18, 62, 82, 131, 133, 135, 151, 183
Prizrën 29
Progon 7
Prushi, Qafe (Pass) 29
public holidays 33, 105, 123, 125
Puka 29, 30, 97
Pulcheriopolis 82

Qemali, Ismail 8, 78, 93
Qeparo 76, 149
Qerret i Epërm 97, 181
Qinamokx 187
Qyteti Stalin 82

radio and television 18, 113, 156, 157, 201
Radio/Televizioni Shqiptar (TVSH) 25, 45, 201
Radio Tirana International 26
Radio Shkodra 91, 93
Radomira 193
Ragusa (see *Dubrovnik*)
railways 30, 42 82, 119, 189
raki 24, 33, 64, 66, 105, 108, 131, 136, 193
Red Cross 179
refugees (see *emigrants*)
religion (see also *atheism, Orthodox, Muslim, Roman Catholic*) 35, 91, 92, 119, 125-126, 128-129, 135, 136, 140, 155-156, 157, 165, 169, 200, 201
rental cars (see *car rental*)
Resnja 29
restaurants 20-21, 50, 67, 73, 78, 79, 81, 84, 88, 91, 93, 108, 133, 144, 146, 149, 157, 160, 165, 166, 172, 173, 175, 180, 182, 193, 195, 198, 200
Revolution of June 1924 93, 181
Rinas Airport 39, 51
Riviera 4
road conditions 27-28, 62, 66, 73, 76, 77, 78, 94, 97, 99, 100, 133, 135, 148, 151, 156, 166, 175-176, 181, 183, 184, 189, 190, 191-192, 193, 194, 195, 197, 199
road tolls 27
rock paintings 65

Roman Catholic (see also *religion*) 6, 7, 46, 57, 92, 95, 98, 167, 168, 195, 197, 198, 204
Romania 5, 161
Rome and Romans 7, 27, 39, 44, 51, 53, 56, 59, 62, 73, 75, 80, 82, 83, 87, 88, 89, 92, 119, 120, 146-147, 158, 160, 161, 163, 173, 193, 199
Rosnje Fortress 96
Rozafa Citadel 89-91, 166, 171-172, 199
Rrësheni 29, 98
Rrogozhina 27, 82
Rubiku 98, 189
Rufai 204
Russia (see *Soviet Union*)
Rustemi, Avni 39
safety 13, 116, 185
Sagiada 29
salaries (see *economy*)
salt 78, 79
Sampistët VII
Saranda 4, 19, 29, 30, 31, 36, 72, 73, 76, 144-146, 148
Sarda 95
satellite television 26, 175
Sazani 78, 199
Savra 126
schools (see *education*)
Scientology sect 55
Scutari (see *Shkodra*)
Secret Treaty of London 8
Selca e Poshtëme 59, 132
Selishta 99, 193
Semani 4, 79
Semani River 4
Senate of Central Albania 53
Serbia, Serbs 7, 10, 39, 51, 52, 78, 82, 87, 88, 95, 96, 188, 193
sexhade 96, 181, 182
Sfetigrad 97
Shala, Tribes of 177
Shala River 177
shared taxi 29, 198
Shëlbumit Mountain 88
Shelcani 59
Shën Vasi 149
Shëngjini 4, 36, 88, 166
Shehu, Mehmet VI, 10, 121
Shiroka 94, 175, 197
Shishtaveci 187
Shkelzen Mountain 96, 179
Shkodra VII, 3, 4, 7, 8, 9, 15, 19, 21, 26, 29, 30, 36, 39, 88-94, 95, 97, 108, 166-175, 178, 196, 199
Shkodra Lake 4, 88, 91, 93, 94, 176, 196, 197
Shkopeti Lake 4
Shkumbini River 4, 56, 58, 59, 82, 127
shopping 31-33
Shoshanit 96
Shpataraku, Konstandin and Athanas 81
Shpati 59
Shpiragu Mountain 82
Shqipe 6
Shqipëria 6
Shqiptar 6
Shtama Pass 100
Shurdhahut Fortress, Island 95, 179
Siberia 60
Siege of Shkodra, The 88

Sicily 49
Sigurimi (secret police) VII, 167
silk 39, 56, 58, 88, 93, 175
silver 31, 33, 56, 57 69, 88, 107, 181, 198
Skampa 56
Skënderbeg, Gjergj Kastrioti 7, 8, 36, 41, 47, 59, 82, 83, 86, 87, 98, 99, 106, 107, 108, 109, 111, 115, 121, 156-157, 161, 163-164, 193, 196, 199
Skopje 187
Skrapar 204
Slavs 5, 7, 59, 60, 62
Slovenia 31
Smiley, David VI, 121, 141
smoking 35, 201
smuggling 196, 200
soccer (see football)
Socialist Party (Socialists) 10, 106
Sofratika 71
Sopoti Mountain 69, 139
Soviet Union VI, 9, 41, 109, 141, 202
Spain 161
spas 58-59, 66, 193
spelling VII, 164
Spile Rock 65
Stafa, Qemal 58, 111
Stalin VII, 41, 113, 119, 151, 173
Sterbeq 196
Struga 29
Sulejman, Sultan 78, 80
swimming 45, 54
Switzerland 6
Synon 78

Tanganyika, Lake 60
Taraboshi Mountain 172
taxi (see also shared taxi) 29, 166
tea, Albanian 22
telephones, telephoning VII, 17, 18, 26, 150
television (see radio and television)
tennis 25
Tepelena 29, 30, 67, 126, 137-139
teqe 46, 49, 66, 85, 100, 107-108, 204
Thanas of Elbasani 81
Thana Lake 4
Thana Pass 29, 59, 132
theater 24-25, 42, 62, 91, 118
Theodosius II, Emperor 82
Theranda 39
Thethi 36, 94, 96, 175-178, 181
Thethi National Park 5
time 33
tipping 34
Tirana 5, 8, 9, 15, 18, 19, 21, 24, 26, 27, 29, 30, 31, 32, 36, 39-46, 56, 58, 75, 80, 82, 87, 88, 98, 100, 103-126, 127, 141, 151, 161, 180, 188, 201-204
Tito 9
toilets 15, 16, 18, 34, 53, 133, 183, 184, 189, 199

Tomori Mountains 56
Tomori, Mount 82
Topias (feudal family) 47
Toptani, Esat Pashe 39, 52
Toptani (feudal family) 39, 43
Topulli, Çerçiz 68, 70
Tosks 5, 58
tour operators 11
traditional dress 31-32, 45, 50, 58, 62, 94, 108, 116, 124, 139, 163, 178, 181, 182, 187, 195, 196, 198
traditions (see customs and manners)
trains (see railways)
travel agencies (see tour operators)
Treaty of Versailles 8
Trebeshinës Mountain 67
Tren Cave 65
trekking 25, 27, 36, 59, 94, 96, 97, 99, 160, 161, 176, 186-187, 193
Trieste 31, 189
Tropoja 10, 95-96, 179
Trpko of Korça 60
turbes 43, 61, 108, 201, 202
Turkey and Turks 5, 7, 8, 25, 27, 30, 41, 42, 47, 48, 51, 52, 53, 54, 57, 58, 59, 60, 62, 64, 68, 72, 73, 77, 78, 83, 84, 87, 88, 89, 92, 94, 95, 100, 107, 108, 111, 146, 147, 158, 163, 194, 198, 204
Turkish baths (see hammam)
Tushemishti 29

Uji i Ftohtë 67, 78, 161
Ukraine 5
Ulkonja 96
Ulza 100
Ulza Lake 4, 100
unemployment 10, 129, 131, 136, 185
UNESCO 69, 135
United States 5, 118, 144, 173
United States Information Service 43, 117
University of Tirana (formerly Enver Hoxha University) 9, 39, 43, 44, 110, 116
Ura Vajgurore 82
Uraka River 98, 190

Valbona 36, 94, 96, 177, 179, 181-182
Valbona River 96, 181
Valeshi 59
Va-Spas 188
Vatican 45
Vau i Dejës 179
Vau i Dejës Lake 4, 94, 179
Velipoja 4, 36, 94, 175
Venice, Venetians 7, 48, 51, 52, 54, 73, 76, 78, 87, 88, 89, 94, 146-147
Vermoshi 94, 196, 197
Vermosh-Velipoja 197

Versailles, Treaty of 8
Via Egnatia 27, 51, 56-59, 82, 131, 132
Vienna 49, 163
visas (see also border formalities) 12, 62, 103-104, 118, 200
Visigoths 7
Vithkuq 64
Vivari Channel 74
Vivari Fortress 74, 76, 147, 148
Vjosa River 4, 66, 67, 137, 158
Vlachs 5, 58, 64, 79, 85, 202
Vlora 3, 4, 7, 8, 19, 26, 29, 30, 31, 36, 52, 78-79, 160, 195, 198
Vlora, Gulf of 78
Voice of America 26
Voskopoja 36, 63-64, 135
Vranina 93
Vrina Plain 74, 146
Vrioni, Omer Pashë 79
Vuno 77

wakes (see funerals)
water (see also mineral/thermal springs) 18, 23, 36, 54, 69, 83, 109-110, 116, 121, 129, 133, 139, 150-151, 153, 156, 161, 164, 179, 180, 184, 199, 201
weapons (see arms)
weather (see also climate) 16, 72, 103, 113, 117, 123, 131, 144, 145, 175, 183, 189, 191, 201
weddings 129, 187, 196
Wilhelm von Wied, Prince 8
wine 24, 33, 66, 78, 133, 136, 144, 146
women's issues 49, 93, 127, 129, 130, 131, 135, 136-137, 138, 159, 175, 177-178, 202
woodcarving 31, 56, 66, 70, 83, 97, 108, 174
Works of Enver Hoxha, The 104, 123
World Bank 45
World Radio TV Handbook 26
World War I 8, 60, 64, 77
World War II VI, 4, 49, 52, 60, 64, 66, 68, 69, 91, 120, 136, 141, 142, 143, 167, 173, 193, 198

Xhani, Mustafa 100

Yalta 173
Yugoslavia 9, 84, 93, 94, 95, 99, 103, 113-114, 121, 144, 177, 196, 197, 203

Zanevia feudal family 68
Zerqan 100
Zogaj 197
Zografu, Constandine and Thanas 64
Zogu, Ahmet (King) 9, 42, 45, 57, 59, 66, 69, 94, 96, 100, 110-111, 119, 121, 139, 161, 175, 181, 194, 195
zoo 45, 123